T0004261

REVIVAL IF...

ROD PARSLEY

CHARISMA
HOUSE

Most Charisma Media products are available at special quantity discounts for bulk purchase for sales promotions, premiums, fund-raising, and educational needs. For details, call us at (407) 333-0600 or visit our website at www.charismamedia.com.

Revival If... by Rod Parsley
Published by Charisma House, an imprint of Charisma Media
600 Rinehart Road, Lake Mary, Florida 32746

This book or parts thereof may not be reproduced in any form, stored in a retrieval system, or transmitted in any form by any means—electronic, mechanical, photocopy, recording, or otherwise—without prior written permission of the publisher, except as provided by United States of America copyright law.

Unless otherwise noted, all Scripture quotations are taken from the Modern English Version. Copyright © 2014 by Military Bible Association. Used by permission. All rights reserved.

Scripture quotations marked AMP are from the Amplified® Bible (AMP), Copyright © 2015 by The Lockman Foundation. Used by permission. www.Lockman.org

Scripture quotations marked ASV are from the American Standard Bible.

Scripture quotations marked CJB are from the Complete Jewish Bible, copyright © 1998 by David H. Stern. All rights reserved.

Scripture quotations marked ESV are from the Holy Bible, English Standard Version. Copyright © 2001 by Crossway Bibles, a division of Good News Publishers. Used by permission.

Scripture quotations marked KJV are from the King James Version of the Bible.

Scripture quotations marked MSG are from *The Message: The Bible in Contemporary English*, copyright © 1993, 1994, 1995, 1996, 2000, 2001, 2002. Used by permission of NavPress Publishing Group.

Scripture quotations marked NASB are taken from the (NASB®) New American Standard Bible®, Copyright © 1960, 1971, 1977, 1995, 2020 by The Lockman Foundation. Used by permission. All rights reserved. www.lockman.org

Scripture quotations marked NIV are taken from the Holy Bible, New International Version®, NIV®. Copyright © 1973, 1978, 1984, 2011 by Biblica, Inc.® Used by permission of Zondervan. All rights reserved worldwide. www.zondervan.com. The "NIV" and "New International Version" are trademarks registered in the United States Patent and Trademark Office by Biblica, Inc.®

Scripture quotations marked NKJV are taken from the New King James Version®. Copyright © 1982 by Thomas Nelson. Used by permission. All rights reserved.

Scripture quotations marked NLT are from the Holy Bible, New Living Translation, copyright © 1996, 2004, 2007. Used by permission of Tyndale House Publishers, Inc., Wheaton, IL 60189. All rights reserved.

Scripture quotations marked TLB are from The Living Bible. Copyright © 1971. Used by permission of Tyndale House Publishers, Inc., Wheaton, IL 60189. All rights reserved.

Scripture quotations from The Passion Translation® are copyright © 2017, 2018 by Passion & Fire Ministries, Inc. Used by permission. All rights reserved. ThePassionTranslation.com.

Copyright © 2022 by Rod Parsley
All rights reserved

Visit the author's website at www.rodparsley.com.

Cataloging-in-Publication Data is on file with the Library of Congress.
International Standard Book Number: 978-1-63641-079-1
E-book ISBN: 978-1-63641-080-7

While the author has made every effort to provide accurate internet addresses at the time of publication, neither the publisher nor the author assumes any responsibility for errors or for changes that occur after publication. Further, the publisher does not have any control over and does not assume any responsibility for author or third-party websites or their content.

22 23 24 25 26 — 987654321
Printed in the United States of America

DEDICATION

*Second Timothy 2:1–2 says, "So, my son, throw yourself into
this work for Christ. Pass on what you heard from me—the
whole congregation saying Amen!—to reliable leaders who are
competent to teach others" (MSG). Or imitate their faith.
It remains my conviction that no divine anointing
ever leaves the earth. It remains available to those
following in its line of legacy. It multiplies.*

*With a spirit of tremendous expectation, I dedicate this volume
to the bold and courageous men and women who are, and
will become, its eager recipients. That which I have freely
received, I now willingly and enthusiastically discharge to my
students, the world changers of Valor Christian College.*

*May the Lord God Almighty deposit and develop within you the
passion and unction, the fire and power of the Holy Ghost. May
you receive and accept His divine call and become that revenant
remnant of revivalists who will steward and release to a weary,
waiting world another Great Awakening for the kingdom of our
God and of His Christ. It is in His mighty name that I bless you.*

*The apex of all Christian endeavor must become to place the
jewel of a soul in the crown of our Savior, that the Lamb of
God who was slain may receive the reward of His suffering.*

CONTENTS

A PARCHED LAND AWAITS US

ALLOW ME TO transport you to a place scientists think may be the driest place on planet earth. The Atacama Desert in northern Chile runs for six hundred to seven hundred miles alongside the Pacific Ocean yet receives no blessing of rain from the world's largest body of water. In most years, this enormous rock-strewn wasteland enjoys scarcely more than a few drops (0.2 inches per year). Instead, an occasional fog rolls in to offer a few precious particles of moisture to quench the parched tongues of the scrappy little creatures—a few species of insects and lizards and mammals—that somehow manage to survive here. The terrain? Mostly rock, dried salt lakes, and ancient lava flows. So barren and inhospitable is this place that NASA comes here to test equipment designed to survive on Mars. And yet...

On March 26, 2015, something extraordinary occurred. Ominous clouds rolled in from the sea. Peals of thunder shocked the graveyard silence. Then the heavens opened. In a mere handful of hours, the vast expanse of sand and rock received the equivalent of *seven years'* worth of rain. But the true miracle was still to come.

Just a few days afterward, local fishermen in passing boats rubbed their eyes and stared at the coast in absolute wonder. For as far as the eye could see, the eternally beige landscape rippled and shimmered with vibrant color. Living lakes of purple, magenta, violet, pink, blue, yellow, and white swayed in unison with the ocean breezes.

Practically overnight the most arid and desolate place on earth had exploded with life. After years of grim barrenness, the desert bloomed. Word rapidly spread, and soon visitors from all around the world arrived at the spot to see the miracle with their own eyes and to try, in vain, to capture its glories with a camera. And all because of the blessing of a single outpouring of rain.

Indulge me now as I take you to another place and time—to the Oklahoma panhandle and the raggedy remnants of a farm in 1939. The Great Depression of the 1930s has loosened its vicious stranglehold on most of America by this time, but not here. Not in the Dust Bowl.

Here in late summer, a leather-faced farmer and his tragically frail wife stand on the front porch of a wood-frame shack half buried in dust on one side. They scan the horizon of a landscape so flat and featureless they can see for fifty miles on a clear day. And they have seen little but cloudless days for eight miserable years now. Standing beside them, their three barefoot children in tattered, flour-sack dresses look upward, searching the faces of their bone-weary parents for any sign of hope or encouragement.

For eight grim, rainless growing seasons heartache is all this gritty farm family has reaped, and hope is all that has sustained them. Indeed, only a mixture of faith, hope, love, and stubbornness have anchored them here on this farm when most of their neighbors and fellow church members long ago gave up, packed up, and drove away westward, even as far as California. For many of those who left, it was April 14, 1935, that dealt the backbreaking blow.

The locals and the history books refer to that infamous day as "Black Sunday." On that Lord's day this family—like thousands of other farm families hanging on by their fingernails in this part of America—returned from church; said "grace" over a meager meal; then began the daily, virtually futile chore of trying to remove dry dust from their house that seemed to accumulate everywhere and cover everything. Around five o'clock a cry of alarm from one of the children sent the couple rushing outside. Approaching from the north they saw a living, churning wall of black devouring everything before it like some hell-born doomsday monster. Wildlife fled in terror and in vain before the coal-dark tidal wave. Birds fell from the sky, and jackrabbits suffocated in the grip of the relentless rolling wall of dirt. Within the hour, the behemoth had blacked out the setting sun and wrapped the family's home in terrifying darkness. Scientists would later estimate that this, one of the worst dust storms in United States history, contained 300,000 tons of prairie topsoil.

The storm passed, and the family dug out yet again and continued the fight for survival. But for many others, this was the last straw. For these, nature's savage attack had extinguished once and for all the flickering flame of hope for better days. Not for this couple. For each of the three years that followed, this God-fearing, churchgoing family bought seed on credit and planted winter wheat in September, hoping the traditional fall and winter rains would nourish their seeds, leading to a May or June harvest that, providing the market price was decent, would settle their debt and provide enough left over to live on for a while. For three more years, as with the four preceding ones, those rains deserted them. Any water-starved green shoots that managed to struggle to the surface quickly died.

Yes, on this day, their situation is beyond desperate. By some miracle, the one surviving feed and seed store in town extended them credit for another attempt at a crop. A few weeks ago, they'd scratched into that hard, dry ground one last time, sowing each handful of seed with salty tears and whispered prayers. Since that day of sowing, they, like Abraham, "who against hope believed in hope" (Rom. 4:18, KJV), had spent many hours standing on that porch. Scanning. Watching. Praying. Contending.

During this afternoon's front-porch vigil, both husband and wife see it at the same time. They turn to look at each other for assurance that their eyes are not deceiving them or that weary hope worn thin does not have them hallucinating. As Elijah said to his servant on Mount Carmel, "Go look again." (See 1

Kings 18.) They too gather their strength and look again. It is real. A line of clouds—white, purple, gray, and green—is fast approaching. Soon, they can actually smell the moisture on the wind. The long-awaited outpouring. A celebration—weeping, laughing, shouting, and dancing—erupts on that wood-plank, dusty porch. Just inside, a tattered King James family Bible lies open to a tearstained page of the second chapter of Joel. A closer look reveals two verses underlined in pencil:

> Be glad then, ye children of Zion, and rejoice in the LORD your God: for he hath given you the former rain moderately, and he will cause to come down for you the rain, the former rain, and the latter rain in the first month. And the floors shall be full of wheat, and the vats shall overflow with wine and oil.
>
> —JOEL 2:23–24, KJV

History will record that the mega-drought that devastated the high plains throughout the Great Depression officially ended in the early fall of 1939 as rains finally returned to the parched land.

ဆ

I write these things to you today because the America I love presently lies in the death grip of another devastating drought, albeit one of a very different type. Ours is a "Dust Bowl" of the spirit. The most fruitful civilization the planet has ever seen withers and shrivels before our very eyes. Having fully embraced postmodern relativism, sexual-revolution hedonism, and a pantheon of false gods, our once-verdant culture has become a moral Atacama Desert. Barren. Powerless. Unable to sustain life. A desolate wasteland that at one time, not so very long ago, was history's greatest garden of human flourishing.

Many times as I've ministered in great churches across this nation, and in my home church as well, I've asked the simple question, "What are we doing?" Eighty-five percent of the churches in America today are in decline.[1] Sixty percent of everyone who will be born again in North America this year will have the experience in a church that is two years old or less.[2] In the largest evangelical denomination in America, the Southern Baptist Convention, baptisms were down to 123,160 in 2020, the lowest number since 1919.[3] The Barna Group says that "If unchurched Americans were their own nation, they'd be the eighth largest on earth."[4]

So the "rain" we so desperately need has a name—one that hits modern ears as hopelessly old-fashioned and outdated. It is *revival*. And it has been far, far too long since we've seen this blessing poured out from heaven. Just as rain is the only cure for drought, revival is our only hope for the current famine of faith.

Yet I often wonder if anyone else has even noticed. Many of God's people, and even the shepherds of His sheep, have grown so accustomed to this dry and barren spiritual climate that they've come to view it as normal. This position has grounded our power, stunted our growth, and rendered us harmless to the kingdom of darkness. Compromise will always take the pressure off, but the cost of spiritual retreat has led millions to a life of peaceful stagnation.

It reminds me very much of the old analogy of the frog who at first is comfortable when placed in the kettle's warm water, until suddenly and without warning he is scalded to death before he can jump to safety.

Some have made peace with the sad and impotent state of modern Christianity. God help us, some have even wholeheartedly embraced and promoted it. They've become satisfied with living without the life-giving "rain" of God as though it's normal, neither expecting nor desiring anything more. After all, rainless Christianity is more orderly. It's less messy. It doesn't make anyone uncomfortable, and comfort has become one of the chief gods of our nation's new pantheon of idols.

We have religiosity, to be sure, in abundance. But in most quarters this is little more than what Paul described to Timothy as "having the appearance of godliness, but denying its power"

(2 Tim. 3:5, ESV). We have some churchgoing too, although not nearly as much as in years past.

During the COVID-19 pandemic lockdowns of 2020 and 2021, millions of American believers became deceived, believing they could "do church" on the sofa in their pajamas. So easy, so undemanding, so complacent and convenient, so benumbed and bleak, so backslidden! Most churches have since reopened, yet many who claim the name of Christ have opted to continue making the couch their permanent church home, complete with snacks and a multitude of interruptions.

Of those who do venture out of the house on Sunday, many seek out the most slickly produced "show" in town. One led by a motivational speaker willing to provide therapeutic bromides that comfort rather than convict and flatter rather than force a confrontation with their stubborn willfulness. I can almost hear their rebuttal now. They chide, "Don't condemn me"—a natural response when the church has replaced "that convicts me" with "that offends me." No longer do we realize that conviction is to our spirits what pain is to our bodies—not the enemy but rather an indication that an enemy has invaded. Without pain, one could cut his foot on a broken piece of glass and bleed to death walking on a beach. Likewise, without the convicting power of the Holy Spirit, one can live in sin and perish without Christ.

In a drought-stricken, rain-deprived culture openly hostile to biblical faith and Mount Sinai's immutable ethical standards, God's image bearers in the earth, His royal priesthood, His holy nation, are more comfortable simply going along to get along. His "peculiar people" aren't at all peculiar in the eyes of a pagan, godless society. We often don't look, speak, walk, or live any differently than those bound for eternity separated from God in a place of torment that your Bible still calls hell.

We find ourselves in this spiritual and moral famine because we have gone far too long without a God-sent downpour and drenching of Holy Ghost power. Some call such a deluge "revival."

Some call it "a move of God." A glorious season of divine rain in the days running up to our nation's founding came to be called a "Great Awakening." As we will see, there is quite a difference between a revival and an awakening, but they both spring from the same fountainhead.

Call it what you like, it is life-giving "rain" from heaven, and we need it now beyond desperation. Indeed, it is the only thing that can save us. I use the word *save* here with great intentionality. Our communities decay and decline into chaos because our churches are dried up and dying. Our churches are in such a state of decay and decline because so many of those within our walls are in absolute need of the convicting power of the Holy Ghost and heartfelt repentance, which alone are the catalysts leading to genuine, authentic conversion. That's right. Though these words may "offend," the fire of the prophetic Spirit within my bones and heart compels me to say this with prophetic clarity and plain speech. The gospel preacher must once again become the anvil upon which the heart of God bursts into language, and through which the voice of the Almighty is made to be heard in all of the indignation that is proper to His outrage!

Keep in mind that the gospel of Jesus Christ is not *inclusive*, it's *exclusive*. Our current culture is baptized in an attempt to be liked by everyone else at the great cost of diminishing their own self-worth and self-distinctiveness. The consensus is to conform and never say anything unpopular, and certainly not to make any waves. Sadly, someone with this standard of mediocrity will never stand up for the Word of God by standing against that which is contrary to biblical truth. The Bible is a rock of offense, according to 1 Peter 2:8, which is not an "inclusive" concept by any means. Nor is Matthew 12:30; in the words of our Savior, "He who is not with Me is against Me." And again, an even stronger admonition from the Lord Jesus from Matthew 7:13–14, "Enter at the narrow gate, for wide is the gate and broad is the way that leads to destruction, and there are many who are going through it, because small is the gate and narrow is the way which leads to life, and there are few who find it."

Unfortunately a large percentage of people on the membership rolls of America's churches are tragically, but simply, not blood-washed and bound for heaven. Jesus said it plainly, and without stuttering, in John 3:3: "Truly, truly I say to you, unless a man is born again, he cannot see the kingdom of God." And to quote the great revivalist Leonard Ravenhill, "I doubt if five percent of professing Christians in America are born again."[5]

May we plead for "showers of blessing," as the hymn "There Shall Be Showers of Blessing" says:

> There shall be showers of blessing:
> This is the promise of love;
> There shall be seasons refreshing,
> Sent from the Savior above.
>
> Showers of blessing,
> Showers of blessing we need;
> Mercy-drops round us are falling,
> But for the showers we plead.
>
> There shall be showers of blessing—
> Precious reviving again;
> Over the hills and the valleys,
> Sound of abundance of rain.
>
> There shall be showers of blessing:
> Send them upon us, O Lord!
> Grant to us now a refreshing;
> Come, and now honor Thy Word.
>
> There shall be showers of blessing;
> O that today they might fall,
> Now as to God we're confessing,
> Now as on Jesus we call!

There shall be showers of blessing,
If we but trust and obey;
There shall be seasons refreshing,
If we let God have His way.[6]

We must have revival in our powerless personal lives. We need it in our loveless homes. And oh, how we need it in our powder-dry and dusty, ritualistic and religious, cookie-cutter churches! Only the rain of revival in all three of those domains holds true hope for transforming our churches, communities, and ultimately our hell-bound culture.

I've experienced revival. Not a slick, well-produced weeklong show designed to draw a crowd with marquee names and flashy concerts of entertainment. No, real revival. I know how it looks. How it sounds. How it feels. Even how it smells. I've felt that life-giving rain upon my face. I've seen dry, lifeless churches and hopeless lives bloom with the vibrancy of heaven overnight, exploding with the eternal fruit of lost and lonely, dying and destitute souls coming to the tree of life—the curse-breaking, soul-cleansing, life-giving cross of Calvary's crucified Christ. Oh, what an extraordinary fragrance emanates from the altar of repentance as one person or thousands of searching, seeking, pleading, praying people rush forward into the holy presence of God Almighty! Coming freely into the loving, forgiving arms of our resurrected Savior. Drawn to His wounded side by the intermediate agency of the mighty Holy Ghost and cleansed by His blood. There to receive eternal life through faith in our Lord Jesus Christ (Eph. 2:8). There to ask, and by grace be granted, His forgiveness, as God our Creator opens the door wide to accept them as His and His alone.

I've watched through tears of wonder, joy, and gratitude as the same mighty Deliverer who rescued Israel from Egyptian bondage; the same Lord of hosts who flattened Jericho's walls through a single, unified shout of His consecrated people; that very same Holy Spirit, poured out at Pentecost, who transformed unlearned and inarticulate men like Peter and John into empire-shaking world changers, swept down aisles of a plain country church, pouring out His glorious power on doctors, lawyers, and professors as well as working men, women, and children. I've wept and I've laughed; I've shouted and I've danced as a deluge of His unmistakable presence and glory swept to hundreds, even thousands, of newly born-again believers as their names were recorded upon the canvas of heaven with a quill filled with the blood of Christ into the Lamb's Book of Life.

Salvations. Miracles. Healings. Deliverances. Restorations. Radical transformation of entire cities and regions with shock waves sent throughout the nation! These are the firstfruits of a mighty revival. We can experience all of that and much, much more, but only *if*...

If *what*, Pastor?

∞

Thirty centuries ago, during the reign of King Solomon, God our Father—the One who introduced Himself to Israel as the "God who healeth thee"—wrote out the prescription for the disease of spiritual and moral famine. It's the very medicine for that which has infected and affected us today. The Lord God foresaw a time such as ours and, in His divine benevolence, advised: "When I shut up the heavens so that there is no rain, or command locusts to devour the land or send a plague among my people..." (2 Chron. 7:13, NIV). Clearly any nation or people dying in a drought, whether natural or spiritual, I'm sure you'll agree, should give careful heed to any words that follow. Here comes our Healer's prescription. Are you ready?

> If my people, who are called by my name, will humble themselves and pray and seek my face and turn from their wicked ways, then I will hear from heaven, and I will forgive their sin and will heal their land.
> —2 CHRONICLES 7:14, NIV

If... Only if!

Oh, how we must pause and listen with great intensity when God Almighty utters that two-letter qualifier, "if," because His promises are always conditional based upon our obedience to His instructions. What keen attention and laser focus are warranted when the commander of heaven's angel armies presents an immutable proposition backed by His infallible omniscience and flawless integrity! When the One who came from nowhere and stood on nothing because there was nothing to stand on, and hung the earth on nothing, according to Job 26:7, and commanded that it remain there, and then spoke entire universes brimming with spinning galaxies into existence, points us to an unchangeable cause-and-effect connection, we are wise to take note.

If My people...

That's you and me, *if* you are redeemed and regenerated by the precious blood of our Lord Jesus Christ. So I implore you to walk with me through the pages that follow as we reveal that prescription and give it the attention it deserves. Time is short. The need is great. And the answer lies not in the White House. Not in the halls of Congress. Not in the deliberation chambers of the Supreme Court. No, God's prescription was written to "My people."

I am old enough to recall a time and place when nearly every church had Sunday night services, and those services were essentially weekly revival meetings. They were evangelistic in their thrust and purpose; accompanied by salvation, healing, and deliverance; and graced by miracles, signs, and wonders. In those seasons of outpouring, we knew that if we brought the unconverted, they would hear the unadulterated, often raw, but real gospel of Jesus Christ preached with power and passion, and we knew that the Spirit of God would be present to convict sinners of their sin and lead them to repentance, and they would be converted. We witnessed this in the long-term effects of lives undeniably changed. Every week we saw people truly become new creatures in Christ (2 Cor. 5:17).

In such seasons we were encouraged, nigh unto *commanded*, to bring the lost, the sick, the bound, the afflicted, and the brokenhearted to receive prayer, salvation, healing, and deliverance. When we did, the ministry those struggling souls received was not some milquetoast "Now I lay me down to sleep" prayer accompanied by a gentle pat on the back. They were ushered to the altar of heaven with a faith and an expectancy rooted deeply in God's great and precious promises. What extraordinary demonstrations of the kingdom of God and the power of the Holy Ghost we witnessed!

If My people who are called by My name...

With groanings too deep for words I long for, I pray for, I *watch* for those times of refreshing again. I know that gathered, truly consecrated believers always stand at the headwaters of revival's healing streams. God's great cause-and-effect equation contains our *churches* as an irreplaceable factor.

My dear friend John Osteen received his eternal reward some years ago, but something he spoke to me once still rings as an alarm bell in my soul. He said, "Rod, the church has become so worldly and the world so churchy, it's hard to tell the difference." Where is our witness? Where is our fire? Where is our energy? Where is our passion? Where is our power? Where are the miracles, signs, and wonders? Where are burdened saints arriving an hour before the church service begins to lie on their faces at the altar, travailing as if in labor, crying, 'God, give us souls or let us die!'" Or, for that matter, where are our altars?

Revival is our only answer. Beloved, God never intended for this extraordinary nation to become a godless, amoral wasteland. The rain can, and I believe will, fall upon this dry land again, and in coming, the outpouring will cause this barren plain to bloom once again. And it will come *if...*

So I write today because I stand on the porch of America's ramshackle house and scan the dry horizon. You hold in your hands a divine mandate written with undaunted hope that you have "come to the kingdom for such a time as this." I pray that the Holy Spirit will use it to rouse you fully awake. To stir a holy hunger in you for another great move of God. To make you as desperate for an outpouring of rain as a Dust Bowl farmer who has staked the whole of his family's future on one last planting.

From the parched deserts of the souls of men and our churches and nation we hear the tortured rattle of death and the silence of the dying. Come stand on the porch with me, like watchers on the wall, and together let's explore the four simple-but-essential "if" requirements that—when fulfilled—will release the life-giving rain of revival upon a nation. As always, the key to a glorious future lies in understanding the past, so we'll begin by examining some of history's greatest outpourings.

Stand a watch with me in hope and expectancy. I do not care to watch and contend alone.

THE CHOICE BEFORE US

Men build our churches but do not enter them, print
our Bibles but do not read them, talk about God but
do not believe Him, speak of Christ but do not trust
Him for salvation, sing our hymns and then forget
them. How are we going to come out of all this?

—LEONARD RAVENHILL, *WHY REVIVAL TARRIES*

SOLOMON—A KING OF incalculable wealth, power, and acumen—
stands in resplendent royal garb. In the morning sun, he glints
and glimmers like a jewel on an elevated platform. He is positioned on one side of the altar in the new eastward-facing temple's inner court. Below him, the gathered elders and elites of
Israel have crowded themselves into the limited space. They are
all here to witness the consummation of Solomon's crowning
achievement and to observe what will turn out to be the apex of
spiritual life in old-covenant Israel. The temple has been com-
pleted, and the day has arrived to bring into its new home that
most holy article of furniture the temple was meticulously constructed to contain. The ark of the covenant, borne on the shoulders of hand-selected priests, is ascending the hill from the City
of David.

Building a majestic and worthy habitation for God's presence
had been his father, David's, lifelong dream. Indeed, David, the
worshipful warrior-king of Israel, spent the final years of his
reign amassing an immense quantity of gold and other priceless

1

materials to finance the monumental undertaking, but execution of the elaborate structure had fallen to the son, not the father, as King David had waged too many wars and shed too much blood in the process. Now the organization and work of more than 150,000 men requiring seven years of construction and painstaking ornamentation by anointed artisans had recently come to its finale. Now the stunning edifice, clad in brilliant white stone and gold overlay, dominates Mount Moriah, towering over the Kidron and Hinnom valleys and shining like the North Star in a dark night sky. All that remains is to relocate the ancient ark and place it with the utmost reverence and care in the most holy place. Even as the priests disappear behind the veil to settle the ark in its hallowed sanctuary, multiple rivers of blood flow down every crevice of the mountain as Solomon and the entire congregation assemble on the summit simultaneously to sacrifice more sheep and oxen than anyone has ever before witnessed in one place.

Suddenly a holy hush falls over the assembly as the priests begin to emerge from behind the curtain. The silence is shattered by the sound of instruments and singing as 120 Levites blow their trumpets and others join with lyres and cymbals. Then with one mighty voice, the Levites commence in singing the opening line from "The Great Hallel," one of the ancient songs of Israel: "O give thanks unto the LORD; for he is good: for his mercy endureth forever" (Ps. 136:1, KJV).

On a future day, Solomon's great-great grandson Jehoshaphat will lead the praise singers of Judah in this exact refrain as they march out to meet an enemy army of overwhelming size. It will seem to be a certain suicide mission, but as the Levites leading the small and piteous army lift up this hymn of praise, the vast and fearsome armies of Moab and Ammon will fall into confusion and disarray and begin attacking one another. Within scarcely more than an hour, Judah's enemies will lay slaughtered across the hilly landscape, without God's people ever even drawing the sword. We might wonder, "Why will they pick *that* particular song as their battle hymn?" Perhaps it was because of what happened earlier on this day of wonders.

As the priests begin their exultant singing, a luminescent silver-white mist begins to fill the room. The very glory, the manifested tangibility of the Lord God Almighty, descends upon the place like a cloud until it completely fills the chamber, blocking out all vision yet filling it with living light. It is as if the Lord of glory, the Creator of heaven and earth, has stepped out of eternity's shadow to bend low to listen, and as He does, the train of His robe fills this temple. The priests have religious duties to perform but are unable to carry them out. One by one, they fall prostrate upon the ground. The weight of divine glory proves far too great for mortal beings to bear. What a moment. When God Himself inhabited the praise of His people.

ᘓᗝ

I too have seen the glory of God fill a house. Certainly, one far more modest than that of Solomon's temple. It may not have manifested as a mist, but it was divine glory from heaven all the same. And as in Solomon's temple dedication, few if any of us in the building could remain upright. When true revival is visited upon a church, it cannot and will not be "business as usual." God's presence in the midst of a people interrupts the ordinary. The weight of His glory often sends those assembled to their knees, and ultimately prostrate on their faces.

It should not surprise us that God's weighty glory and victorious power fell on both occasions in which His people sang with grateful hearts of His goodness and mercy. His *goodness* and His *glory* are inextricably linked! Recall Moses on the cloud-shrouded heights of Mount Sinai (Exod. 33:18–23). There Moses pleads for a glimpse of the glory of the One with whom he has been pleading on behalf of all Israel. The Holy One's response is that Moses cannot see His face and live, but He will hide the man sent to deliver Israel in the cleft of a rock and pass by so that he might catch just a glimpse of His trailing train of glory. Jehovah

3

specifically said, "I will make all my goodness pass before thee" (Exod. 33:19, KJV).

Do you see it? Moses asked to glimpse God's *glory*. God said, "Here is My *goodness*." Solomon and the Levites sang of God's goodness, and His glory filled the room. We do well to keep this in mind as we dedicate our overdone high-tech, flashy, state-of-the-art, computerized, and dare I say, built-on-borrowed-money faux houses of worship. "Except the LORD build the house, those who build labor in vain" (Ps. 127:1).

Although I've never tackled a project remotely as ambitious as Solomon's magnificent hilltop habitation for the holy ark of God, I know a little about constructing houses and buildings in general—including houses of worship. My father, James, was a custom home builder, and my mother, Ellen, was a real estate broker, so growing up I had a front-row seat to witness both the practices and pitfalls of bringing a blueprint vision to brick-and-mortar life. I carried a lot of their passion for construction with me into ministry. And throughout my more than four decades as the pastor of World Harvest Church and the launches of more than a dozen affiliated schools, ministries, and outreaches, I have had the opportunity to indulge that passion. I thoroughly enjoy being immersed in the minutiae and process of building. My extraordinary wife, Joni, does *not* share this enthusiasm. (It's true what they say about opposites attracting.) I've overseen the construction of massive tabernacles, schools, studios, ministry centers, office spaces, gymnasiums, cafeterias, and ministry support complexes through the journey from thumbnail sketch on the back of a napkin all the way through to completion and dedication to the glory and service of the Lord Jesus Christ.

But there has never been a building dedication like the one Solomon presided over three thousand years ago. Certainly no edifice has since been erected that is of greater significance. I pointed you to that remarkable event, recorded in 2 Chronicles, chapter 5, for a reason. I need you to see what God spoke immediately afterward. As chapter 6 reveals, following the outpouring of God's glory Solomon spoke a blessing over the people, then addressed a long and sincere prayer, one that fills nearly all forty-two verses of that chapter. Chapter 7 then brings us Jehovah's answer to that royal prayer.

The first portion of that response was given not in the form of words but in the presence of fire. Exactly as had been the case with Moses and the wilderness tabernacle five centuries earlier, heavenly fire poured out and consumed the offerings upon the altar. Oh, how long it had been since an Israelite altar had been visited by fire from heaven. But here it was once more, just as in days of old. An outpouring. As is always the case, fire from heaven sparked a revival in the house.

> And when Solomon finished praying, fire came down from the heavens and consumed the burnt offering and sacrifices, and the glory of the LORD filled the temple. And the priests were not able to enter into the house of the LORD, for the glory of the LORD filled the LORD's house. And all the sons of Israel saw when the fire came down and the glory of the LORD came on the temple, and they bowed their faces low to the ground on the pavement, and they worshipped confessing, "The LORD is good, and His mercy endures forever."
>
> —2 CHRONICLES 7:1–3

When the God of heaven pours out His glory, the resulting revival very often produces an outpouring of grateful worship and extravagant giving on the part of His people. And so it does here. Even though countless consecrated beasts have already been sacrificed by the people on this day, it is now Solomon's opportunity to give his offering.

> King Solomon sacrificed twenty-two thousand oxen and one hundred and twenty thousand sheep. So the king and all the people dedicated the house of God.
>
> —2 CHRONICLES 7:5

Seven days of feasting and celebration followed this extraordinary day of days. Then, on the eighth day, God speaks once again. The infallible Scriptures tell us plainly that this divine dictation is a direct response to Solomon's petition. (See 2 Chronicles 7:12.) That very night, the Lord God appears to the earthly king of His chosen nation with a word of inspired counsel and direction. Indeed, this is far more than advice. It contains a life-changing and history-making promise of eternal importance.

The God of heaven and earth chooses to speak in explicit simplicity here. I tend to follow His example and do the same. I have, at times in the last forty-plus years of ministry, been called a preacher who "tells it like it is" and have often been introduced as being a "straight talker." I have even been accused at times of being too blunt in my proclamations of God's eternal truth. Not diplomatic enough for some with delicate sensibilities. It's been said that I am an equal opportunity offender! I can only say that I come by this unapologetic plainspokenness honestly. As in this case, my God and King could at times fall into all of these accolades though they be minted as slurs.

In the dark watches of the night, the God of Israel comes to Solomon with a direct message for the entire nation. Here Jehovah employs the eloquence of simplicity. He speaks in direct terms so there can be no misunderstanding. Second Chronicles reveals those holy and immutable words which must be proclaimed in this present hour, and they demand to be heard. They represent the Holy Spirit's clarion call to you, me, and every person who claims the name of Jesus Christ:

> Then the LORD appeared to Solomon in the night and said to him: "I have heard your prayer and have chosen this place for myself as a house of sacrifice. When I shut up the heavens so that there is no rain, or command the locust to devour the land, or send pestilence among my people, if my people who are called by my name humble themselves, and pray and seek my face and turn from their wicked ways, then I will hear from heaven and will forgive their sin and

heal their land. Now my eyes will be open and my ears attentive to the prayer that is made in this place."

—2 Chronicles 7:12–15, esv

Again, I emphasize, God could not have spoken more directly or clearly. He employs no prose, nor poetry. He leaves no room for prophetic interpretation nor creative speculation. No hinting. No implying. We find no opaque metaphors nor cloudy imagery. He plainly states a four-part prescription for healing and restoration of a drought-stricken people:

"I need My people who are called by My name to (1) humble themselves, (2) pray, (3) seek Me, and (4) turn from their sin."

There we have it, distilled to its clearest transparency, preserved for us and history in black ink on white pages.

Upon more devoted examination the immutability of the divine commitment is revealed, and as is the case with all of God's great and precious promises, this extraordinary proclamation is *conditional*. The Lord God's promises are ever and always conditioned upon our obedience to His Word, command, or instruction. Anyone familiar with computer programming understands the nature of an "If-Then" statement in computer code. The coding stipulates that "if" a certain condition is met "then" a specific action will be taken. If...then...

Here the grand designer of the universe's software writes an "If-Then" string of code into the way things will work for God's people in every situation, in every time and every place. This is the eternal declaration and decree of our eternal Father, who cannot lie (Titus 1:2)! He solemnly and simply promises, "Anytime My people do these four things in concert, I will hear them, I will forgive their sin, and I will heal their land."

This is His pledge. His oath. The guarantee of our holy and changeless God. Still, some might question, "Can God truly be counted on to fulfill a promise made three thousand years ago in a place halfway around the world?" The Bible is filled with affirmative answers to that question. I cite just a handful here for your consideration:

> Let us firmly hold the profession of our faith without wavering, *for He who promised is faithful.*
> —HEBREWS 10:23, EMPHASIS ADDED

> *The Lord is not slow concerning His promise,* as some count slowness. But He is patient with us, because He does not want any to perish, but all to come to repentance.
> —2 PETER 3:9, EMPHASIS ADDED

> Blessed be the LORD who has given rest to His people Israel according to all that He promised. *Not one word of His promises which He gave by the hand of Moses His servant has failed.*
> —1 KINGS 8:56, EMPHASIS ADDED

Add to these the declaration of Deuteronomy 7:9 where we recognize that this promiser is "the faithful God, who keeps covenant and mercy with them who love Him and keep His commandments to a thousand generations." Some calculate a generation to be forty years. If that is the case then a thousand generations is forty thousand years and we have another thirty-seven thousand years to run on the shelf life of that divine guarantee. Let us also remember what both the prophet Isaiah, under the old covenant, and the apostle Peter, under the new, made sure all generations to come would understand concerning the promises of God: "The grass withers, the flower fades, but the word of our God shall stand forever" (Isa. 40:8; see also 1 Peter 1:24–25).

I have absolutely no doubt that I am on solid scriptural footing to encourage you to place the full weight of your confidence and trust in this ancient and immutable promise—the assurance that if...only *if*...we as God's people will (1) humble ourselves, (2) pray, (3) seek His face, and (4) turn from our sin, then Jehovah God will still and forever hear us, forgive us, and heal our land!

Put another way, God will faithfully and unfailingly send the refreshing rain of heaven-sent, Holy Ghost revival if only we will take the simple prophetic, profound, and powerful steps prescribed in this conditional promise.

Hear the same truth from the apostle Peter recorded in Acts 3:19: "Repent and be converted, that your sins may be wiped away, that times of refreshing may come from the presence of the Lord." It's even more clear from The Passion Translation: "And now you must repent and turn back to God so that your sins will be removed, and so that times of refreshing will stream from the Lord's presence."

I'm sure you experienced it. There was a great deal of preaching, citing, and pointing to 2 Chronicles 7:14 beginning in the tumultuous year 2020 as Americans, in dismay and alarm, witnessed a trifecta of trouble. A global pandemic, civil unrest tearing our cities apart, and political polarization of a degree not seen since the Civil War erupted and spilled an ocean of blood. This widespread appeal to 2 Chronicles 7:14 was absolutely appropriate. And I took encouragement in seeing so many leaders from so many different streams of ministry directing God's people to this ancient yet timely promise of God.

At the same time, I also believe we have yet to fully explore this verse's breadth and depth, and there are hidden treasures and veins of golden wisdom within it yet to be mined and discovered. Indeed, this verse is like a flawless, exquisite diamond with a multitude of facets. The more we examine it, from fresh angles and in differing lights, the more we see what we had not seen before. Each new encounter reveals dazzling beauty and deepens our awe.

With humility, and even fear and trembling, I have set myself here to the task of helping us explore many of those facets. It will in no way be exhaustive, for with divine, living truth that is an impossible task. But I do believe it will be illuminating, motivating, and I pray, transformative.

Before we begin in earnest, I will remind you that God began

His conditional promise with the words "If My people...," not "If the people of the world..." No; it is you and me and all those who claim the name of Christ as Lord and Savior to whom this offer of grace and glory is perpetually extended. It is written to those of us within the church, not those outside of it looking in. But could it be that there is more than we've previously perceived in the Father's decision to choose those specific words, "My people, called by My name"?

Years ago my wife, Joni, asked herself this same question. After a season of fervent prayer and exploration by the Spirit, the Holy Ghost illuminated her understanding. She recorded her powerful revelation and spiritual insights in a blog post. What she wrote impacted me so profoundly that I quickly invited her to read that post before a full tabernacle on a Sunday morning. It had the same effect on the congregation that day as it did on me. So now, with her permission, I wish to share a condensed version with you for your prayerful consideration.

Regarding 2 Chronicles 7:14, Joni wrote:

> I have heard the scripture and I have read it countless times. I've heard preachers refer to it while particularly preaching about America and its need for revival....Yet I still felt like there was something I was missing [when rereading the full chapter]....I discovered a prevailing theme throughout which plainly dealt with covenant, consecration, and obedience....What did God mean by the phrase "will heal their land"? Most interpretations I've heard refer to this as healing our countries, but could there be more?...Besides our countries, what land is He talking about?...One definition [of *land*] that stood out to me described *land* as "a realm, a domain, and a portion distinguishable by boundaries and ownership."...My land is not just America but is *my* portion, my domain, the realm of my existence and everything within its boundaries as well as what I own. Now imagine all these things and examine their current state. How needy is my portion? How strong

is my domain? Is the realm of my existence and everything within its boundaries well and sound? Is everything I own in good shape? With that, is there a need for healing anywhere? My answer is an emphatic yes! God's answer is also emphatic. Do as He commands. All He asks is that we turn. When we turn our hearts toward God, we turn our backs to the world. Certainly we desire this healing that God wants to give us, but what does that mean? Healing is defined, "to make sound or whole, to restore to health, to patch up a breach or division, and to restore to original purity or integrity." Our portion, our domain, what we own, the realm of our existence and everything or everyone within the boundaries of our lives can be healed. Furthermore, it can be restored, purified, made sound and whole, undivided, and unbroken.[1]

Yes, our national "domain" is in a severe drought. This we well know. It seems all the old pagan idols and gods of Babylon, Egypt, Greece, and Rome are worshipped in every city and town in America, only under modern new names. Oh, how parched our decadent, godless culture is in this hour. But I suspect you could use some rain in your own life. That's why on the pages that follow we will examine the magnificent jewel of 2 Chronicles 7:14 not only for keys to cultural and national revival, but to quench our thirst for personal revival as well.

What about your realm? Your portion? Your domain? Before we can talk about a revived nation or a revived community or church, we must ask, "Do I need to experience a revival in my life and family?" Before we turn to the larger question of reviving our nation, our culture, our churches, we must begin with reviving me. Reviving you. Bringing and releasing Holy Ghost rains of healing and blessing to your domain and everything within its boundaries. I write from a deep desire to see you in ongoing, perpetual revival. It's possible. I can testify of it from personal experience.

Being outdoors is a personal passion, so I know that when

you're making your way through a dense forest, the old paths are usually the most reliable, even if they've overgrown with vines from lack of use. So we'll begin by walking the most ancient of all paths to revival, those we find in the biblical record. There have been many great outpourings throughout history. We'll mine those for insight and direction as well. From there we'll move on to an exploration of how we—as individuals, churches, and a nation—can fulfill the critical "*If*" of 2 Chronicles 7:14.

At each stop along the way I'll do my best, with perhaps some artistic license, to give you a front-row seat to some of the key moments in great moves of the Spirit of God from the past. It is absolutely vital that you come to share my desperation, hunger, and passion. It is indeed our only hope.

This is the choice before us. God so values freedom that He gives us the opportunity to choose. As for me and my house, we choose for our domain to exist in a state of perpetual revival. You can experience perpetual personal revival, as well. *If* and only *if* you obey the command of the Lord in 2 Chronicles 7:14, I believe God will send a drenching downpour of Holy Ghost rain and revival such as you and the world have never experienced before.

The proof of desire is pursuit. In a season of drought, let us become so passionate in our pursuit of His glorious presence that we become as David, and with burning lungs and parched lips, cry out even now, "As the deer pants after the water brooks, so my soul pants after You, O God" (Ps. 42:1).

If we meet these divine stipulations—and God would not have extended the offer if we were incapable of meeting His command—*then* we will experience something truly extraordinary in our lives, in this great nation, and in our world.

PART ONE

&

HE HAS REVIVED BEFORE

There is a sense in which revival is like a prairie fire ignited by a bolt of lightning from the heavens. Without organization, advertising, or even sometimes human leadership, revivals have altered hearts of men, the social attitudes of millions, and the destinies of nations.

—Richard Owen Roberts

Chapter 1

BIBLICAL REVIVALS

IS REVIVAL A biblical concept? After all, a search of the biblical text for the word produces no results. The closest we come is Psalm 85:6 wherein the psalmist, in the midst of a spiritually dry season for the nation of Israel, cries out to God in deep desperation, "Will You not revive us again, that Your people may rejoice in You?"

No, you won't find the specific word *revival* in your big King James family Bible, but you will find the concept running throughout its pages like a golden thread from Genesis to Revelation. As we have already seen, it is there in 2 Chronicles 7:14 in God's conditional promise to heal our land. It is there in David's Psalm 51 prayer of heartrending repentance for his own personal sin. In sorrow and contrition he asks for revival when he says, "Restore to me the joy of Your salvation, and uphold me with Your willing spirit" (Ps. 51:12). It is there in 1 Kings, chapter 18, in Elijah's declaration to the apostate King Ahab, as four hundred humiliated prophets of Baal lie dead by the river Kishon at the base of Mount Carmel: "Go, eat and drink, for there is the sound of a heavy rain" (1 Kings 18:41, NIV). The powerful and unrestrained voice of Elijah and the people's rejection of Baal and his prophets brought an end to a three-year drought and an even longer period of spiritual barrenness and torrid idolatry.

Revival is very much at the heart of the event directed and conducted under the leadership of Ezra and Nehemiah, in which a remnant of Judah is restored to the land after seventy years of Babylonian captivity, then rebuilds the ravaged temple and restores the protective walls around Jerusalem.

Oh, yes, extraordinary, history-changing revivals appear consistently throughout the biblical narrative. Yet I cannot help but contrast these mighty and restorative moves of God among His people with what passes for "revival" in our day. I see the word used freely and frequently—often in advertisements in Christian media. "Come join us six months from now for our great revival meetings!" As if one could predict that divine lightning strike and plan a revival for a certain week or two on the calendar a year in advance. I'm concerned that we have accepted mechanical irrigation for divine intervention!

Some years ago the *Rocky Mountain News* reported a story regarding a severe drought in the Denver area. The farmers of the area had become distraught because the ground was dry as powder, and they knew if they didn't receive the necessary rainfall soon, the crops that they had sown in the fields would certainly wither and die, and they would lose the entirety of their income.

Those hardworking men and women of agriculture agreed to hire a "rainmaker" whose job it would be to fly his airplane into the clouds and seed them with dry ice to cause them to pour forth the moisture they were so desperate for. They were in such despair that they paid him $500,000 to begin, and he would receive another $500,000 if he was successful in the endeavor.

The rainmaker did his due diligence and scientific inquiry before he ascended into the clouds that first day, but unfortunately his efforts failed. The *Rocky Mountain News* reported the next day, "Rainmaker fails." He tried again the next day, and the report following that attempt read, "Rainmaker tries again and fails."

The farmers decided it was time to cease their arrangement with the rainmaker, but he pleaded with them for a three-day extension, and they agreed. Now the headlines read, "Rainmaker gets extension." He tried again. The first day, nothing. Second day, nothing. Third day, nothing. At last, the headlines of the *Rocky Mountain News* read, "Rainmaker fired."

Not two days later, the heavens billowed out, lightning began to flash out of dark-throated storm clouds, and raindrops the size of nickels began to fall. They had what we used to call a "toad-strangling gully washer"!

It is time in the realm of the Spirit, and in the modern church, that we do away with such artificial rainmakers who cost an exorbitant amount of money and make a great deal of noise but produce no rain. Charles Haddon Spurgeon declared, "Without the Spirit of God we can do nothing; we are as ships without wind, or chariots without steeds; like branches without sap, we are withered; like coals without fire, we are useless; as an offering without the sacrificial flame, we are unaccepted."[1]

We are required as never before to seek the face of our God and in our poverty declare, "Only You can send the rain of our deep necessity!" May dry and thirsty hearts rend the heavens with cries for the Almighty to drench our parched souls and powerless existence with a deluge of Holy Ghost rain that cannot be produced by mechanical irrigation but only by divine intervention.

I do not wish to offend, but I find my subject so vastly important that I cannot help but be straightforward in my communication. The stakes are far too high to risk my message and mandate being obscured by disingenuous diplomacy. You simply cannot schedule an outpouring of God's power. You can only pray, believe, and fast for it in the ways we will explore in this chapter and beyond. The truth is, much of what passes for revival in this season is nothing of the sort and bears no resemblance to the genuine article. Our organized, streamlined, computerized, carnal, and convenience-based form of Christianity has failed repeatedly to produce an authentic revival! We cannot manufacture revival with elaborate stage lighting, fog machines, and talented musicians with record deals. Preachers without passion to study the Word of God are nothing more than performers who may be able to thrill, enthrall, and at times, even inspire. But this is not revival. Yes, you can fill massive church sanctuaries, basketball arenas, and even stadiums with warm bodies with attractions such as these. But you cannot fill them with the convicting and convincing power of the Holy Spirit (John 16:7–10). Everyone will have a good time and possibly even feel somewhat better, but little, if any, life change will have taken place.

Much of this is little more than quality Christian entertainment. And please understand, I have nothing against Christian entertainment. We need it as a wholesome, un-defiling alternative to the sea of sewage being profusely pumped into our living rooms and minds via the ever-proliferating streaming media services. No, there is nothing wrong with entertainment, per se; however, it must not be conflated with revival. Entertainment feeds the soul (mind, will, and emotions) and can even energize the body. But it does not, cannot, will not touch the spirit. Only deep can call to deep (Ps. 42:7).

I am concerned that we have raised an entire generation of church attenders who have never once tasted the fruit of true revival. Most modern Christians would recoil from the reality that history reveals that actual revival attracts far more critics than fans. Skillful showmanship and salesmanship can stir the emotions. But emotions are fleeting; they evaporate like the morning dew. Only Holy Ghost interventions that penetrate to the "inner man"—the spirit—can produce truly transformed men and women. And only men and women thus changed at the spiritual level can shake cities. Hearing that a presentation was "soul-stirring" is not a compliment in my book. Our souls have been stirred enough. We have blended flesh and soul into an unholy and ungodly amalgamation with our born-again spirits. We are weak and powerless and spiritually sick and stunted from consuming the concoction. We need to hear Holy Ghost–anointed preaching that shakes and stirs our slumbering *spirits* awake.

During a season of such widespread spiritual drought, many spirits in the pews may actually be more dead than asleep. That's why revival is our only hope. You don't have to be an English major like my daughter Ashton Blaire to perceive that the root word of revival is *revive*, which the dictionaries define as to "bring back" to life.[2] Diving down yet another layer, our word *revive* combines two Latin words: the first, *re*, meaning "to bring back"; the second, *vivere*, meaning "live."[3]

To re-vive clearly means to bring back to life again. The implication is that the dead thing was previously alive and is currently in need of resurrection. With a heart of deep sorrow I must report that the previously-alive-but-now-dead thing is much of the church in America. But she can live again. We ought to raise our unified voices of desperation and repentance as one mighty chorus and cry out in the powerful and prophetic words of the old, neglected hymn "Revive Us Again" that rang from the wooden rafters of the old camp meeting tabernacles of my youth.

In the light of that definition, please allow me to ask a question: How many authentic revivals have you experienced? How many of the Christian "events" you've attended—perhaps with thousands or tens of thousands around you—restored you to life and did for you what a phone booth did for Clark Kent? How many brought you back from an inactive, unused, non-productive state and propelled you into a new season of fruitfulness, fulfillment, and fire in the kingdom of God and of His Christ?

There's a seldom-used word that literally means "someone who has been dead but has been made alive once again." Such a person is a *revenant*.

True revivals produce a resurrected army of revenants. Revived, restored, and reanimated by the same power that shattered the gates of hell and raised our Lord Jesus Christ from the dead, these revenants spill out of the pews and into the streets and marketplaces. They are inspired rather than daunted by the words *impossible, incurable, insurmountable,* and *insufferable*. They cannot be discouraged, and they refuse to quit. These revived, revenant saints—infused with the anointing, authority, acceptance, and ability of God—become a disruptive force, annoying the complacent, offending the apathetic, and appalling the image-conscious.

An authentic move of the Holy Ghost ruffles feathers and shocks the dignified sensibilities of both the coldly religious and the godless and worldly. As the late British revivalist Arthur Wallis correctly observed:

> Revival is...God revealing Himself to man in awful holiness and irresistible power....If we find a revival that is not spoken against, we had better look again to ensure that it is a revival.[5]

A revenant insurgency carries with them the keys to earthly cities, regions, and nations because they belong to the One who holds the keys to death, hell, and the grave. What they bind on earth is bound in heaven, and whatsoever they loose on earth is loosed in heaven (Matt. 18:18).

This and this alone is the hallmark of real revival. The dead, lifeless, and barren burst forth with life and fruitfulness just as a desert blooms in response to rain. My hope is that by now I have been able to stir a hunger within you to see such a glorious visitation of God with your own eyes. To feel it and be changed forever by it. My prayer is that you are experiencing a growing, unquenchable thirst to be not only a witness to such an outpouring of Holy Ghost power, flowing forth in mighty torrents from heaven itself, but a fully engaged participant, that you have opened your inward man to drink deeply of heaven's holy rain.

As I noted at the opening of this chapter, there is much to learn from the revivals recorded in our Bible. So let us take hold of that golden thread and follow it to some stunning lessons of divine wisdom for inviting and stewarding the destiny-altering, history-making, life-giving promise of revival.

಄

Israel's glory years were short lived. After four hundred years in the land of promise, the twelve squabbling sibling tribes had finally united under Saul. The kingdom expanded both in territory and might under David. Then, for a season, David's son Solomon elevated the nation to even higher glories and international prestige. With neighboring Egypt, Assyria, Babylon, and the Hittites all simultaneously in decline and disarray, for a brief but shining hour Israel stood head and shoulders above them all—and could have continued to do so had Solomon not fallen prey to the twin seductresses: pride and hedonism.

The Lord Jehovah, through Moses, had graciously provided a guide to the kings of Israel more than four centuries before her first king ever wore a crown. The Book of Deuteronomy is God's grand, comprehensive covenant treaty for the nation, outlining the terms and blessings for faithfulness and the penalties for rebellion. It was His gift to Israel and her leaders on the eve of their entering the land of promise—a deeply loving but stern guide for flourishing as a nation and a culture. The final seven verses of chapter 17 are specifically aimed at that distant future day when Israel would enthrone kings. In verse 15, the Almighty decrees that He will choose their kings from "among your brothers." In other words, no foreigner would rule over them.

He then gave three very specific commands, which were neither optional nor flexible, to the future kings of Israel in the two verses that follow. Those commands were as follows:

1. "He shall not accumulate horses for himself or cause the people to return to Egypt in order that he accumulate horses" (v. 16).

2. "He shall not acquire many wives for himself, lest his heart turn away" (v. 17).

3. "Nor shall he acquire for himself excess silver and gold" (v. 17).

If you know your Bible, you may already be ahead of me here. In the years that followed that glorious revival outpouring at the dedication of the temple, Solomon proceeded to violate all three of these ordinances in the extreme. He amassed personal wealth to a degree that astounded visiting kings and queens. He did indeed seek to import military hardware from Egypt, particularly horse-drawn chariots, to enhance the power of his armies. (See 2 Chronicles 1:14, 16.) But most devastatingly of all, he forged marriage-covenant alliances with hundreds of neighboring pagan nations and tribes by taking wives from among the daughters of their kings. In spite of all God's solemn warnings about alliance with Egypt—the nation that had enslaved His people and out of whose hand God had delivered them with mighty and miraculous signs and wonders—Solomon married a daughter of Pharaoh himself. This marriage signified, at best, an alliance between the two nations and, at worst, that Solomon was making Israel a vassal of her former oppressor.

We don't have to speculate about the impact of those ungodly marriages upon Solomon's heart, character, and destiny. First Kings chapter 11 spells it out in heartrending specificity:

> But King Solomon loved many foreign women in addition to the daughter of Pharaoh, women of the Moabites, Ammonites, Edomites, Sidonians, and Hittites....He had seven hundred wives who were princesses and three hundred concubines, and his wives turned his heart away. For when Solomon was old, his wives turned his heart away after other gods, and his heart was not perfect with the LORD his God as the heart of David his father had been. For Solomon went after Ashtoreth, the goddess of the Sidonians, and after Molek, the abomination of the Ammonites.
>
> —1 KINGS 11:1–5

The biblical scribe summarizes this scathing multi-count indictment in the very next verse:

Solomon did what was evil in the sight of the LORD and did not fully follow the LORD as his father David had done.

—1 KINGS 11:6

Solomon indulged the exact three things God, through Moses, had warned against. What pride, rebellion, and outright foolishness on the part of "the wisest man of the Old Testament." What a travesty of leadership, and what a tragedy for Israel. And how many preachers of the gospel in our day have fallen by touching and willfully partaking of these same three forbidden fruits—the gold, the glory, and the girls?

All are simply different forms of the same abomination: idolatry. And indeed, the verses that follow this litany of shame recount how Solomon's wives seduced him to turn from worship of the one true and living God to the flesh- and soul-driving worship of demonic powers. The one who had been granted the honor and prestige of constructing God's holy habitation on Mount Moriah turned his talents toward building shrines for practices that included child sacrifice, right in the shadow of the temple of our glorious God:

> Then Solomon built a high place for Chemosh, the abomination of Moab, in the hill that is close to Jerusalem, and for Molek, the abomination of the children of Ammon. He did the same for all his foreign wives, who burned incense and sacrificed to their gods.
>
> —1 KINGS 11:7–8

A prophecy of apostasy as spoken of in 1 Timothy 4:1 should never surprise us: "Now the Spirit clearly says that in the last times some will depart from the faith and pay attention to seducing spirits and doctrines of devils." Second Thessalonians 2:3 gives us fair warning: "Do not let anyone deceive you in any way. For that Day will not come unless a falling away comes first, and the man of sin is revealed, the son of destruction." The Lord Jesus Himself foreshadowed that before the great and terrible day of the Lord, there would be a great falling away. (See Matthew 24:9–12.)

Having gained the knowledge of the truth, let us remain watchful and vigilant against the spirit of deception. Jude 3 urges us to contend for the truth (fight with all of our strength and might). The admonition to fight presupposes an opposite and opposing enemy. We must remain rooted and grounded in faith, immovable and impenetrable.

There must be birthed in our hearts and in the church a desire for change. There is an unholy alliance that has boiled to the surface in the simmering cauldron of ecumenical religion where everything is a church and everybody is a preacher. Apostasy produces the careless. Idolatry produces cowards because they never see their man-made and flesh-fashioned god move a mountain, fill up a valley, or make a crooked place straight.

The apostate church today will continue its frigid and rigid indifference to a true move of God's Spirit in the earth even as the true apostolic church continues to seek true revival and prepare the earth for the imminent return of our Lord and Savior, Jesus Christ.

The generational seeds of the apostasy that Solomon had sown sprouted almost immediately. He wrote the Book of Proverbs to pass along to his sons the wisdom he'd received from his father, David. Yet biblical history reveals that none of that wisdom was embraced by his boys. May this serve as a constant and unavoidable reminder for Christian parents and preachers in this most critical hour that your children are paying far more attention to what you *do* than to what you *say*.

Almost immediately after Solomon's death the kingdom split in half, north and south, weakening both. Solomon's deadly pattern of tolerating idol worship and spiritual compromise continued for both for much of the next two hundred years, but especially in the northern kingdom, whose steady descent into paganism reached its nadir with the infamous duo Ahab and Jezebel.

The decline of covenantal faithfulness was less rapid but no less relentless in Judah, the southern kingdom. One of several low points came during the reign of King Ahaz. In his debauched sixteen-year tenure as king, this direct descendant of David—the man after God's own heart—plunged Judah into unprecedented depths of demonic idolatry. In the time of Ahaz, the "high places" of demon worship that Solomon had constructed to please his hundreds of pagan wives became more popular than God's holy habitation. Solomon entered into an alliance with Egypt, but Ahaz went much further, actually making Judah a subservient vassal of Assyria. To pay the necessary tribute to this pagan nation, Ahaz looted Jehovah's temple of its gold cladding and ornamentations. The holy brazen altar was literally set aside. In its place, a pagan altar to a pagan demon was given the central location in the holy place. In both natural and spiritual terms the glory, the tangible manifestation of God's presence, had departed. Perhaps the darkest day of Judah's darkest, blackest season came as Ahaz forced one of his sons to "pass through the fire." That's right; he burned his own son alive as a sacrifice to Molech (2 Kings 21:6).

Oh, how far that extraordinary nation, created by God and for His purpose, fell in less than 250 years! Solomon inherited a land at the peak of her illustrious glory and power. Her primary house of worship was pure, resplendent, and graced with the very glory and fire of the Lord God Almighty. Solomon's backsliding sent them down a path that led to every sort of wretched wickedness and demon-possessed perversion. They descended from being the envy of nations to being a shriveled shell, powerless and utterly dependent upon a godless neighbor for their own protection.

Before we shake our heads in disgust at a society that would tolerate and embrace the horror of child sacrifice, we should pause and reflect that millions of so-called American Christians have been tolerating the very same murderous atrocities since 1973. Since *Roe v. Wade* was wrongly decided, over 63 million innocent babies' lives have been extinguished as of this writing.

No funeral nor flowers to even mourn their death. As a culture, we've been legally sanctioning the sacrifice of preborn infants on the altar of sinful lusts and bankrupt consciences of convenience for nearly fifty years. Thankfully, the Supreme Court has recently overturned the Roe decision with the Dobbs ruling, which will return decisions about abortion to state legislatures instead of nine unelected justices. It will not stop abortion on demand, but it will go a long way toward affirming limits to the deadly practice.

We should be mindful that America, too, is only a little less than 250 years since her founding. How desperately far we have fallen in moral collapse and spiritual decay. Compromise, while it may alleviate and take the pressure off, in the end will always result in stagnation and spiritual ruin. Yet I am hopeful for our nation. This hope springs, in part, from what transpired next in Judah. Revival came.

I suppose that every king desires a successor of his own flesh and blood to carry on his legacy. Thus Ahaz did not sacrifice every son. From his birth, Hezekiah was groomed to ascend the king's throne upon his father's death, but as we know, it is not uncommon for a young man to rebel against his father's values. In this case, that was a very good thing. Second Kings 18 discloses that when Hezekiah, son of Ahaz, arose to his place on the throne in Jerusalem at age twenty-five, he "did what was right in the sight of the LORD, according to everything that David his father had done. He removed the high places, broke down the sacred pillars, cut down the Asherah poles, and crushed the bronze serpent that Moses had made, for until those days the children of Israel had made offerings to it" (vv. 3–4).

We're also informed that he "trusted in the LORD…there was no one like him among all the kings of Judah or among those who were before him. He clung to the LORD. He did not depart from following him." And as a result, "The LORD was with him. Wherever he went, he prospered" (vv. 5–7).

Nearly two and a half centuries of self-inflicted, suffocating spiritual drought in Judah came to a sudden close as the glorious, thirst-quenching, life-giving rain of revival began to fall in Hezekiah's time. One of his first initiatives as king was to cleanse the holy temple of God of all the defiling altars and shrines that had been accumulated and functioning there. The second was to order the priests and Levites to prepare to conduct the sacred Passover sacrifice and ordinances. The Scriptures do not divulge how long it had been since Judah had last obeyed God's command to observe Passover, but we know it had been so long that no one among the priesthood had an idea how to perform the divine directive. Nor did they have any of the necessary materials to accomplish the task. So unprepared and untaught were they that they missed the God-designated date, Nisan 14, the first month in Israel's civil calendar. Passover was eventually celebrated, but a month late. One of the foremost hindrances to a move of the Holy Spirit is an inability to discern the timing of God. In order to miss the will of God, one must only be unaware of the proper time. God is a God of time, of seasons and of cycles.

Too many believers never seem to find the center of the circumference of the perfect will of God because they simply don't discern or understand the spiritual cycles or seasons. We do not *find* the will of God. We should wake up in it; we should learn to live in it. Acts 17:28 reminds us, "In Him we live and move and have our being." Friend, if we don't move in Jesus, we dare not move at all.

When my children, Ashton and Austin, were younger, they didn't descend the staircase each morning in a reverent manner and present themselves before my wife, Joni, and me with bowed heads, outstretched hands, and trembling lips inquiring, "Oh, dear gracious father and mother, what is your will for us today?" They didn't do that because they knew what our answer would be: "Get your fine selves upstairs, make your beds, get your book bags with your homework done in them and bring them back down, fix your breakfast cereal and eat it, then put your dishes in the dishwasher before you head off to school for the day." You see, finding and living in the perfect will of God isn't a complicated matter. The only way for them to have missed our will would be to have their alarms set to the wrong time or their calendars on the wrong day.

How indispensable and of utmost importance the observance of Passover was and is to our Father God! We now know that every element and aspect of the Feast of Passover, with the sacrifice of a spotless lamb at its center, was a harbinger pointing to the appointed time when the sinless Son of God would surrender His life on Calvary's cruel, mean, biting beam, there to become the propitiation as the spotless "Lamb of God, who takes away the sin of the world" (John 1:29). Hezekiah clearly perceived the centrality of Passover in the eternal, redemptive plan of God because he sent a letter throughout Judah, as well as to the estranged Israelite remnant of the northern kingdom, pleading with all his heart for them to return to Jerusalem and to the mountain of God. He wrote:

> Sons of Israel, return to the LORD of Abraham, Isaac, and Israel that He might turn to the remnant who has escaped from the king of Assyria. Do not act like your fathers and brothers who were faithless before the LORD God of their fathers, and He appointed them for horror, as you observe. So now do not harden your necks as your fathers, but give yourselves to the LORD and come to the sanctuary that He has consecrated permanently. Serve the LORD your God so that His burning anger might turn away from you all. Because if you return to the LORD, your brothers and children will find compassion before those who have taken them captive, in order to return you to this land. For the LORD your God is gracious and compassionate. He will not turn His face from you *if* you all return to Him.
> —2 CHRONICLES 30:6–9, EMPHASIS ADDED

There that word appears again. *If*... As we'll discover in every revival we examine, the salvation, healing, deliverance, anointings, miracles, signs, and wonders that flow forth in every outpouring are ever and always conditioned upon a "yes" of obedience on the part of God's people. The invitation is divinely extended. But the initial step always belongs to us. "Because if you return to the Lord..." you will invariably be met by a God who is "gracious and merciful," willing and eager to pour out the rain of revival upon your weary and worn, parched and dry soul. *If*...

Another precursor to revival is the willingness of God's people to rise up out of their comfortable homes and familiar routines to assemble (Heb. 10:25). In this case, the people responded to Hezekiah's invitation. For example, verse 11 of 2 Chronicles 30 reveals that members of the distant tribes of Asher, Manasseh, and Zebulun chose to "humble themselves and came to Jerusalem." We have already seen, and will continue to do so, that humility is the language of honor and is at the very heart of the divine prescription for revival. And what an outpouring of renewal and restoration they experienced as a reward. For seven full days they celebrated the Passover enveloped in God's glory with music, singing, and sacrifices to the Lord.

Everywhere idol worship and pagan altars were found, those revenant people destroyed them. This is another of those *"If"* conditions outlined in 2 Chronicles 7:14. The people, en masse, turned from their wicked ways. Multitudes of Israelites from across Judah and from the long-estranged northern tribes like Ephraim and Issachar made their way to Jerusalem to obey the command to celebrate the Passover feast for the first time in their lives. At the end of the week, the spiritually resurrected Israelites could not tolerate the thought of it ending, so they extended the celebration for another seven days. Herein lies another hall-mark of true revival. God's people have no desire to leave the house of God. The Israelites developed an appetite, a deep thirst, a craving for the holy presence of God that overshadowed every-thing that had previously distracted them. They had no time for the rigors of dead, dry religion nor the husks which the swine did eat. The very thought of returning to the past state of normalcy was rejected with rigor and resignation, and their new normal was approached with eager anticipation and expectation!

What an extraordinary season of refreshing, renewal, and reset. What restoration! What recovery! And it all began with a blazing wildfire ignited by a single revived life. As our historical tour continues, we'll be reminded that one lone individual is often all that's required. In this case, that "one" was a young man whose father was so depraved that he sacrificed one of his own sons to the demon-idol Molech. Yet as we'll continue to see, our great God needs only for the lightning bolt of His will to strike a single, solitary dry and desperate heart to spark a mighty revival—and youth is no disqualification.

℞

Igniting a revival is one thing. Sustaining one is another. I have discovered that living in ongoing, perpetual revival requires intentionality and passion. It demands determination and daring. Rarely in history has it been sustained beyond a single generation. Thus we should not be surprised to learn that Judah quickly reverted back to its evil, idolatrous practices upon Hezekiah's exit from the scene. The wise father's body was barely buried before his son and successor, Manasseh, set out to restore and rebuild every single one of the high places of worship and altars of sacrifice Hezekiah, in the heat of revival, had torn down.

Just how wicked was this son? The witness of Scripture says that "Manasseh made Judah and those living in Jerusalem to wander and to perform more evil than the nations that the LORD destroyed from before Israel" (2 Chron. 33:9). His personal sins chronicle a long and sordid life of debauchery. Among his demon-inspired proclivities were a devotion to witchcraft, sexual perversion, gross immorality, and sacrificing his own sons on the altar of false gods. Hezekiah failed to raise up a son willing to tend the flames of revival. Manasseh's son was no better. The Word of God declares that King Amon did what was evil in the sight of the Lord and sacrificed to all the idols that his father had made, and that he "did not humble himself before the LORD" (vv. 22–23). So corrupt and hated was this grandson of Hezekiah that his own servants conspired to murder him.

Two wicked kings in succession ruled the nation out of which God had chosen to bring forth the Messiah, the Savior, His only begotten Son, into a sin-cursed world. For forty-seven years Jacob's prodigal son wallowed in the pigsty of depravity and rebellion. The sand in the hourglass of God's restraint and patience had already run perilously low. His holy prophets had begun warning of impending judgment, and indeed the destruction of the city and the captivity of the nation lay less than fifty years in the future. Yet there must have been some silver-haired intercessors in Judah praying for the nation. Perhaps a weathered company of saints old enough to remember the glorious days of Hezekiah's revival were fasting and imploring heaven for one last refreshing. Maybe a consecrated remnant remembered God's 2 Chronicles 7:14 promise delivered way back in the days of Solomon and began to fast and seek the face of the Lord in earnest. Revival has never and will never be manifested unless and until God's people become impassioned and humble, faithful and fervent, devoted and desperate in prayer.

What we do know with certainty is that only two years into Amon's reign he was cut off, leaving behind an eight-year-old firstborn son named Josiah. This unlikely child, blessed, appointed, and anointed of God, would bring the rain of revival to the parched and barren landscape of the nation once again. Perhaps the prophet Isaiah glimpsed this particular outpouring when he wrote, "...and a little child shall lead them" (Isa. 11:6). Oh, for such a child. Only *if*...

My study of the history of revival strongly suggests that children or young people are quite often the catalyst for great moves of God's Spirit. Back in 1972, as a gangly freshman in high school, I experienced that truth personally and powerfully.

At the time, I was a fifteen-year-old living in a quiet little suburb of Columbus, Ohio. I'd rarely been much farther away from home than to see relatives a couple of hundred miles south in the hills of northern Kentucky. As the close of the school year approached, my excitement rose in anticipation of an event I was scheduled to attend in Dallas. Explo '72, organized by a young, emerging organization called Campus Crusade for Christ, was a six-day event for youth from across the nation.

For four nights, tens of thousands of us slept in sleeping bags on the floors of new, but quite unfinished, apartments. For the duration of the conference we sat transfixed in several different venues while some of the most prominent influential and evangelical leaders of that day spoke with judgment-day honesty and urgency of the need for believers to get serious about the Great Commission, and gave us practical instruction in personally sharing our faith. I can still see the small, yellow-gold booklet used in our training. It was *The Four Spiritual Laws*. In the afternoons, we hit the streets of Dallas to put theory into practice. We eagerly shared the good news of the gospel of Jesus Christ, about wholeness and heaven, with any warm body who would hold still long enough to listen.

Every evening we attended events in the huge, iconic Cotton Bowl. I was overwhelmed to hear men like Billy Graham and others proclaim and extol the power of the gospel to save sinners. And yes, they actually used the words *sin*, *sinfulness*, and *sinner* in their preaching. How inspiring it was for us to be challenged to consecrate our gifts, our energies, and our lives—for the rest of our lives—to extending that hope to the millions upon millions waiting to hear and accept it as we had.

The week culminated with a gospel concert featuring some of the most iconic "Jesus music" artists of that day. Larry Norman. The Archers. Johnny Cash. Kris Kristofferson. The Disciples singing, "I Don't Know Why Jesus Loves Me." I can still hear the voice of the legendary songwriter and vocalist who became my dear friend, Andraé Crouch. I love and revere the historic hymns of the church, but for teenagers in 1972, having contemporary, more popular-styled music that exalted and brought glory to the Lord Jesus was electrifying. Nobody knows exactly how many people jammed into that Cotton Bowl those nights. The official capacity in the stands is nearly one hundred thousand. That night the stands and the playing field were filled and overflowing with young, on-fire, passionate believers. It was unlike anything I had ever seen or dared to even imagine.

What I didn't comprehend at the time was that I was participating in a history-making event—one that launched Campus Crusade for Christ into national prominence. All I knew was that it had changed my life and left the indelible handprint of God upon my heart, which at this very moment is still crying out for more. I have no doubt that many thousands of other young people in those meetings would give the same testimony. That week focused the entire arc of my life and ministry. It lit a fire within me that I've never allowed to be extinguished. I've been tending it, fueling it, protecting and spreading it for nearly fifty years, and I pray that, God being my help, I will never stop. For a surety, revivals often begin in the tender, open, and enthusiastic hearts of the young.

But the Savior did tell us that the kingdom of heaven belongs only to those willing to come as a little child (Matt. 19:14). And Paul reminds us that God delights in using the things the worldly "wise" perceive to be foolish to confound them, and in using people viewed as weak to confound the "mighty" (1 Cor. 1:27).

Josiah was but an eight-year-old child when called upon to assume the throne of Judah. At that moment the professional political pundits probably gave him little to no chance of even surviving, much less succeeding. Yet he would eventually be used of the Lord God to lead a sweeping national revival. The Bible emphatically states that "[Josiah] did what was correct in the eyes of the Lord, and he walked in the ways of David his father and did not turn either to the right or left" (2 Chron. 34:2). When he was still only sixteen, Josiah "began to seek out the God of David his father; and [when he was twenty] he began to cleanse Judah and Jerusalem from high places, Asherah poles, idols, and carved and cast images" (v. 3).

You will recall that one of the key "*If*" stipulations of 2 Chronicles 7:14 is that the people of God must turn from their wicked ways. So this vital season of repentance and reform set the stage for a glorious revival. Eventually, the young king, still in his twenties, tasked several men with the duty of cleansing and restoring the holy temple of Jehovah. This was of absolute necessity because his ungodly grandfather, Manasseh, had sanctioned the abomination of idol worship to once again defile God's sacred and sanctified house. During this restoration, a priest named Hilkiah discovered something quite peculiar: a long-forgotten artifact from a previous era of faithfulness. He came across a dust-and-cobweb-covered scroll containing the Book of the Law—the words God Almighty Himself had dictated to Moses on Mount Sinai more than a thousand years earlier.

God had personally descended from the pavilions of heaven to reveal His commands which "*If*" obeyed would cause His people to flourish and thrive. Those precious words had been disrespected, disregarded, and discarded. The holy, heavenly wisdom and direction of the ages was found lying in filth, buried under the rubble with other despised and desecrated objects. Shoved aside to make room for pagan altars where God's handpicked people bowed themselves down in demon-fueled and sexually charged worship to Baal and many other false gods.

We ought not be too quick to pick up stones to cast at that generation of God's elect. Have not many of God's people today done something similar? Has the inspired, immaculate, infallible, inerrant Word of God been just as neglected and forgotten in many, if not most, households? How many thousands of Bibles gather dust under a pile of worldly magazines? Have not whole churches, and even entire denominations that carry the name of Jesus Christ in their very identity, tossed aside the sacred Scriptures and replaced them with pop psychology and the idolatrous fads of our depraved popular culture?

Is it any wonder, then, that we see these staggering statistics from a recent study: "Of an estimated 176 million American adults who identify as Christian, just 6% or 15 million of them actually hold a biblical worldview." The study also reveals that "while a majority of America's self-identified Christians, including many who identify as evangelical, believe that God is all-powerful, all-knowing and is the Creator of the universe, *more than half* reject a number of biblical teachings and principles, including the existence of the Holy Spirit" (emphasis added).[6]

If that's not bad enough, another study exposed that more than 60 percent of born-again Christians in America between the ages of eighteen and thirty-nine believe that Buddha, Muhammad, and Jesus are all valid paths to salvation.[7]

Yes, Josiah was born into a culture in desperate need of and bankrupt of revival. But so were we!

At this divinely orchestrated rediscovery, King Josiah, possessed of the spirit of revival, ordered that the book be read in his presence. Hearing the eternal Word of the living God proclaimed did in Josiah what it always does to softened hearts and contrite spirits. It cut. It convicted. It convinced. Then it kindled a flame and caught a nation on fire.

Upon hearing the living, heart-penetrating words of truth, Josiah tore his clothes and humbled himself before the God of all that was, is, and is to come. Then he gave the order for every man, woman, and child in Judah to assemble together. Hebrews 10:25 admonishes us to "not forsake the assembling of ourselves together." Not for us to "gather"—a gathering is simply a group of disjointed, disconnected, dislocated, and diverse parts without function. To assemble is different altogether. I have vivid memories of all-too-many Christmas Eves that Joni and I stayed up most of the night "assembling" those "must-have" toys for Ashton and Austin. You know the ones I'm referring to, with all the little pieces and parts, with nails and screws and pins. All of the parts were "gathered" in their respective boxes, but our "calling," our responsibility, was to "assemble" them together as one functional unit. The Spirit of God is "assembling" His church, bone to bone, sinew to sinew, flesh to flesh. And when we are fully assembled, we will experience the Spirit of God breathe upon dead bones once again!

Standing outside the temple, overlooking the confused and curious throng below, Josiah, the king himself, read aloud to them the same sacred, life-giving, revival-birthing, flame-fanning words of eternal truth that had been read to him. As it unfailingly will, the living words of the sovereign Creator of the universe, boldly proclaimed, had the same explosive effect upon the hearts of the people.

> The king stood in his place and made a covenant before the LORD, to walk after the LORD, and to keep His commandments and His testimonies and His statutes with all his soul, to perform the words of the covenant written in this book....And all his days they did not turn away from the LORD God of their fathers.
> —2 CHRONICLES 34:31, 33

Sitting is a contented posture. Where you sit, you intend to stay. Tens of thousands of church congregations across America are sitting stagnant, desperately waiting to hear God's divine edict proclaimed in just such power and raw, unadulterated purity. Oh, if only those who stand in our pulpits today would return to an unapologetic declaration of God's standards and commands.

If... Only if!

As unlikely as this might seem, the witness of Scripture is clear and sure. A mere child ignited one of the most powerful and profound revivals in the history of Israel. Let us "never despise one of these little ones" (Matt. 18:6, CJB) nor look down upon our youth (1 Tim. 4:12). Let us take hold of the horns of the sacred altar of prayer and plead with God over the divine destiny of our children, for they too may become the catalyst for a mighty move of God, a revival, an awakening. Pray over them, prophesy to them, teach and train them in kingdom realities. They don't need another trinket of technology. They need the transforming power of God! And under God, do not send them, but take them, to church. If you must choose between church and Little League or cheerleading or dance or a hundred other perfectly wholesome activities—choose church! If parents would put God first and lead their children in full surrender to the lordship of the living Christ... *If...* Only *if!* We'd live in a perpetual state of revival!

౭

With both Hezekiah and Josiah, the revivals they began were national in scope. But make no mistake, revival can be personal as well. Indeed, one of the reasons I have poured out my passion onto these pages is to equip you to experience your own *personal* revival. (We'll explore that more in chapters to come.) However, we see biblical examples of both kinds of revival in the life of the prophet Jonah. You know his story well. Even the unchurched and unbelieving can tell you the broad outlines of the Jonah narrative, so I won't recount it in detail here.

The prophet received a divine directive to go and warn the people of Nineveh—a pagan Gentile city near the border of the northern kingdom, Israel—of impending divine judgment should they refuse to repent of their damnable depravity and demonic debauchery. For a variety of personal reasons, Jonah was in no way inclined to obey the command of the Lord, and so he attempted to escape by running hard and fast in the opposite direction. You know what happened next. While fleeing by boat, a great storm arose, and Jonah was swept overboard and subsequently swallowed by a great fish. In terms of types and symbols, this represents Jonah's "death." Indeed, Jesus Himself used Jonah's time in the belly of the whale as a metaphor for His own three days in the "belly" of the earth (Matt. 12:38–42). Just as Jesus conquered death and was resurrected, Jonah, too, experienced a form of resurrection when he was regurgitated onto the shore right on Nineveh's doorstep! You could say Jonah was a revenant.

I would remind you that the very word *revival* speaks of being made alive again from the dead. So it is doubly appropriate to say that Jonah experienced personal revival here. Jonah repented, submitted to God's will, and was restored to fellowship with God. Jonah then, in obedience, declared the strong and stern word of the Lord to the Ninevites. And they responded en masse! Imagine it. A large, prominent pagan city entered into mass repentance before the Most High God for a season. Remarkable! From this we can take great encouragement that no American city is too reprobate or too far gone to experience the flame of revival. The convicting, convincing power of the Holy Ghost is well able and more capable to pierce the most stone-cold hearts and draw sinners to the cross of Christ and God's ever-abundant mercies. But if... Only *if*!

By the way, I recall a time as a much younger preacher when I delivered a sermon based on the Jonah passage. In those days, I was subject to bursts of enthusiasm, and I got excited, ran long, and had to cut the message short. After the service Mother Parsley lovingly said, "That was a powerful message, son. So anointed. But next time, try to get Jonah delivered from the belly of the great fish. It'll make a very good closing!"

As Scripture has shown countless times, our God's heart is to revive individual lives of men, women, and children and then use the fire and passion they carry from the altar to set everyone around them ablaze with His glory. This is essentially what happened in each of the Old Testament examples we've examined thus far. So hold on, because the prophetic and powerful pattern continues right into the New Testament and beyond.

જી

The apostle Peter was at the low point of his life, filled with shame and completely estranged from Jesus, his friend and Lord. Has any believer ever been in as desperate a need of revival as was Peter following his oath-swearing denial that he even knew Him? Not once, not twice, but three times, all prophesied by the Lord Jesus (John 13:38). Peter had repudiated and rejected the

One who had chosen him, taught him, and loved him. All this after his boastful, prideful statement at the triclinium, "I will lay down my life for Your sake" (John 13:37). And oh, what mercies and miracles this broken man had witnessed at the hands of his friend.

He'd watched the Son of Man wipe blindness from Bartimaeus' eyes, straighten the stooped, and feed a multitude with nothing more than a boy's sack lunch and a spoken blessing. He'd stood in spellbound wonder as the Lord gave a grief-stricken mother back her son with nothing more than a simple touch on his casket. Peter had seen his mighty Master command the wind and waves. He'd watched Him walk up on the water and, when beckoned, had even received the faith to walk on the water himself. Then, as now, "faith comes by hearing, and hearing by the word of God" (Rom. 10:17).

Yet in the vulnerable hour of his Master's greatest need, he deserted Him. In the very moment his friend most needed to know He was not alone, Peter had done more than abandon Him. He had repudiated Him.

He'd fled. Cowered. Hid himself away while Roman soldiers led the Lamb of God away to a long and torturous night of brutal beatings and ultimately the unspeakable cruelties of death by crucifixion on a Roman cross.

What a disastrous downfall. Only days earlier Peter was convinced that he had reached the pinnacle and purpose of his life. In an electrifying moment, the Spirit of God had revealed to him that his friend and leader was none other than the Messiah of all humanity Himself. Indeed, this backward fisherman from the hillbilly north was a key member of His inner circle! In response, Jesus had proclaimed that He would build His *ekklesia*—His assembled army—on the very revelation that Peter had been given! Peter could imagine his glorious future stretching out in front of him. The Messiah would soon take His deserved place on David's throne in Jerusalem, and Peter would be at His right hand.

That was the plan. Until it wasn't.

When the Lord Jesus took His place, not on the regal throne but standing accused in front of the Sanhedrin, on trial and facing almost certain death, Peter's courage collapsed like a house of cards. Confusion filled his mind and panic gripped his soul. In a matter of days Peter had plummeted from the heights of confidence into a black chasm of fear, shame, and self-loathing. Lost in a sea of regret, he returned to the only thing he felt confident about. He returned to the place and life he'd known before the carpenter from Nazareth walked into it and changed everything. It was almost as if those three years of his life were but a dream and evaporated. It was a type of apocalyptic living death. But we know the One who can revive the dead. The One who once presented a series of parables about a lost sheep, a lost coin, and a lost son now came looking for a lost and lonely, perplexed and puzzled friend.

You likely know the story. Peter and a few of the other disciples were fishing on the Sea of Galilee when their revenant Lord appeared on the shore. There was a flash of recognition, at which Peter rebaptized himself, leaping into the water and hurriedly swimming to his Savior. The revival of a failed man's heart had already begun. After a breakfast of fish, the process continued in a private and profoundly meaningful conversation between the two:

> Jesus said to Simon Peter, "Simon, son of John, do you love Me more than these [others do—with total commitment and devotion]?" He said to Him, "Yes, Lord; You know that I love You [with a deep, personal affection, as for a close friend]." Jesus said to him, "Feed My lambs." Again He said to him a second time, "Simon, son of John, do you love Me [with total commitment and devotion]?" He said to Him, "Yes, Lord; You know that I love You [with a deep, personal affection, as for a close friend]." Jesus said to him, "Shepherd My sheep." He said to him the third time, "Simon, son of John, do you love Me [with a deep, personal

affection for Me, as for a close friend]?" Peter was grieved
that He asked him the third time, "Do you [really] love
Me [with a deep, personal affection, as for a close friend]?"
And he said to Him, "Lord, You know everything; You
know that I love You [with a deep, personal affection, as
for a close friend]." Jesus said to him, "Feed My sheep."
—JOHN 21:15–17, AMP

Peter had buried himself in a tomb of self-loathing shame. But
the voice of the Master saying "Come forth" brought him back to
life. Throughout this chapter we've seen how one truly repentant
and revived individual can spark a much larger, broader revival.
So we must take note that, not too many weeks after this lakeside
revival meeting, Peter and 119 others would find themselves in
a house in Jerusalem awaiting a promise of power from another
world. When that promise accompanied by a mighty rushing
wind arrived, they all, including Peter, received a supernatural
infusion of resurrection power. Literal tongues of fire rested
upon each one of them.

The terrified man who had thrice denied he even knew the
living Savior walked out of the room, head high and shoulders
squared, into the center of the city to boldly and bravely proclaim Jesus as Christ to the very throng that had only weeks earlier clamored to Pilate for His crucifixion. He lifted his gravelly
voice like a trumpet, carrying an anointing that in all likelihood
had never been heard before. He gave a clarion call and preached
the gospel of Christ in its entirety for the first time in human
history. After fearlessly calling the people out for having crucified the very Son of God, Peter concluded by giving the altar call
with this heart-arresting appeal:

Repent and be baptized, every one of you, in the name
of Jesus Christ for the forgiveness of sins, and you shall
receive the gift of the Holy Spirit....Be saved from this
perverse generation.
—ACTS 2:38, 40

Who were the congregants assembled for this inaugural sermon of the church age? Well, amidst the crowd of Jewish zealots who had raised their accusing voices in unison and demanded Jesus' death there were likely dozens, perhaps hundreds, of gawking, rough, and rugged Roman soldiers. Some of these surely had participated in Jesus' scourging and crucifixion. Given the makeup of this audience, how many would you expect to openly, publicly repent and surrender to the gospel's message? One, maybe? Or two, perhaps? A few more might have stealthily approached to ask questions after the crowd dispersed. This is what all reason and logic would suggest. But that's the point: revival transcends reason. The convicting, convincing power of the Holy Ghost defies all logical expectancy. As the ensuing verses reveal, "that day about *three thousand souls* were added to them" (v. 41, emphasis added). That's quite a response to an altar call given by a novice preacher. Never, ever underestimate the mighty power of the holy anointing of God graced upon a humbly submitted man or woman.

Even better, these weren't just three thousand emotional "decisions." These were three thousand repentant people who had been "converted" and baptized in the very fiery presence of God Almighty! These were new creatures that the world around them and hell beneath them had never encountered before. They were instantly transformed, born-again firebrands of revival!

If... Only *if* our altars (if there are any left) could be flooded and our churches filled with men and women who were truly convicted of sin and convinced of righteousness as these surely were! They were three thousand genuinely revived, revenant souls, for as we read also:

> They continued steadfastly in the apostles' teaching and fellowship, in the breaking of bread and in the prayers. Fear came to every soul. And many wonders and signs were done through the apostles. All who believed were together and had all things in common. They sold their property and goods and distributed them to all, according to their

need. And continuing daily with one mind in the temple, and breaking bread from house to house, they ate their food with gladness and simplicity of heart, praising God and having favor with all the people. And the Lord added to the church daily those who were being saved.

—ACTS 2:42–47

Again, that's an astonishing altar call for a first-time preacher given the nature of that crowd. But that is the very nature of revival. It makes the improbable possible. Speaking of the improbable...

This is just not the way we mere mortals would have crafted the story. Yet our infinitely creative Creator wrote it so that the world-changing, empire-shaking, hell-destroying church had its beginning with a crude and unlearned fisherman who only weeks earlier was terrified by a young lady who simply asked him if he knew his leader. The movement that would sweep the world and remake civilization itself was launched by a traitor who denied the One to whom he'd pledged loyalty unto death, then walked away from his calling and back to his old life. But revival came to his shattered soul.

That's the unrivaled, transforming power of true revival. And beloved, that power didn't end in the first century. Oh no. As we're about to see, the glorious *if* promise of 2 Chronicles 7:14 has never been repealed. And throughout history those who have taken God up on His extraordinary offer have experienced and enjoyed that life-giving rain in overwhelming, tangible abundance.

Chapter 2

SNAPSHOTS OF
HISTORICAL REVIVALS

CAN A PRAYER meeting change the course of history? I know with certainty that it can because it happened. On a Wednesday morning, August 13, 1727, something broke through from the grand dimensions of heaven invading this fallen, broken, blue-marble planet—something so potent that it would ultimately alter the course of world events and transform the eternal destinies of countless millions. Indeed, much of what we now understand as missionary methods and strategy was birthed in the glory of that gathering. This stunning event transpired in Herrnhut, an obscure little hamlet in a remote corner of central Europe near what is today the intersection of the borders of Germany, the Czech Republic, and Poland. A little background will help you understand the meaning and power of this extraordinary out-pouring, now commonly called the Moravian Revival.

Herrnhut was a village of refugees. For several years, Bible-believing, Christ-following Protestants had been finding refuge from persecution in the domain of a righteous German nobleman named Count Nikolaus Ludwig von Zinzendorf, or simply Count Zinzendorf. He was a remarkably distinguished man and had been set apart and marked by the Almighty from a very early age. At only four years of age, Zinzendorf drew up and signed a cov-enant vow to God. In a childish scrawl he wrote: "Dear Savior, do Thou be mine, and I will be Thine."[1] And to think there were no light shows, ice cream, Bozo the clown, nor Fufu the dog to entertain him in children's church.

Several years later, while still in his teens, Zinzendorf found himself in Dusseldorf art gallery standing transfixed before a massive painting of the crucified Christ. What, no screaming guitars and pounding drums? No pizza party or movie? Beneath the painting hung a plaque that simply but with resounding truth read, "This have I done for thee; What hast thou done for me?" Moved to live a life that would answer that haunting question, Zinzendorf recommitted his life to Jesus Christ and adopted these words as his creed and vow: "I have one passion: it is Jesus, Jesus only."[2]

Zinzendorf came to real, saving faith in a time of tremendous spiritual upheaval across Europe. The Protestant Reformation had touched many nations that continued to be dominated by Roman Catholic monarchs fiercely loyal to Rome. Pockets of born-again, Bible-believing, and frequently Holy Spirit–filled Christians had sprung up all over the continent. Many of these faced brutal persecution and staunch attempts at suppression. One of the earliest of these suppressions was leveled against the followers of Jan Hus (anglicized as John Hus) in Bohemia, now a part of the modern Czech Republic. In 1415, one hundred years before Martin Luther nailed his "95 Theses" to the door of the Castle Church in Wittenberg, Hus was burned at the stake for the cause of Christ. Hus' execution led to a revival of biblical faith in Bohemia and Moravia that produced a movement called the Unity of the Brethren, or simply "the Brethren."

Three centuries later, around 1720, intense persecution of the Brethren in Moravia led a large number of them to look for a refuge of safety for their families—a place where they could pray and worship as the Holy Spirit and Word of God directed their consciences. They found just such a refuge on the vast estate of young Count Zinzendorf. They named their new religious refugee community Herrnhut, meaning "The Lord's Watch."

The revenant believers there built a humble assembly building, and in 1727 a group of men began to meet there regularly to receive Holy Communion together. These gatherings were compelled by a rising spiritual hunger for God's divine presence that they all were experiencing. Oh God, how we need such a stirring among us today. If... Only *if*!

As the men—many of whom were only in their late twenties—continued to congregate and seek the face of God together, their gnawing sense of dissatisfaction only grew. May our satisfaction, as was theirs, become our dissatisfaction with the current presence and power of our King upon and manifested through us. As one body of believers, they began to sense there was more in God, more *of* God, than they were experiencing.

Then on Sunday morning, August 10, three days before the divine deluge and breakthrough, a guest preacher, a man named Rothe, came to speak to the assembly. An escalating sense of spiritual expectancy in the community resulted in a house packed to the rafters with men, women, and children. Midway through his sermon, Rothe abruptly stopped mid-sentence, dropped to his knees, and began praying with new fervency and intensity. The startled congregation stood in absolute silence for a moment or two; then, one by one, they too fell to their knees and began to cry out in great power at the throne of God. Soon the entire room was united in Holy Ghost–inspired intercession. They continued unabated in earnest until well after midnight. By the holy unction of God's Spirit, the believers of "The Lord's Watch" were learning to "watch and pray" (Matt. 26:41).

Think about that for a moment. A small but serious group of believers knelt upon a hard, wooden floor and fervently prayed for more than twelve hours without complaint or coffee break. They were completely unconcerned about getting to the local restaurant before all the hot rolls were gone. They didn't take a break for dinner. No one checked their cell phone or watch. There was no nursery, no giant screen nor video. No padded pew, no ornate architecture, no board meeting nor annual budget. But they modeled what the old Baptist and Pentecostal saints I grew up with called "praying through." The seeds sown in those prayer meetings would bear fruit swiftly. Only three days later, the noon Holy Communion gathering that had for months only consisted of a handful of men was now filled to overflowing with men, women, and children. As they entered, there was a corporate "knowing" that something was different, something had changed; the very atmosphere seemed to vibrate. The floorboards of that little church had been saturated by the anointed tears of genuine intercessors, crying out with all of their hungry hearts for a move of God.

Later, not one of the people who were present on that momentous day could begin to adequately describe what had transpired. It was a glorious, joyous, rapturous blur. One chronicler wrote that they walked out of the meeting "hardly knowing whether they belonged to earth or had already gone to Heaven."[3] All that those in attendance could verbalize with certainty was that the Holy Spirit of the living God had been poured out upon them in a way that reminded them all of the day of Pentecost described in Acts, the second chapter. And this was no fleeting, fleshly, emotional frenzy. Those who emerged from that humble house of worship were forever changed, and they had become carriers of a Holy Ghost contagion infecting others with the same passion and fervency that had been miraculously imparted to them. Revival is contagious.

In the days, weeks, and years that followed, that remote Moravian community of roughly three hundred souls would become a global force of missionary evangelism, with Zinzendorf leading the way. The late, great historian of Christian missions Dr. Gustav Warneck wrote this concerning the long-term effects of the Moravian revival: "This small church in twenty years, called into being more missions than the whole Evangelical Church had done in two centuries."[4]

It should not surprise us to learn that the twenty-seven-year-old Count Zinzendorf himself, the one who as a teen had vowed to make "Jesus only" his life's sole passion and pursuit, was present on the very day of this historic outpouring. Nearly three decades later, on the anniversary of the revival's beginning, he attempted to explain to a gathering of curious British Christians what preceded and produced the earth-shaking divine visitation in that meeting.

> On this day twenty-seven years ago the Congregation of Herrnhut, assembled for communion...were all dissatisfied with themselves. They had quit judging each other because they had become convinced, each one, of his lack of worth in the sight of God and each felt himself at this Communion to be [in] view of the noble countenance of the Saviour.[5]

On another occasion, Zinzendorf also recalled:

> The Saviour permitted to come upon us a Spirit of whom we had hitherto not had any experience or knowledge. Hitherto WE had been the leaders and helpers. Now the Holy Spirit Himself took full control of everything and everybody [emphasis in original].[6]

Before we continue, I am compelled to pause here and ask that you would examine the above details and statements in the light of the fourfold *if* of 2 Chronicles 7:14. Please recall that the stipulations to be met that result in God's promise fulfilled are that God's people would (1) humble themselves, (2) pray, (3) seek His face, and (4) turn from their sin. Is it possible that this seemingly insignificant and small fellowship of believers fulfilled their end requirements and therefore became the recipients of this divine promise?

"Humble?" We just read Count Zinzendorf testify in his own words that they all came with an overwhelming sense of unworthiness and that they were utterly "dissatisfied with themselves."

"Pray?" These were a praying people who had just experienced a remarkable Holy Spirit–led, orchestrated, and empowered season of gut-wrenching, soul-disturbing, hell-dethroning intercession.

"Seek His face?" The young men were meeting practically daily to partake of Holy Communion together in order to better connect to the living God and to rightly discern the body of His precious Son in and through a revelation of the elements.

"Turn from their sin?" One revival historian records, "The brethren had been judging one another; doctrinal disputes were common; heated arguments that threatened division and discord were the order of the day."[7] Much of the prayer that preceded the revival was prayer of repentance. Indeed, that long, anguished day and night of praying that preceded the outpouring of the Spirit by three days contained prayers of confession and contrition. Tears of sorrow and remorse baptized that altar.[8]

Why would, why should, we marvel that these believers experienced a mighty, world-shaking outpouring of revival? After all, these God seekers followed our Father's "*if*" prescription to the letter. Of course, He responded by fulfilling His promise! He always has, He always will. He is faithful. He is true. He watches over His word to perform it (Jer. 1:12)!

The Moravian Brethren had endured centuries of brutal persecution for their faith. They persisted, and therefore they prevailed in victory and triumph. Their forefathers had joyfully endured loss of homes and lands, imprisonment, and torture for their devotion to the Lord Jesus and the inerrancy and accuracy of His eternal Word. Now, here in small and obscure Herrnhut, "The Lord's Watch," the descendants of those who had "loved not their [own] lives even unto death" (Rev. 12:11, ESV) had watched the Lord God pour out a fresh baptism of His Holy Spirit. As on the day of Pentecost, that fire from heaven filled them with both the deep desire and the empowerment to become His witnesses to the "uttermost parts of the earth." Virtually overnight they became the world's evangelists and missionaries. By the hundreds they would carry red-hot embers from that fire to wherever the name of Jesus Christ was least known, including Greenland,

South Africa, Australia, and even Tibet.[9] Naturally, these long-suffering saints carried the compassionate heart of Christ for the oppressed. So as missionaries they specifically targeted much of their ministry to suffering or enslaved groups of people.

Historians of the Moravian movement record that on October 8, 1732, two such missionaries stood on the deck of a ship sliding out of Copenhagen harbor, bound for the plantations of the Danish West Indies. Those young men, Johann Dober, a potter, and David Nitschmann, a carpenter, were forsaking the comforts and familiarity of home and family to bring the light of the gospel to the most dehumanized and suffering people on the planet and, in Christlike surrender, putting themselves in their place. The Moravian histories record that as the ship slid away from her moorings, the two looked to their friends and families remaining at the dock and lifted up a cry that would instantly become both the motto and the motivation for Moravian missionaries all over the world: "May the Lamb that was slain receive the reward of His suffering!"

Oh, what a tidal wave of transformation that Wednesday outpouring produced in the extraordinary Moravian believers. A love for Jesus Christ and an all-consuming, breathtaking passion to see precious, created-in-the-image-of-God people perishing without the saving grace of the Lord and facing eternity separated from Him in a place called hell come to know Him as Savior is the hallmark of a revived people. To fan the flames of that revival as well as provide heavenly support to the missionaries who would soon be heading out across the world, those who remained in Herrnhut devoted themselves to ceaseless prayer. In fact, only two weeks after the outpouring of revival, twenty-four men and twenty-four women committed themselves before God to spending one hour each day in prayer and consecration. These inspired intercessors divided the twenty-four-hour day among themselves and launched a round-the-clock prayer vigil that continued for one hundred years!

The Moravians eventually even developed their own seal—a

sort of coat of arms—to signify their movement and mission. The seal featured the image of a lamb carrying a flag emblazoned with a red cross on a white field. Surrounding the image in a circle were the words "Our Lamb Has Conquered. Let Us Follow Him."

Some of those ember-carrying, firebrand missionaries followed Him to New World shores of what would become the United States.

Like floating embers from a forest fire, carried upon the wind for miles and igniting other blazes, the revival-born fervor of the Moravians spread to other groups and denominations, inspiring them to implore heaven for lost souls and for the power of the Holy Ghost. As we'll see on the pages to come, many of those sparks landed in the United States. For example, Schoenbrunn and Gnadenhutten were the pioneering Moravian missionary outposts in unsettled Ohio. These historic places are just one hundred miles east-northeast of Columbus, where I live today and the area in which I grew up. But my family heritage is rooted a few hundred miles in the other direction—in eastern Kentucky. Many of my most precious, profound, and powerful childhood memories run back to those deep, dark hills and forests. Some of my most transformational encounters with God as a young man took place there too. And not far from that rocky soil, in 1801 the flames of revival ignited a white-hot inferno in a place called Cane Ridge.

❧

"Lord, make it like Cane Ridge." No more than a morning's drive from the fountainhead of my family's lineage in eastern Kentucky is the site of a revival of astonishing power and intensity. The events that transpired in those days of glory thrilled the faithful and terrified sinners. This monumental move of God left such an indelible mark that for many years afterward revival-hungry, presence-driven saints across the nation cried out for God Almighty to send a visitation of the Holy Ghost to them in an equivalent outpouring as He did for a small, backcountry church at the turn of the nineteenth century.

In the summer of 1800, minister Barton Stone attended a revival in Logan County, Kentucky, led by James McGready. Encouraged by the demonstration of God's Spirit at the event, the sweeping harvest of souls, the redemptive impact, and the resulting cultural shift he witnessed in the local community, Stone commenced planning for a similar revival at his own modest church back home in Cane Ridge the following year.

Of course, a move of God cannot simply be planned and scheduled into existence. As G. Campbell Morgan, the mighty revivalist and eyewitness to the great Welsh Revival which would break out almost exactly one hundred years after the events at Cane Ridge, once wrote: "We cannot organize revival, but we can set our sails to catch the wind from Heaven when God chooses to blow upon His people once again."[10] It's true; you can't organize a revival. But you can position yourself for just such an expression from heaven by simply submitting yourself to the ancient "*if*" requirements of 2 Chronicles 7:14.

The dates of Barton Stone's meetings ultimately arrived. Keep in mind that this was long before the days of mass-marketing advertising and social and broadcast media. The invention of the radio was more than one hundred years away at this time. Word of the revival meetings spread predominately by word of mouth, which to this day remains the most effective means of promoting the gospel. Nevertheless, by Saturday evening, the second night of the weekend-long camp meeting (so called because attendees would travel by wagon and camp out in the surrounding woodlands for the duration of the revival), the number of people who arrived at this little backwoods church to hear the gospel of Christ proclaimed under supernatural Holy Ghost power with its accompanying demonstrations of miracles, signs, and wonders was estimated to be near 30,000! The largest city in the state of Kentucky at the time, Lexington, had a population of under 1,800. Today Lexington's population is roughly 320,000. So in proportional terms that revival meeting was the equivalent of more than five million people showing up for a church gathering today! This was God. This was glory. This is what we desire, intercede, and preach for today. If... Only *if*!

Gospel meetings were certainly not unheard of in that day and time, but for unexplainable natural reasons, word about the Cane Ridge outpouring spread like a California wildfire blazing across Kentucky, Ohio, and Tennessee, seeming to supernaturally capture imaginations and ignite spiritual hunger in every corner. A divine force drew them. They were compelled by an inward desire to come, and come they did by the tens of thousands. They threw a few days' supplies into their wooden wagons and set out upon tortuous wilderness roads at great personal peril in search of just a glimpse of the glory of God poured out from heaven in the lumbering Kentucky hills. Please understand, this is no evangelistically spun tall tale amplified by two hundred years of storytelling. What transpired at Cane Ridge was nothing short of an awful, alarming, life-altering advent of God's Holy Spirit reminiscent of what the thundering prophet called for in Isaiah, chapter 64:

> Oh, that You would rend the heavens and come down, that the *mountains* might shake at Your presence, as when the melting fire burns, as the fire causes the waters to boil, to make Your name known to Your adversaries, that the nations may tremble at Your presence! When You did awesome things for which we did not look, You came down; the *mountains* quaked at Your presence.
> —ISAIAH 64:1–3, EMPHASIS ADDED

A local atheist skeptic at the time, James Finley, described what he witnessed when he visited Cane Ridge to attempt to disprove its authenticity. Even as a "secret agent" of hell, sent to see why tens of thousands had gathered in the Kentucky woods, he wrote:

The noise was like the roar of Niagara. The vast sea of human beings seemed to be agitated as if by a storm. I counted seven ministers, all preaching at one time, some on stumps, others in wagons and one standing on a tree which had, in falling, lodged against another. I stepped up on a log where I could have a better view of the surging sea of humanity. The scene that then presented itself to my mind was indescribable. At one time I saw at least five hundred swept down in a moment as if a battery of a thousand guns had been opened upon them, and then immediately followed shrieks and shouts that rent the very heavens.[11]

Finley later wrote, "I fled for the woods and wished I had stayed at home!"[12] But when revival breaks out the relentless "hound of heaven" will not be denied when He sets His sights on a sinner. Finley turned around, no doubt compelled by the Holy Spirit. Shortly he, too, succumbed to the flood of conviction, repented, and was saved. How saved? Bible saved! He became a new creature (2 Cor. 5:17). No "Now I lay me down to sleep" prayer. No thirty-second confession with no contrition. No, he was truly born again (John 3:17). He was eternally changed into a new man and became a traveling Methodist circuit preacher spreading the same glorious gospel he first heard at Cane Ridge.

Mighty moves of God's Spirit are rarely quiet, tidy, dignified affairs. Throughout the camp meeting there were reports of men, women, and children falling to the ground shrieking. People sang, danced, groaned, and wept bitterly. Those receiving salvation in full pardon from their sins became hysterical and were overcome with involuntary bodily shakings that would later be referred to as "the jerks." Peter Cartwright, who was converted to Christ Jesus as a teenager at Cane Ridge that weekend and who later became a Methodist missionary, described this demonstration of the Holy Ghost in these words: "I always looked upon the jerks as a judgment sent from God, first, to bring sinners to repentance; and, secondly to show professors that God could work with or without means, and that he could work over and above means, and do whatsoever seemeth him good, to the glory of his grace and the salvation of the world."[13]

The apex of all Christian endeavor must become to place the jewel of a soul in the crown of our Savior so that the Lamb slain may receive the reward of His suffering.

However one may seek to intellectualize, explain away, or dismiss phenomena like "the jerks," the fainting, the mourning, the laughter, the baseball-stadium-sized crowds, or the mass salvations of the lost and dying destitute throngs of humanity, it can never be disputed nor denied that God Almighty Himself came down in an awe-inspiring, skeptic-silencing, atheist-converting, life-altering, history-making visitation of the Holy Ghost in the wooded mountains of Cane Ridge, Kentucky, that mighty and monumental weekend—and it was far from being the only American outpouring of that era. The nineteenth century overflowed with very similar demonstrations. The fire of God-inspired, heaven-sent, authentic revival did not fall only on country folks. As we're about to see, America's great cities were disturbed, stirred, and affected as well. And like fingerprints and snowflakes, each move of God has its own DNA.

୨୦

Many outpourings are noisy and characterized by an extended season of bold, high-energy proclamation of the gospel. But not all of them. Some are graced of God by being prayer-driven rather than preaching-driven. At times the only manifestation of which we become aware is that of humble and obedient saints quietly, consistently imploring heaven on behalf of those lost without the saving power of the living Christ.

Such was the case in the Fulton Street Revival of 1857, a "largely forgotten chapter of American church history," during which some calculations show that "as many as 3 percent of the population of the United States may have been converted during what came to be known as the 'Businessmen's Awakening.'"[14] There, a New York City businessman named Jeremiah Lanphier found himself with a broken heart overflowing with compassion for the desperate, lost souls all around him. Those "without Christ, being aliens from the commonwealth of Israel, and strangers from the covenants of promise, having no hope, and without God in the world" (Eph. 2:12, KJV).

In the fall of 1857, Lanphier, a layman with a heart for God, received the divine deposit of an idea, a heavenly download by the Spirit of God. His inspiration involved holding a weekly hour-long prayer meeting at Old Dutch North Church in downtown New York City. In that day lower Manhattan was nothing like what we see today. The first mayor of New York City was elected only two years earlier. The city resembled more of a Wild West frontier town with mud streets and plank-board sidewalks. An abundance of saloons played host to drunkards and prostitutes, tenement houses were jammed to the rafters with impoverished immigrants, and rampant lawlessness was fueled by large criminal gangs. In the very same year Lanphier received his God-idea, downtown New York City experienced major riots. The first of these, the terrible New York City Police Riot, involved rival police forces and was triggered by efforts to rein in widespread corruption among the police. One month later the Dead Rabbits Riot sprang from a massive brawl between two criminal gangs in the Five Points district in Lower Manhattan. This bloody event served as the context for Martin Scorsese's 2002 film, *Gangs of New York*. The Five Points district lay only a few blocks north of the church where Lanphier began to hold prayer meetings. This should be our response to the current unrest in our culture… Only *if!*

It should not come as any surprise that Lanphier became burdened for the lost, desperate, destitute souls that he encountered around him every day. In obedience, he distributed handmade flyers throughout the area. These said only:

> Wednesday prayer meeting from 12 to 1 o'clock. Stop 5, 10 or 20 minutes, or the whole time, as your time admits.

Lanphier then ascended the staircase leading to the third-floor room the church assigned for his use and simply waited. That was all. He had no marketing team. There was no social media campaign. No church committees made plans over pastries and coffee. He was just one man desperate for revival with a fistful of crude flyers. Oh, *if* only...

If only we had such men and women in *our* bone-dry day of hatred and division, of violence and corruption. Ordinary believers with attentive ears attuned to the Master's voice. Only *if*...God could locate a people willing to humble themselves and pray. What might happen in our time? Perhaps we can take some insight and encouragement from what happened on Fulton Street. Let's never forget the admonition that prayerlessness is sin—perhaps the most common and widespread sin in today's church.

At noon on that first Wednesday, Lanphier found himself completely alone. Nevertheless, he began to pray. At 12:10 he remained alone. By 12:20 not a soul had joined him. Finally, at 12:30, the welcome sound of footsteps came from outside the room. His first prayer partner had finally arrived. By the end of the hour there were six men in that room praying in agreement for the Lord God Almighty to reach even one with the glorious gospel of the living Christ. It is, after all, all about the one (Luke 15:4). The first refreshing drops of Holy Ghost rain in the Businessman's Revival had begun to fall.

The next week there were twenty intercessors gathered. The following week their group swelled to forty. Some stayed for only five minutes, but the majority used their designated lunch hour and spent it all pleading for souls dying without Christ. In a very short time, Lanphier and his new brothers in spiritual arms sensed once a week wasn't enough. They agreed to begin meeting every day. They also established four simple rules to guide and order their precious, Holy Ghost–empowered hour of prayer each day:

1. The leader was limited to ten minutes.

2. Other speakers and those leading in prayer were limited to five minutes.

3. There were to be not more than two consecutive addresses and prayers.

4. No controversial points were to be discussed.[15]

These guideposts were adopted to guarantee that this divinely orchestrated group was assembled for one singular purpose—prayer. These men were supremely focused upon pleading with heaven for God's Spirit to pour down on them and to, by His omnipotent mercy and grace, forgive the sins and save for eternity the unbelievers around them. This was not about debating controversial topics nor arguing over doctrinal differences. Nor was it a platform for grandstanding or selfish ambition. Far too great a number of "modern" preachers are afflicted with a malady that compels them to hold forth at length anytime a crowd gathers. And the larger the crowd, the stronger the compulsion. The boundaries of godly wisdom adopted by Lanphier and his brothers in prayer assured them that as their movement grew, they would remain common men, humbly bringing their requests before the God whose ear is ever attuned to the prayers of the righteous.

A mere three weeks after Lanphier held that inaugural prayer meeting with local New York City businessmen, the stock market crashed, sending economic crisis and chaos across the country. Banks locked their doors, and the entire nation overnight descended into the worst financial crisis of its young life. This became known as the Panic of 1857. History reveals that financial uncertainty arrests the attention of people like few other things can. Fear and lack always seem to turn human eyes toward the heavens.

I am compelled to believe that our omniscient, all-knowing, all-wise, all-powerful God knew exactly what He was doing when He placed it upon the heart of a single businessman to invite others like himself to pray at noon rather than eat.

Within six months, in the midst of gross immorality, cruelty, and depravity, there were ten thousand men meeting every day across New York City bringing their heartfelt and conscience-compelled petitions before the throne of God. Of course, ten thousand men couldn't meet with such regularity for prayer in a city like New York without word getting out. Before long, newspapers had picked up the story, bringing news of the prayer revival to churches in other major cities. As one report explained the exponential results of the lone disciple's decision to obey the Holy Spirit's leading on his heart: "Soon, every northern city had prayer meetings. Eventually, the revival spread to the South. Upwards of a million souls were converted to Christ across America because God used one ordinary man named Jeremiah Lanphier, who started a prayer meeting on the third floor of a dying church."[16] Life often springs forth from a dying place, and often the coals of yesterday's visitation, breathed upon by God's Spirit through prayer, ignite the flames of a new revival!

If you know your United States history dates, you may have already anticipated another timely aspect of the blazing revival of prayer begun in 1857. Within a few short years a bloody, cataclysmic Civil War would be visited upon America. More than 700,000 would perish. A nation would be torn in twain. Clearly, not only was God intent on rescuing the eternal souls of men, but in retrospect I believe He was reaching out to a nation before disaster descended, and before nearly three-quarters of a million souls would be swept into eternity. We will never know this side of heaven how many that lost their lives in the Civil War avoided eternity in hell because of a revival of prayer that enveloped the nation in the years just prior to the clamor of war. Oh, what a merciful God we serve! He is not willing that any should perish but that all should come to repentance (2 Pet. 3:9).

This is the desire of God through revival. He delights in awakening hearts and altering eternal destinies. He's eager to heal broken bodies and divided families. He is ever waiting to pour out the balm of Gilead and heaven's mighty power if only... *if* only His people will humble themselves and pray. In 1857, He found such a person, and then such a people, in the most unlikely place—in downtown New York City among a group of businessmen during a season of suffocating spiritual darkness.

What the Lord God did in New York, He has brought from elsewhere many times. But one of the most significant and unique outpourings arrived on the scene roughly fifty years later in another unlikely spot—the coal country of Wales.

ℚ

Five decades and an ocean away from the events at Old Dutch North Church in lower Manhattan, in a little church in a small Welsh village called Cardigan, the sparks of revival are about to ignite. An evening service is underway, and the pastor has just asked his congregation if anyone would like to stand up and give testimony to what the Lord has done in their lives recently. In response everyone just stares at their shoes, scrupulously avoiding eye contact with the preacher. The unresponsiveness drags on uncomfortably for what seems like an eternity. The pastor, clearly with a bit of a stubborn streak and a high tolerance for awkward silence, is prepared to wait. Nothing. Eventually, the graveyard quiet of the meeting hall is broken by the scrape of shoes on a wooden floor and the soft rustle of a dress. Eyes turn to see an ashen young girl standing. Her name is Florrie Evans. With a meek and trembling voice she responds, breaking the stalemate: "If no one else will, then I must say that I love the Lord Jesus Christ with all my heart."[17]

Now recall the words of the prophet Isaiah, "And a little child shall lead them" (Isa. 11:6). The purity and sincerity of this single, simple expression of love for the Savior shatters something in the room. Whether it was pride, complacency, or timidity muzzling the adults in attendance, it has now vacated the premises. Like a tiny crack in a dam, this courageous girl opens the way for a deluge of testimonies about the furious love of God, gratitude for His ceaseless mercies, and how the Holy Spirit has been speaking to penitent hearts. Here in the fall of 1904, a small but significant outpouring has been loosed among the working-class poor of this meager coal mining village. Yet our great God intends to bring refreshing rain of revival to more than this single hamlet.

Word of the revenant quickening soon reached a young theological student named Evan Roberts. That same year, he was enrolled at a Bible college, studying for ministry, in Newcastle Emlyn, ten miles away. When he received the news, he immediately abandoned his studies and headed for Cardigan. On October 31, at his home church's Monday night prayer meeting, Roberts, drenched in the oil of anointing, stood up to speak. He opened his mouth, lifted his voice, and the nation of Wales was never again the same.

Roberts purposed to awaken his fellow countrymen to their need for salvation by grace through faith (Eph. 2:8). His consuming passion and hope was to persuade them to publicly confess their sins and proclaim Jesus as their Savior (Mark 8:38). We should not be surprised at the simplicity of both the message and the method Roberts employed to initiate what would become a nationwide awakening, for Paul the apostle testifies:

> This is the word of faith that we preach: that if you confess with your mouth Jesus is Lord, and believe in your heart that God has raised Him from the dead, you will be saved, for with the heart one believes unto righteousness, and with the mouth confession is made unto salvation. For the Scripture says, "Whoever believes in Him will not be ashamed."
>
> —ROMANS 10:8–11

Stand up and unashamedly confess Jesus Christ as Lord and Savior. As Kenneth Nehemiah Edet has said, "The simplicity of the gospel is its awesome power and the power of the gospel is in its awesome simplicity." It's that simple! We must guard ourselves from ever tumbling into the religious pitfall of overcomplicating the gospel. We require no million-dollar advertising budget nor cutting-edge graphic presentations. We have no reliance upon complex psychological terminology nor complex theological discourses to effectively communicate the great and glorious gospel of our King. I suspect many pastors and church leaders of our day would be stunned to learn how little preaching was actually done in Wales during this massive revival. Consider the words from an account of the outpouring given at the time:

> Three-fourths of the meeting consists of singing. No one uses a hymn-book. No one gives out a hymn. The last person to control the meeting in any way is Mr. Evan Roberts. People pray and sing, give testimony, [and] exhort as the Spirit moves them....
>
> An indefinable influence pervades the country, and awakes to action in the services through the mere reading of a passage, or the singing of a well-known hymn, or the inelegant prayer of a [coal miner] or a country maiden. The ministers, even when in sympathy, take little part...the meetings, often prolonged through the whole night, seem to conduct themselves.[18]

The account continues:

> The enthusiasm was unbounded. Women sang and shouted till the perspiration ran down their faces, and men jumped up one after the other to testify. One told in quivering accents the story of a drunken life. A working [man] spoke like a practiced orator: and one can imagine what a note the testimony of a converted gypsy woman struck when, dressed in her best, she told of her reformation and repentance. At ten o'clock the meeting had lost none of its ardor. Prayer after prayer went up from these Welsh hearts with almost dreary persistence. Time and again the four ministers who stood in the pulpit attempted to start a hymn, but it was all in vain.[19]

It is impossible to exaggerate or overstate the far-reaching effect and raw and dynamic power of this remarkable and miraculously uncommon move of God's Spirit. An outbreak of the manifested tangible presence of the living God in a small church is certainly a glorious thing. After all, all of heaven rejoices when a single sinner repents and comes to the cross (Luke 15:10). But a true revival that shakes and stirs, that transforms and transfigures an entire nation is remarkable and glorious beyond human description. Often, we've witnessed the phenomenon of great revivals beginning with one or two humble, obedient people with a burning passion for the presence of the Lord and a heart for the hopeless, helpless, and hell-bound. In this case, the igniting spark of a bold little girl and embers fanned by a fervent and forceful seminary student became a wildfire of redemptive change so intense that practically scarcely a home or business in the nation of Wales was left untouched by its flame. Theaters were deserted. Bars shut down. Athletic events were postponed because everyone wanted to be at church. Alcohol sales declined significantly, while pocket-size New Testaments were being sold on every corner.[20]

Countless stories and testimonies emerged from those days of glorious visitation of the Spirit of God. One of my favorites involves horses. (I am a lifelong ardent enthusiast of all things equine.) For years, the local coal miners had trained the horses pulling the carts to obey specific profanity-laced commands. Now, under the influence of the wave of holiness washing over the land, the miners found themselves convicted by the Holy Spirit to abstain from such filth. They had to retrain the horses to understand a new, wholesome vocabulary. The revival had spread even to the beasts of burden![21]

I am a pronounced advocate of the local church. I am proud to be a pastor, friend, and mentor to thousands of other pastors across this wonderful nation, as well as globally. However, I admit that I am both challenged and encouraged by something that G. Campbell Morgan, an eyewitness to that great move of God and perhaps my favorite gospel preacher since the New Testament, said about the Welsh Revival:

> What is the character of this revival? It is a church revival.
> I do not mean by that merely a revival among church mem-
> bers. It is that, but it is held in church buildings...I have
> been saying for a long time that the revival which is to be
> permanent in the life of a nation must be associated with
> the life of the churches.[22]

I long for, pray for, look for, and will continue to contend for a revival among the churches of America. I believe that invaluable, biblical keys are put forth in this very book. But we have addi-tional revivals to explore and much more to discover concerning the means and methods by which the Lord God moves when His people follow the 2 Chronicles 7:14 guideposts on the divine roadmap of revival.

Cane Ridge taught and informed us that God is more than willing and able to move in remote places. But few places are more remote and isolated than a small group of islands just off the northwestern coast of Scotland.

ಬಿ

About forty-five miles off Scotland's far northwest coast is a chain of interconnected islands called the Hebrides. In the mid-twentieth century, with an ocean between the islands and the rest of civilization—and mainland Britain still rebuilding itself after the Second World War—it was probably easy to put the farmers, fishermen, and sheepherders of these tiny North Atlantic islands out of mind. But our great God had by no means forgotten them.

That was the promise that two elderly women of the Hebrides held on to in 1949 when they began fervently praying for the Spirit of God to descend upon the whole of their island. I sus-pect by now you are beginning to discern an unmistakable pat-tern where revival is concerned. I don't know if any significant move of God has ever emerged that did not begin with one or more selfless, self-denying saints fully surrendering themselves to a burden for the lost in prayer.

By the way, have you a burden for the lost souls in your family, a burden for those surrounding you every day, whom, should this be their final twenty-four hours upon this earth or should some disease or accident claim their life or should the trumpet of God sound, would spend eternity separated from you and our God in hell? If you have no such burden, pray for it now and unceasingly.

In the Old Testament the prophet Amos, whose very name in Hebrew means "burden bearer," is a type and shadow for us of how the Lord Jesus is our burden bearer, and how we are expected to help one another in the body of Christ. Galatians 6:2 admonishes us to "Bear one another's burdens, and so fulfill the law of Christ." A burden upon the heart of a believer is a pre-requisite for revival. It places in the soul the heaviness of a great weight of godly love and compassion for the lost. Indeed, a deep revelation of all that awaits the unrepentant is the terrifying sign-post over the entryway to Satan's abyss in Dante's *Inferno*: "All hope abandon, ye who enter here."[23]

A burden is that divine enduement of God's Holy Spirit which alone can produce the unnatural compulsion of interces-sion. Think not that the burden for souls is imparted only for the masses of the world, for it is most often graced upon us for "the one," a single lost sheep. The visitation of a heavenly burden cannot be manufactured. It must be sought in prayer and is car-ried in hope. For the revenant Christian warrior, a burden is the result of devotion to God's Word and prayer. It is fostered by surrender, fasting, devotion, and consecration. A genuine burden produces a Holy Ghost compulsion to reach the unreached, rescue the dying, and save the perishing from eternal separation from God. Oh, that we all may receive just such a burden and experi-ence both its crushing and comforting heaviness and weight. Oh, dear Lord, only *if...*

Such was the burden carried by two elderly sisters, Peggy and Christine Smith, one eighty-four years old and the other eighty-two, one nearly blind and the other severely bent over from spinal stenosis. These godly women had become deeply burdened for their community. As a result, they spent hours every night praying in agreement for an outpouring. They refused to be refused, to give up or let up until God answered.

After some time, as well as a God-ordained chain of events, a Scottish preacher named Duncan Campbell arrived at their island for a planned two-week visit. He didn't leave for two years. He could not. A true and consecrated man of God doesn't walk away from a move of God to satisfy his own agenda or fulfill his own calendar.

It was said of Duncan Campbell that he carried such a profoundly powerful anointing that if you were walking beside him, whether on the town streets or out on the lonely moors of the Hebrides, he would remove his hat, have you take off yours, and he'd invite you to kneel, then and there. After doing so, the presence and glory of God would invariably come upon the both of you, and such fervent Holy Ghost–driven and inspired prayer would weigh down upon you that there the two of you would remain, rooted to that very spot for hours.

Prior to Campbell's appearance there, it is thought that most of the people of the Hebrides were quite religious but not truly saved. Those who attended Sunday school would memorize large portions of Scripture. Some families read the Bible and prayed together, but did so out of a sense of duty, obligation, and tradition. These dry and routine, powerless and passionless mechanical observances were not born of hearts set ablaze for the Word or zeal for their Savior and His kingdom. I must say that many modern churchgoers fall into this identical sad circumstance. There is a verifiable danger to having "head confessions" replace "heart conversions." We have faulty conversions because we preach a faulty gospel. We find ourselves at the infancy of the twenty-first century exactly where William Booth, founder of the Salvation Army, said we were in the twentieth century: "The chief dangers which confront the coming century will be religion without the Holy Ghost, Christianity without Christ, forgiveness without repentance, salvation without regeneration, politics without God, and heaven without hell."[24]

After Campbell's first service, nothing of note had taken place, and their time together in the church ended at 10:45. However, later that night, God poured Himself down upon them in a way no one could have foreseen. A young deacon who had glimpsed by the Spirit a coming move of God in the Hebrides told Campbell, "Don't be discouraged, it is coming. I already hear the rumbling of heaven's chariot wheels. We will have another night of prayer and then we will see what God is going to do."[25]

So the deacon and others immediately gathered together to call upon heaven, paying no attention to the hour of the night, which they felt to be no barrier to their desire and God's call. At about 3:00 a.m., God's fiery chariot swept down upon them, its flames rapidly engulfing the entire island. Dozens lay prostrate on the floor in waves of supplication. Men and women lay by the roadside suddenly and without expectation, possessed by the Holy Spirit alone, under conviction for their own sin, crying out for God's mercy and grace. Reports came to Campbell of a crowd that had spontaneously assembled outside the church, despite having received no invitation, drawn only and completely by the glorious "hound of heaven" loosed by God in response to prayer and devotion.

The very next night, busloads arrived from every town and village on that island, crowding the church far beyond its capacity. When asked why they had suddenly bought their bus ticket that day and come to the revival, hundreds could offer no answer or explanation other than they had a stirring in their hearts to go to the village of Barvas (where the church was located).

Years later, when reflecting on the events of those sovereignly orchestrated days in the Hebrides, Duncan Campbell would recall that 75 percent of the converts during that time came from outside the church. When people arrived in town, they would simply fall on their faces under the convicting power of God. Others would be going about their workday routines when suddenly, without warning, they would collapse to their knees, weeping before God and begging Him to forgive their sins. Others reported similar experiences while lying in their beds asleep. The convicting, drawing, heart-softening glory of the Holy Spirit was present and evident to anyone and everyone on that heaven-saturated island.

Perhaps evangelist and writer Rume Kpadamrophe best articulated the awakening:

> Revival had come. God came down and shook the little island of Hebrides. I've watched testimonies of people who saw the literal shekinah of God descending and resting on houses even as dishes clattered under the weight of the glory. Some claimed they saw a ship but there was no sea where they saw the ship. It was indeed heaven on earth. The revival lasted for two years. It is said that over 90 percent of the island was saved.[26]

ℬ

We have only scratched the surface. We stand upon the shore with the sea in front of us. Countless times in history—from the day of Pentecost nearly two thousand years ago until this very hour in certain corners of our world—God has poured out His Spirit in power. Saving power. Redeeming power. Healing power. Delivering power. Keeping power. There are scores of other tremendous outpourings I could have described here.

I could have thrilled your soul with details of what John and Charles Wesley were used of the Lord to help usher in at Oxford, England. Now known as the Methodist revival in the early 1700s, the outpouring would shake and reshape both the British Empire and the United States. Had I the time and you the patience, I could have revealed astonishing stories of great revival preachers of the colonial era like Jonathan Edwards and George Whitefield. Or great revivalists of the 1800s like Charles Finney, Charles Spurgeon, and D. L. Moody. I could have written at length about the world-changing Azusa Street Revival in Los Angeles at the beginning of the twentieth century. That move of God's Spirit lasted for nearly ten years and gave birth to the modern Pentecostal movement. In the twentieth century, anointed revivalists like Billy Sunday, Aimee Semple McPherson, and then in the post-war years, my pastor and mentor Dr. Lester Sumrall, Dr. Oral Roberts, and of course the late Dr. Billy Graham were all used so mightily of the Lord God Almighty to spark and sustain robust and power-packed revivals.

The students at Asbury College in Kentucky experienced two major outpourings in the twentieth century, separated by twenty years, that caused ordinary chapel services to last for several days. I witnessed and was privileged to preach at the first open gospel meeting in over seventy years in the former Soviet Union in 1991 at only thirty-one years of age, along with Dr. Lester Sumrall. In this meeting, dozens of people rose from their wheelchairs, and hundreds of soldiers still wearing their Red Army uniforms ran to the altar in open repentance to receive Christ and were baptized in the Holy Ghost.

The point is, God's passion to possess what He paid so dearly for—the price of His only begotten Son's untainted and unblemished, spotless blood—has not waned or subsided! God so loved the world that He gave His only begotten Son (John 3:16). Souls are ever and always the heartbeat of God. And through examining the chronicles of revival in the earth we are beginning to understand that when souls become our heartbeat as well, heaven rains down upon the dry earth.

If my people...*if*!

God has not changed! The writer of Hebrews shouted it: "Jesus Christ is the same yesterday, and today, and forever" (13:8). The problem is not with the living God; the problem is, as always, with us. The problem is the church. We need to be revived! We need to humble ourselves before God and pray to our Father, who answers by fire. We must wholeheartedly seek the face of the Lord Jesus and turn completely, entirely from our sins of omission and commission.

Have you noted a pattern in these revival histories we've explored thus far? In every case, the revival began with a single individual. A single revived individual. Nation-shaking, culture-transforming, history-making revivals begin with one individual in personal revival. So I must ask you:

Could you be that "one"? Are you willing? Are you prepared to experience the refreshing, revenant rain of personal revival? If... Only *if*!

PART TWO

&

WILL YOU BE REVIVED?

We must wake ourselves up! Or somebody
else will take our place, and bear our cross,
and thereby rob us of our crown.

—William Booth

Chapter 3

IF MY PEOPLE...
WOULD HUMBLE THEMSELVES

Is IT POSSIBLE to live in ongoing, perpetual revival as an individual? Can a person experience revival as a lifestyle rather than just a few weeks of elevated fervor and passion for God once every few years? Many believers have been taught and trained to answer those questions with a "no." But I believe they are wrong.

I know beyond all doubt that it is possible to live in constant revival because I have personally experienced that overwhelming blessing of outpouring for many decades. I say this with a humble and thankful heart for such divine grace extended and certainly not as a boast but rather a simple testimony of what is possible. So why do such a large number of believers doubt and dare not even dream of that possibility?

Many who were reared in church are familiar with the term *mountaintop experience*. In their youth they were excitedly and with great anticipation sent off to a summer camp of some sort and returned to their home churches fired up, on an emotional high, and having freshly been born again or rededicated their lives to Christ. Then they were usually warned about the fleeting, temporary nature of the "mountaintop experience." Their fervor was quenched as they were instructed that you can't live on the mountaintop. At times even misappropriating passages such as Peter's enthusiasm on the Mount of Transfiguration as a proof text (Matt. 17:1–8), they were advised that you can't remain in that state of passion and power all the time or even much of the time. Eventually you must go back down into the "valley" of daily life and to a more "normal" lifestyle of defeated and dull tragic Christianity.

But I must ask you: From the day of Pentecost forward, did the apostle Peter live a lifestyle of defeat or demonstration, or of reversal or revival? I would submit to you that he lived in passionate, powerful, fruitful outpouring of the glorious manifestations of the Holy Ghost until the very day he joyfully submitted to martyrdom for the cause of Christ, just as His mighty Savior had predicted he would.

At the end of the day, all any of us have is our testimony. And my testimony is that a believer can live in this broken, fallen, twisted, sin-ravaged world in a near-constant state of revival. I have done so across six decades of Christian living and more than forty years of gospel ministry. Growing up as a Baptist boy, I was perhaps exceptionally privileged to sit under pastors who boldly declared the truths of God's Word without apology or compromise. Men like C. A. Newman, Richard Presnell, Tommy Moore, and Andrew Workman preached against the rebellion of sin as they upheld the precious blood of Calvary's crucified Lamb as its only antidote.

I recall a decisive series of revival meetings during my early teen years when God was dealing with my eternal soul with immeasurable intensity. These were days of divine destiny for me. I attended every night and didn't seek secrecy in the back rows of the house of God, but rather planted myself as near on the front pew as possible night after night for weeks, often weeping as the Spirit of the living God convicted me, purged my willfulness, drew me, shaped me, spoke clearly to me, marked me, and called me. I owe so much to the powerful preaching to which my young heart was exposed in that most critical season. I continually thank God that my parents took me to churches led by pastors unafraid to offend the delicate sensibilities of the modern, comfort-addicted Christian.

My initial encounter with that rare brand of revival that can be sustained for a lifetime came when I was seventeen years of age. As profoundly grateful as I am for my Baptist upbringing, it was not going to bring me into a life-transforming collision with the power of Pentecost. It was then, under the preaching of Dr. Bill Basansky, that I experienced the mighty baptism of the Holy Ghost. The authentic Book of Acts version! Then and there I discovered that what Jesus had spoken to His disciples was without question absolutely true. The Master had commanded them to wait in Jerusalem until they were filled with power from on high. Then, and only then, would they carry His life-transforming, history-making, destiny-altering power and become His witnesses to a lost and dying world.

A Holy Spirit–baptized people receive two things: (1) a hungry heart to reach lost souls; and (2) supernatural, passionate power to win them to Jesus Christ. One of the great evidences that America's churches are *not* in revival is the nonexistence of preaching to and the rampant complacency and apathy toward those lost and dying without Christ. This is reflected in the dwindling of those called to and fulfilling the fivefold ministry gift of the evangelist (Eph. 4:11). On a typical Sunday morning there will be an altar call all right, but more than likely it will be extended for the members to receive prayer for whatever light affliction they may be experiencing at the moment. What is increasingly more rare these days in our largest, fastest-growing "churches" is a sermon crafted from the heart of God and anointed of the Holy Ghost to convict sinners of their sin, and the resultant prayer-soaked altar call that invites the lost to repent and receive the mercy and grace that our Father is ever so eager to extend through His Son's atoning blood.

Please don't misunderstand; I'm not condemning the practice of praying for and encouraging believers at church. Indeed, according to Hebrews 10:25, we are commanded thus: "Let us not forsake the assembling of ourselves together, as is the manner of some, but let us exhort one another, especially as you see the Day approaching."

But our churches must once again become preeminently about advancing God's kingdom by reaching those added to the church daily—not by adopting them from other churches, but by them accepting Christ. It is no accident that among our Commanding General's final orders before ascending into heaven and taking His seat of honor at the right hand of the Father was His Great Commission to go into all the world and make disciples. Sadly and surprisingly, 51 percent of United States churchgoers say they've never heard of the term "the Great Commission."[1] Evangelism—from "the guttermost to uttermost"—is our primary and prevailing assignment. And the Holy Ghost and His abundant, extravagant gifts are essential to carrying out that mission with maximum results and effectiveness.

Oh, that we, with unified voices, might cry out and plead for heaven's rain to fall upon our dry and parched souls and services, for it is our only hope. It is also one of the key reasons I've been able to live in ongoing revival. Am I always in revival because I have a passion for souls? Or do I have a passion for souls because I remain in revival? I'm not sure I can say with certainty which is the *cause* and which is the *effect*. But what I do know is that a passion for souls has characterized my life and ministry since the day God's holy fire immersed me in power, and I can pinpoint the very day and hour that it became immovably and irreplaceably rooted in the depths of my identity in Christ.

I was in my office at World Harvest Church, signing letters after an exceptionally long and taxing day. I wasn't doing anything particularly "spiritual." I wasn't coming off a twenty-one-day fast. I hadn't spent the previous hour with hands upraised in worship. I hadn't just gotten off the phone with Dr. Lester Sumrall. I was just carrying out a simple, mundane task that happened to be on my to-do list for the day. As I left my office and entered the familiar hallway that leads to my study, I was suddenly overwhelmed by a strong presence of the Lord. The next thing I remember was being on my hands and knees with my head under a chair, weeping as though I was heartbroken.

As indeed I was, after God asked me this question—or these questions.

"Why do you do what you do?" His voice thundered in my consciousness. "Why do you conduct services? Why do you sing songs? Why do you have a youth program, or a children's church, or a nursery?"

I knew that God never asks a question to which He does not already know the answer. I wept and waited.

After some time, He gently spoke these words: "The apex of all Christian endeavor must become to place the jewel of a soul in the crown of our Savior, so that the Lamb of God slain may receive the reward of His suffering."

This statement did not come from my mind. It was not something I'd recently read. The only explanation was that it was directly downloaded from heaven, and that my overly busy mind had to be momentarily taken "offline" in order for the download to take place. This thirty-five-word sentence is not a question. Nor is it framed as a suggestion. This is not God offering some food for thought. It is a plain statement of fact. A declaration. A clarifying, focusing mission statement.

Of course, you may recognize a couple of phrases in that proclamation as coming from the Moravian missionaries. As we've seen, the battle cry for Moravians putting themselves into unimaginable hardship and danger in order to reach the most neglected and forgotten lost souls was, "May the Lamb that was slain receive the reward of His suffering!" Those Moravians, freshly set ablaze and burning with the fire of revival, perfectly captured the beating heart of the Savior of all men with that riveting statement. They understood well what many pastors and Christians today do not, namely, that we serve a God whose heart is captured in perfect relief in three parables delivered consecutively by His Christ. A lost sheep, a lost coin, and a lost son. In each case the "lost" item is urgently and exhaustively sought. No effort was spared in restoring the lost one to its rightful owner. Jesus both punctuated and illuminated the "lost coin" parable with these words: "Likewise, I tell you, there is joy in the presence of the angels of God over one sinner who repents" (Luke 15:10).

The Moravians understood the enormity of the price God and His spotless Son paid to restore such sinners to Himself. They belong to Him. They are bought and paid for at incalculable cost. So of course the almighty God would declare to me and, in turn, ask me to declare to this dying and depraved, seeking and self-centered generation that "the apex of all Christian endeavor must become to place the jewel of a soul in the crown of our Savior, so that the Lamb of God slain may receive the reward of His suffering."

Embracing and absorbing this truth into your innermost being and everyday consciousness will keep you ever connected to the heart of God. It will keep you in revival.

So yes, I know that I know with certainty that it is possible for an individual to live in a perpetual, ever-renewing and deepening move of God. I can testify. In explaining how and why, I would be remiss if I did not mention the influence of one incomparable man of God upon my life among the many to whom I'm in eternal debt. Leonard Ravenhill, the fiery, eloquent, and plain-spoken British evangelist who lived the final decades of his life in East Texas, received his incorruptible crown in 1994, but his voice still echoes in my soul. His relentlessly burning passion for lost souls, for holiness among God's people, and for revival itself marked me forever. At each stage of my development as a minister of God's grace—from boyhood to adulthood—he was used to stir and challenge, convict and inspire me. Any book by this anointed, thundering prophet is well worth your time, but perhaps his most impactful work, upon me and the church world, is titled *Why Revival Tarries*, first published in 1959 and reprinted scores of times, with over a million sold.

Ravenhill was not one to pull his punches. (Perhaps some of this rubbed off on me. I certainly hope so.) In the opening chapter of *Why Revival Tarries* he issues this indictment against the preachers of that day. (Keep in mind this was written over six decades ago.)

> But who now "earnestly contends for the faith once delivered to the saints"? Where are our unctionized pulpit crusaders? Preachers who should be fishing for men are now too often fishing for compliments from men. Preachers used to sow seed; now they string intellectual pearls.... Away with this palsied, powerless preaching which is unmoving because it was born in a tomb instead of a womb, and nourished in a fireless, prayerless soul.[2]

Every word is true and remains more relevant than ever today to bring forth a remnant of revenant preachers, churches, and saints. Yet the key to revival does not lie solely with our pastors and preachers. It lies equally with you and me. I must, therefore, propose the same question the Lord Jesus asked the lame man at the Pool of Bethesda who had lain there paralyzed for thirty-eight years. The Savior caught the man's eye and asked, "Wilt thou be made whole?" (John 5:6, KJV). My question to you is, "Will you be revived?" Will you walk the clear and divinely marked roadmap given to us in 2 Chronicles 7:14 with me? As with all things related to your experience in God, the choice is yours. God so values your freedom that He gives you the power to choose. Will you? If your answer is yes, then let's embark on our pilgrimage down that prophetic path to awakening.

ಬಿ

After even this briefest of reviews of the revival history, it should be clear now. We can't experience true revival in the world, in our nation, in our communities, or even in our churches, until we experience it personally—as individuals. Authentic outpourings of God's grace and power are not only about the unchurched but also about the church. But Holy Ghost fire will not blaze in the church until it ignites our individual hearts. That's you. That's me. Oh, how God values the "one"!

We really don't comprehend the value of a soul in the eyes of God. We simply don't. Jesus sought the downcast and the outcast. He came to seek and to save that which was lost. He was speaking of Himself when He told those stories about the lost sheep, the lost coin, and the lost son. He was revealing His heart. People are not sinners because they sin; they sin because they're sinners. The answer is not to talk to them about their sin. Every sinner knows all too well about their sin. Instead, talk to them about your sin, and about how He met you just as you were, loved you, lavished His grace upon you, forgave you, and resurrected you as a new person. Cleansed. Restored. Made whole. Tell them, as the anointed reverent psalmist of Israel did, that He heard your cry and lifted you out of the shame and depravity and bondage and pain and filth of your own sin. Tell them how He set your feet upon a solid rock and gave you a new song of praise to sing (Ps. 40:1–3).

Too many new church planting and growth strategies seem more like corporate expansion plans than organic, Holy Ghost–directed blueprints. They train would-be pastors to seek out the wealthiest part of town. The mantra becomes location, location, location rather than prayer, prayer, prayer. Jesus modeled no such concepts. Oh, that His Spirit would direct our paths and we would build it according to the pattern given to us in the mountain of His presence.

Too many new "works" seek to attract the "up-and-comers" with light shows, world-class music, and carnivals. Charles H. Spurgeon said, "If you have to give a carnival to get people to come to church, then you will have to keep giving carnivals to keep them coming back."[3] Having glimpsed the Father's heart, I cannot reckon this to be God's prescription for New Testament church growth. At times, I wonder what we are growing—egos or the kingdom of God's Christ. God, give us the passion of Christ for all men and women, for boys and girls, the hurting, bruised and battered, the abandoned and shut-in. Send us first to those You would seek first. May we lead them to Your cross.

May we see them get washed in the blood and filled with the Holy Ghost. The power of Jesus to transform sinners is the most glorious miracle witnessed by humanity and yet it is the most underappreciated, least-marketed, and rarely preached message in Christendom.

Lots of preachers and believers seem eager to minister to celebrities, the wealthy, the lovely, and the "influencers" of our social media age. But God is looking for individuals who are willing to see the people the world overlooks. People with no influence. People who can do nothing for you. I mean actually *see* them through the lens of Calvary as God does.

As I said in *The Cross: One Man...One Tree...One Friday*, "For churches needing to appeal to an image-conscious public, holding the cross high is poor marketing—bad branding."[4] Personally, I thank God for a lady preacher who was conducting a revival meeting in a small cinder block building. (This was back in a day when our particular denomination did not ordain women to minister the gospel. I'm not sure where that would leave the two Marys in Matthew 28:1 and 10.) She pleaded along with a scruffy and skinny eight-year-old boy who had walked down the aisle with tears streaming down his freshly scrubbed face. She prayed for what seemed like an hour with me at the altar, and I was the only person who answered the salvation altar call that night. She was not looking for borrowed prestige. She wasn't looking for a celebrity convert. She was genuinely and deeply interested in "the least of these" (Matt. 25:40). That night, I was the least one in the room of less than fifty people. What moved her? She had a compulsion to place another jewel of a soul in the crown of our Savior. She had an inward desire to serve an infallible leader possessing irresistible power based upon absolute truth. At the conclusion of her loving and powerful intercession for me, she asked how I felt. My answer came easily: "I feel like I've had a bath in Mom's number three washtub with her homemade lye soap—but on the inside." I was clean, washed by His blood, and I had been wonderfully born again.

She earnestly prayed for me, an insignificant child with nothing to offer her, because she spiritually comprehended the inestimable value of a solitary soul. She understood that someday that eight-year-old boy might be graced to win millions to the kingdom of God and His Christ. She was convinced that it was truly all about the one, and through the wisdom of God's Word she knew that we're all going to live forever somewhere.

Again, she possessed the revelation of and understood the value of the "one." She demonstrated the power of "one"—one willing witness reaching one reachable soul. God has always been about the *one*. The individual. The lone person willing to say yes to life amidst a vast crowd of walking dead. And beginning with only that one revived person, God can revive an entire nation.

I cannot help but recall an incident in the life of a nineteenth-century British revivalist named Henry Varley. Now, don't feel embarrassed if you have never heard of him. Few people have. But Varley befriended Dwight, a young American wrestling with the call of God to preach the gospel.

One day in conversation, Varley looked at the young man and said, "Moody, the world has yet to see what God will do with a man fully consecrated to him."[5] The words hit the young believer like a lightning bolt. Conviction, humility, complete surrender, and of course, an outpouring of personal revival followed. Dwight Lyman "D. L." Moody became one of the most effective preachers of the gospel of that or any era, used by God directly and indirectly to change millions of eternal destinies. Even less famous in this woefully uninformed culture is Moody's Sunday school teacher, Edward Kimball. When Moody was eighteen, Kimball led Moody, who had been raised in a Unitarian household, to genuine saving faith in Jesus Christ. In the eyes of the world, Moody was a "nobody" when a Sunday school teacher led him to the cross, and an older evangelist led him to lay his life on the altar for souls. One, reaching one.

There are two valuable lessons for us here. First, we're never more like our Savior than when we search for that lost "one" that

Christ Jesus longs to recover to Himself. Second, and equally important, you are a "one" He loved, sought out, and by the sacrifice of His Christ, redeemed. His great desire is to fill you with His purpose and power. In other words, His quest is to pour Himself out upon you in individual, personal, radical revival.

෭

What does perpetual personal revival look like? It can certainly take on varying forms, but I am convinced that a common denominator is a sensitivity of heart toward and fellowship with the Holy Spirit and consistent, contrite gratitude toward both our Father and His Son.

When I think about living with a tender heart toward God, my mind instantly goes to my precious wife, Joni. She is another reason I am convinced that it is entirely possible to live in a state of ceaseless outpouring. I've had a front-row seat for watching her live that way across nearly four decades of marriage. That tenderness of heart was on full display one day as I noticed her weeping. Tears were not dropping onto the pages of her well-worn, marked-up Bible. Her tears were not falling onto the altar at our church. No, the tears streaming down her lovely face and dripping from her chin were landing in our kitchen sink filled with dishwater. She did not know I was watching.

Concerned and curious, I intruded on what turned out to be a holy moment and asked why she was crying. In reply she explained, "I just realized that as I fulfill my calling as a wife and mother, God receives it as worship. He has visited me here in the everydayness of my life, and I am overwhelmed by His love and presence."

This is the Master's mark of a believer in revival presence. He or she realizes God's heavy hand of presence upon him or her everywhere and in everything. You are no doubt familiar with the words of Romans 12:1–2, most likely memorized from the King James Version, but allow me to refresh your memory: "I beseech you therefore, brethren, by the mercies of God, that ye present your bodies a living sacrifice, holy, acceptable unto God, which is your reasonable service. And be not conformed to this world: but be ye transformed by the renewing of your mind, that ye may prove what is that good, and acceptable, and perfect, will of God." This exhortation is evergreen. We are well served to ponder it often. Yet these familiar lines take on fresh dimensions of meaning in *The Message* paraphrase:

> So here's what I want you to do, God helping you: Take your everyday, ordinary life—your sleeping, eating, going-to-work, and walking-around life—and place it before God as an offering. Embracing what God does for you is the best thing you can do for him. Don't become so well-adjusted to your culture that you fit into it without even thinking. Instead, fix your attention on God. You'll be changed from the inside out.
>
> —Romans 12:1–2, *MSG*

Please note that we're not alone in following this admonition. What Paul is encouraging us to do here, God is fully empowered to prepare us to accomplish! Of course, the decision is ours. God never violates our freedom to choose, but once the decision is made, you will find God's "grace to help" (Heb. 4:16).

Also note that what is to be offered here is "your body." Most scriptures deal with our minds and spirits. They speak of *spiritual* things. But in referencing our bodies, the Word of God is speaking to our natural lives. Earthly, mundane things. Your sleeping, eating, going-to-work, and walking-around life! The exhortation is to place these before God as an "offering" or, as the King James Version witnesses, "a living sacrifice." That is profound. "Living" to me denotes vibrancy, vitality, energy, motion! I often say that I want to live out loud. Our great God desires for us to thrive in this earth, not simply survive in it. There has been a divorce in the church where we separate the perceived *spiritual* aspects of our relationship with the living Christ from perceived *natural* aspects of that relationship. I've got good news for you: God Almighty, through the intermediate agency of the Holy Ghost, wants to become actively involved in your "every-dayness"! This is the life-altering, presence-producing, prophetic, lovely, and powerful revelation Joni received while just washing some dishes.

Are you ready to become immersed in profound personal revival? Are you ready to have your dry soul revived with an out-pouring of Holy Ghost rain? My hope is that I have stirred in you a desire to experience this glory not only for a brief, fleeting season, but that it will become your lifestyle. If so, then the pathway forward is well marked. As we've seen, God Himself established the signposts for us in 2 Chronicles 7:14. And our divine directive on this journey is to take a hard right turn toward humility.

ɞ

If my people, which are called by my name, shall humble themselves...

If! As with all virtues, humility has an opposite: pride. It should not surprise us that revival and restoration begins with humility, because all "falling away" begins with pride. Pride sent the archangel Lucifer plummeting from the heights of glorious splendor near the very throne of God to very depths of hell itself. When that same devil, as a serpent, sought to draw and deceive the crowning jewel of creation, mankind, into treason and rebellion, the appeal was advanced directly to Eve's pride. "You will be like God, knowing good and evil," the vile deceiver whispered with venomous words (Gen. 3:5).

"Humble yourself" is the first command given to ignite revival. Pride is the primary roadblock to the fuel supply necessary to sustain it. The Lord Jesus, the master storyteller, once shared a parable about a humble yet despised tax collector. He brilliantly contrasted this humble man with a pompous, prideful Pharisee. In Luke's account Jesus says:

> Two men went up to the temple to pray, the one a Pharisee and the other a tax collector. The Pharisee stood and prayed these things about himself, "God, I thank You that I am not like other men: extortioners, unjust, adulterers, or even like this tax collector. I fast twice a week, and I tithe of all that I earn." But the tax collector, standing at a distance, would not even lift his eyes to heaven, but struck his chest, saying, "God, be merciful to me a sinner." I tell you, this man went down to his house justified rather than the other. For everyone who exalts himself will be humbled, and he who humbles himself will be exalted.
>
> —LUKE 18:10–14

One man was thoroughly impressed with himself and boastful in his religiosity. The other was so secretly ashamed of his sin he dared not even lift his eyes from the floor. One was drowning in a pool of self-righteousness. The other was utterly convinced that he was undeserving and in desperate need of God's mercy.

None of us wants to be that Pharisee. We see Jesus' approval and want to be the tax collector—the humble sinner whom Jesus exalts as justified. Of course, we would all tell ourselves we would choose humility over pride. But do we?

James 4:10 offers a lifeline of hope and encouragement to those who recognize their spiritual bankruptcy: "Humble yourselves in the sight of the Lord, and He will lift you up." The apostle Peter seconds this motion and echoes the immutable principle when he writes, "Humble yourselves under the mighty hand of God, that He may exalt you in due time" (1 Pet. 5:6).

As God's children, redeemed by the spotless blood of Calvary's Lamb and granted eternal life, we are citizens and ambassadors of the kingdom of God. Yet we choose to live every day in another kingdom belonging to God's sworn enemy. Jesus Himself once called Satan "the prince of this world" (John 14:30, KJV). Though we are no longer of that kingdom, we remain in it. We must, therefore, at all times and in all ways, resist the temptation to devolve into the value system of that kingdom, where pride isn't vanquished as sin but is lionized as virtue. In that insolvent system, meekness is mocked as weakness. The aim is never to serve, but to be served. When pride sits upon the human heart, success means being envied by as many people as possible. What a hellish existence such a system of bankrupt values spawns.

The revenant believer, however, must remember that the principles and values of God's kingdom are diametrically opposed and mutually exclusive to those of the domain of darkness from which we were rescued. That's why the Word enjoins us to be *in* the world but not *of* it. Jesus told His disciples, "If you were of the world, the world would love you as its own. But because you are not of the world, since I chose you out of the world, the world therefore hates you" (John 15:19). How about that for a Sunday sermon series!

In stark, jarring contrast to the pride-driven principles of this world, kingdom principles often seem like a paradox. In the kingdom of our God the way up is down. We lead by serving. We increase by giving. We experience abundant life by dying to ourselves and our selfish desires. In His kingdom promotion is achieved by assuming a posture of humility—down on our knees, knelt at His altar, with our eyes gazing upon our own spiritual poverty and our hands uplifted in absolute surrender to our glorious King and holy God!

In the light of this, should we marvel or be mystified that God says, "If my people...will humble themselves..."?

After all, to be revived is to be restored to life, which in turn presupposed that something had to be taken through the process of death. In Colossians, Paul wrote that we are to "put to death the parts of [our] earthly nature" (Col. 3:5). Exactly what needs to die? Above all, it is our pride, or what 1 John 2:16 calls "the pride of life." Pride is the most formidable of foes, and we must vanquish its fortresses to see the heavens rent opened and receive a personal outpouring of revival. We must humble ourselves before our magnificent, mighty, indescribably holy and infinitely wise God, our Creator.

That defines the what of the matter. Now let's explore the how. Put another way, how do we humble ourselves before the mighty hand of God as 2 Chronicles 7:14 compels?

જી

It was C. S. Lewis who said, "Pride is spiritual cancer: it eats up the very possibility of love, or contentment, or even common sense."[6] Humility begins by simply and honestly recognizing our need for God's constant guidance in our lives. Pride snarls, "I've got this figured out." "I need no help." "I am self-sufficient." "I know where to go and how to get there." It's certainly not a coincidence that we men are legendary for our refusal to admit when we're lost and simply stop and ask for directions. What is the driving force of such stubbornness? Pride!

The alcohol addiction recovery group Alcoholics Anonymous (AA) lists as step two of their very successful Twelve Steps recovery program: "We...came to believe that a Power greater than ourselves could restore us to sanity."[7] That's a humbling admission of great need.

You may have never struggled with an addiction to alcohol, but don't fool yourself as the prideful Pharisee did—you still are completely helpless to restore yourself. Of course, the higher, greater "power" referenced in the Twelve Steps is generically referring to our Mighty God, Creator of heaven and earth. And it goes without saying that Christ Jesus is the ultimate and only answer to any of life's questions. However, for the believer, there is a related "authority" to which we must constantly submit ourselves in contrition and humility. I'm referring to the absolute, unquestionable authority of God's living Word. The almighty God and His Word are indivisible. In 2 Timothy 3:16 the apostle makes it undeniably clear: "All Scripture is inspired by God and is profitable for teaching, for reproof, for correction, and for instruction in righteousness."

If your heart aches for a refreshing river of revival to flow in your life with great force, and thirsts for a fresh outpouring of

Holy Ghost power to break upon your soul, you must begin by humbly submitting yourself in unquestioning surrender to the authority of God's Word. When your daily news feed and academia, the pundits and politicians all chant a rebellious harmony and God's Word stands in stark opposition, who will you believe? To what paradigm will you submit? Do you truly live by a thoroughly biblical worldview? Or do you cave under cultural pressure? Years ago, I wrote:

> As Christians, the Bible is our standard and code of conduct. It is the bedrock of our faith and the foundation upon which to build our future. However, in our present society, we have refused to sacrifice our carnal desires to receive the heavenly blessing of delving into its pages. We've allowed radicals in the minority who can shout the loudest to set the course for our future. Our "Christian" conduct is carnal. We've substituted the Word of Truth for false doctrine. It is time to rediscover God's Word again![8]

Now, recall the revival in Judah under young King Josiah. After hearing the wondrous words from the God of Abraham found in the recently discovered Book of the Law, King Josiah "tore his garments" (2 Chron. 34:19). He then immediately demanded that every other person in the kingdom be required to come to hear God's infallible Word read aloud in their hearing. Although Josiah was the most powerful and high-ranking individual in Judah, he threw himself under the authority of God's Word in humble realization and open declaration of his desperate and overwhelming need for the guidance, wisdom, and blessing of the Lord God Almighty.

We saw that when King Hezekiah restored the Passover celebration and ushered renaissance and revolutionary revival throughout the nation, he "clung to the LORD" (2 Kings 18:6). At this pivotal moment, what are you "clinging" to? Small children cling to their parents when they require comfort or protection.

Extreme rock climbers literally cling for dear life to every crevice and outcrop of a mountain for survival.

Oh, that we might cling to the solid rock, the unfailing and unspoken Word of God with such desperation! What a difference we would see were we to hold to those living, life-giving, victory-sustaining words as if our very lives depended on it—because in actuality, they do! God, grant us the strength to, in humility, submit even our intellects to the wisdom of Your inerrant Word, for human wisdom is corrupted (1 Cor. 1:18–21), but the Word of the Lord is incorruptible seed (1 Pet. 1:23, KJV). Your physical brain will deceive you. Logic will disappoint you. Your human senses will defraud you. The Book of Proverbs confirms the reality:

> Trust in the LORD with all your heart, and lean not on your own understanding; in all your ways acknowledge Him, and He will direct your paths.
> —PROVERBS 3:5–6

Fulfilling the *if* requirement of humbling ourselves begins by submitting our intellect, our value system, indeed our every decision to the infallible, inerrant, incorruptible Word of the living God. My wife, Joni, lives in a perpetual renewal and revival. Her favorite verse in the sixty-six books of her Bible sets the tone for her extreme passion for her Savior's presence. That revival-producing verse is Micah 6:8: "He has told you, O man, what is good—and what does the LORD require of you, but to do justice and to love kindness, and to walk humbly with your God?"

৪৩

Humbling ourselves also involves becoming brutally honest in the confession of our sin and sinfulness—something very popular in the Bible but very unpopular in today's me-centered pulpits and, therefore, the church's self-centered attenders. It was just this type of self-abnegation that fueled the Holy Ghost fire during the Welsh Revival that we examined in chapter 2. Some outpourings are prayed down. Others are preached down. But in a very real sense, the Welsh Revival was "confessed" down. Evan Roberts' message to his Christian fellow countrymen in Wales was simple: confess your sins to one another and proclaim your need for Jesus Christ as your personal Savior. It's true. Its effect was astonishing. One of the mightiest revivals the world has ever known was inaugurated and sustained not by elaborated and embellished expositions of the Bible by fire-breathing orators, nor the so-sought-after miracles, signs, and wonders. The fuel of that awakening's inferno was the public confessions of personal sins by ordinary working men and women, beginning with a tender-hearted young girl's simple profession of love for her Savior. But the Welsh outpouring was no isolated incident.

In 1970 real revival broke out in a chapel service at Asbury College, a Christian college just outside Lexington, Kentucky. The regular chapel service began with the school's academic dean giving his testimony. He then invited the students to share their own salvation experiences. One courageous student responded. Another followed, then a third, and a fourth. One report gleaned from eyewitnesses tells the story: "Gradually, inexplicably, students and faculty members alike found themselves quietly praying, weeping, singing. They sought out others to whom they had done wrong deeds and asked for forgiveness. The chapel service went on and on."[9] This routine and mundane chapel service—mandatory for students—was scheduled to last just fifty minutes. Instead, it continued without interruption for 185 hours—running twenty-four hours a day for an entire week. But for such showers we plead. If... Only *if*!

By the time the fiery storm subsided and the chapel service ended, the revival had spread like a Holy Ghost contagion far beyond the walls of the chapel or even the confines of the campus. As word of what was taking place at Asbury College broadened, so did sparks of the revival. They floated from that campus, carried on winds of the Spirit, kindling fires of awakening across the United States and foreign nations. Two thousand-plus witnessing teams were sent from Asbury to 130 churches and college campuses throughout America. As with the Welsh Revival, this mammoth move of God began with open confessions of sin and professions of faith from humbled hearts.

Authentic, revival-sparking humility before the Lord involves an innate and clear recognition of our personal sinfulness—acknowledgment of how very far from the mark we often fall. In the Old Testament, this acknowledgement of sin was unmistakable. It was paramount in every act of worship, and it's woven into the fabric of the practices of the nation.

Recently, as I have been urging a return to placing altars back into our churches and homes, I rediscovered what was historically known as "the mourner's bench," also known as "the mercy seat." It was originally instituted by John Wesley. Placed in a prominent location in the sanctuary, the bench would be used for anyone present under the conviction of the Holy Spirit to go and sit or kneel. A minister would then approach the penitent to inquire of their need and hear their renouncing of sin and pray with them for salvation and forgiveness. I was able to locate one of these historic prayer and confession mourner's benches and placed it in my personal study. It reminds me of the call of God to humility every day.

In Leviticus chapter 4 and Numbers chapter 15 we find explicit instructions for bringing the "sin offering." This involved bringing a perfect, unblemished animal for sacrifice, after which some of the blood of that animal would be sprinkled on the horns of the altar. The annual Day of Atonement (Lev. 16) was another occasion during which everyone was commanded to bring a sacrifice to the priest. This sacrifice was meant to ceremonially "cover" the sins of the previous year. In both cases, if you saw someone carrying a lamb or goat to the tabernacle, it was clear to everyone that a "sinner" was coming to "confess" his sinful state. There was no attempt to hide or disguise it. The profession was, purposefully and by nature, very public.

Most believers understand that the Lord Jesus was and is

our sin offering. They know that He was what both the Day of Atonement and Passover sacrifices were pointing to. Jesus, operating as both heavenly High Priest and sacrifice Lamb, sprinkled His own guiltless blood upon the mercy seat in the heavenly tabernacle of which the tabernacle of Moses was only a pitiful, shabby copy (Heb. 9). Jesus Christ became the ultimate and final atonement, making any further sacrifice at the cross or any other altar unnecessary.

Sadly, to their own demise and the shame of their spiritual leaders, many in the church are completely unaware of their deep and abiding need to still openly and regularly seek forgiveness through repentance. Romans 10:10 says, "For with the heart one believes unto righteousness, and with the mouth confession is made unto salvation." In too many places today, regular confession of our sins at the altar has been abandoned for a life of make-believe, one in which church attenders are deceived into thinking there is no longer any need for confession or repentance because of unscriptural teaching on the subject of grace. In the words of A. W. Pink, "It is not the absence of sin but the grieving over it which distinguishes the child of God from empty professors."[10]

No longer do we desire an altar to repent of our lying, deceiving, manipulative spirits. No longer do we seek an altar to confess our own cover-up. It's all just too public. There are no beauty filters to camouflage our blemishes. The reigning and ruling demonic leviathan of pride will never permit you to publicly reveal the depth of your depravity and your desperate need of confession and repentance. We're too image conscious to humble ourselves at the foot of the cross—the place where the masks must be discarded and all pretensions of self-sufficiency be cast aside. Rarely do we cry out for God to meet us at the mercy seat anymore. The trek to the altar is no longer well worn. Our smooth knees testify of our allegiance to our idolatrous self-worship.

Is it any wonder we are spiritually impoverished and chronically powerless? May I tell you when you can stop asking for God's forgiveness? When you stop sinning! Your Bible and mine assures us that day will not come until our ultimate glorification in heaven. The apostle Paul, author of nearly a third of the New Testament, said regarding himself, "I am carnal, sold under sin. For what I am doing, I do not understand, for I do not practice what I will to do, but I do the very thing I hate" (Rom. 7:14–15). If Paul recognized and professed his ongoing need for mercy and grace, how much more should we?

Watchman Nee said, "Now is the hour we should humbly prostrate ourselves before God, willing to be convicted afresh of our sins by the Holy Spirit."[11] Are you daily "convicted afresh" of your sins?

What is the principal barrier to the open confession of sin? Pride! That's why "humble yourselves" is the first, un-skippable waypoint on the road to revival. And it is precisely why there is deliverance and empowerment in confessing our sins not only to God but also to each other. Certainly, when we confess our sins to Him, God "is faithful and just and will forgive us our sins and purify us from all unrighteousness" (1 John 1:9, NIV). But what truly crushes the pervasive inundation of stubborn and stiff-necked pride is confessing our sins to one another. Authentic accountability that produces honest humility arrests the attention of the Author of awakening and is displayed when we get real with each other about our rebellion and willfulness. This is what fueled the Welsh Revival. The people there lived the scriptural command in James 5:16, "Confess your faults to one another and pray for one another, that you may be healed." The believers in Wales were saved from their sins when they confessed their sins to their Savior, but they were *revived* when they confessed to one another.

When King David was confronted by Nathan concerning his adultery with Bathsheba and his subsequent first-degree murder of her husband, Uriah, David did not merely fall at the altar and plead for God's forgiveness privately. He also wrote a song about it that he then gave to the choirmaster to sing so his sin would be on open display and never forgotten. That song is now referred to as Psalm 51, in which David wrote, "I acknowledge my transgressions, and my sin is ever before me. Against You, You only, have I sinned, and done this evil in Your sight" (vv. 3–4). For three thousand years, millions have been reading David's confession. That is about as public as it gets.

Not even Israel's greatest king kept his most shameful sin a secret from others, though he certainly had the power to do so. Perhaps that is why God called him "a man after My own heart" (Acts 13:22). Nothing nails pride to a cross like open, transparent confession of our sins to one another. Parents can and should model this for their children and teach them the difference between being sorry and biblical repentance. Every sin is a sin against God, but often our sins are also against the people we love the most. What an impact it would have on children to see a father or a mother reach across the dinner table and say, "Honey, I'm sorry. What I did was hurtful. I was wrong, and I ask for your forgiveness." What kind of indelible imprint would it leave on a young teen who sees Dad walk the aisle, kneel, and confess with tears the ways he has not walked "in a manner worthy of the calling" of being a Jesus follower (Eph. 4:1)? What would it take to do that? Humility. "If My people, who are called by My name, will humble themselves..." *If!*

ॐ

There is another way we can fulfill the nonnegotiable revival requirement of humbling ourselves. We do so every time we submit our wills to God's will. Before I continue, please know that the Lord never asks for our will to be broken. One with no will would be of no use to the kingdom or the world. Rather, He asks for our will to be consecrated to and submitted to His divine will.

In all of history the ultimate revenant life would have to be that of our Lord Jesus Christ. Not because He had to repent of and die to His sins as we must, but because He literally died and three days later was revived. Though the same could be said of

Lazarus, he eventually succumbed to death while on this earth. This was not the case with our Savior, whose resurrected body ascended to heaven and now rules from His rightful throne.

As in every other aspect of living the Christian life, the Lord Jesus is our instructor and example. He modeled and demonstrated complete submission to the will of our Father every moment of His glorious and exemplary advent. He modeled it in His willingness to condescend to this blue-marble planet and become as one of us:

> Let this mind be in you all, which was also in Christ Jesus, who, being in the form of God, did not consider equality with God something to be grasped. But He emptied Himself, taking upon Himself the form of a servant, and was made in the likeness of men. And being found in the form of a man, *He humbled Himself* and became obedient to death, even death on a cross.
> —PHILIPPIANS 2:5–8, EMPHASIS ADDED

Jesus modeled humility and self-abasement throughout His earthly ministry, declaring that He only did those things He saw the Father doing (John 5:19) and only spoke what He heard the Father saying (John 12:49). He spoke in human terms, "My food is to do the will of Him who sent Me" (John 4:34). He carried this posture of humble submission to the Father's plan right through the Garden of Gethsemane—see Him there under the full light of a Passover moon against a rock, praying until His facial capillaries burst and spill sinless blood upon His tortured brow; hear Him as He cries out, "Father, not My will but Yours be done!"—and all the way up Calvary's cruel and craggy, rough and ragged hill. There He willingly lay down upon a cross and gave His healing hands to the nailer when, but for His humbling and submission to the Father's will, He could have called ten thousand angels to destroy the world and set Him free.

Oh, that today we would cry to our Father for the strength of character and willingness of spirit to pray that powerful prayer

of consecration, yea of submission, to the will of our Father. If...
Only *if*! Proverbs 14:12 convicts and convinces us, "There is a
way that seems right to a man, but its end is the way of death."
Our will, as good-intentioned, well-founded, and prudent as it
may seem to us, can lead only to destruction if it is not directed
by and rooted in the will of our Father and God. We must die
daily and intentionally choose God's will over our will. His ways
over our own. His values over our preferences. His laws over our
desires, His kingdom over our possessions, His sacredness over
our status. This is a type of humility that qualifies you and posi-
tions you for a raging storm of Holy Ghost refreshing to wash
you clean and propel you into the splendor of personal revival.

When the living God brought awakening to Wales, Evan
Roberts was about a year into his study at the Ministers' Training
College at Newcastle Emlyn. Certainly, he could have responded
to God with any number of selfish excuses—something modern
churchgoers have become professionals at. He could have said,
"I simply can't; it wouldn't be wisdom. It would make no sense
for me to interrupt my studies now and risk losing everything
I've achieved thus far. Oh, I'll do it, but just not right now. Let
me finish up my degree, then I'll gladly go wherever You want."
Instead, according to one writing of the revival at the time, "Little
more than a month ago Evan Roberts was unknown, studying so
as to prepare for the Calvinistic Methodist ministry. Then came
the summons [from God], and he obeyed. He insists that he has
been called to his present work by the direct guidance of the
Holy Ghost."[12]

"Not my will, heavenly Father," Roberts said, "but Yours, be done."

When it was time for Moses to pack up the tent and move
the moaning and groaning Israelites closer to the Promised
Land, he pleaded with God, "If Your Presence does not go with
us, do not bring us up from here" (Exod. 33:15). What a staggering contrast to modern church services, planned to the second
and orchestrated by a click track. Oh God, for a divine disturbance of Holy Ghost disruption. A return to utter betrayal of our

self-confidence and assurance. Away with our insular plans and programs which have inoculated us against the unrivaled spontaneity and creativity of the moving of God's Spirit among us. If... Only *if*!

True humility before God means not desiring to move a single muscle, sing a song, or utter a word unless it's under divine direction. It is at the nail-scarred feet of Calvary's crucified Lamb that we must pray in humility of heart and submission of spirit until our will aligns with the Master's. We must make our way to that place where if we don't move in Jesus, then we dare not move at all. Again, our great God does not desire to break our will but to give us a will submitted to His authority, whereby we can reach the unreached, tell the untold, and change the world.

Please understand, the will of God is not a mystery or a deeply hidden secret. He delights in making His will known. It fulfills His Word. It aligns with His peace. It's hard to miss. In fact, any believer who delights in the Lord and sincerely desires to follow Him will naturally find themselves abiding therein. Unless you are in rebellion and apathy, you'll go to bed tonight and awaken tomorrow in the center of the circumference of His perfect will!

The fundamental solution lies in the beloved invitation hymn published in 1896 that led us in professing: "All to Jesus I surrender, all to Him I freely give; I will ever love and trust Him, in His presence daily live."[13] It truly is just that simple.

෯

Often, humbling yourself involves something other than confession of sin or surrender of will. At times it requires what is referred to as "a sacrifice of praise." I have been graced with a long-standing intimate acquaintance with this form of sacrifice.

Many years ago, when our son, Austin Chandler, was diagnosed with Asperger's syndrome, a high-functioning form of autism, the doctors told us, "Your son has an incurable neurological condition for which there is no treatment, no cure, and no hope." As the initial shock of what the specialists said was a "life sentence" began to wane and we began to process the implications of those words, it became clear that the road ahead for us as his parents would not be what we had anticipated as a young couple dreaming of our future family.

I was unsure of what I was supposed to do—as a husband, a father, a child of God. What I did know was that Hebrews 13:15 instructs us to "continually offer to God the sacrifice of praise, which is the fruit of our lips, giving thanks to His name." The psalmist wrote, "He who offers a sacrifice of thanksgiving honors Me" (Ps. 50:23, NASB). So, with these eternal truths in mind, I found myself a week later high atop one of the Rocky Mountains, alone with my swirling thoughts, my roiling emotions, and my God. There I found some fallen trees and constructed a crude altar. I then carved my son's name into that place of intercession and consecration and declared to God, "Here at this altar, today, I offer up to You this sacrifice of praise." At that moment, something born of glory broke through my confusion and I was instantly and forever changed. I have never been the same.

All genuine sacrifice is born of thanksgiving, but not all thanksgiving involves a sacrifice. It is easy to be thankful for the many and varied good and perfect gifts in our lives—the new position, the beautiful home, the unforgettable vacation. The true test of a thankful heart of praise is often revealed at midnight, in the midst of hardship. In profound disappointment. When our hearts are breaking. Paul instructs us in 1 Thessalonians 5:18, "In everything give thanks, for this is the will of God in Christ Jesus concerning you." I read the verse to mean that pure praise is born from pain—even when our pride and self-will would shout that we have every reason to be bitter, angry, resentful, even unforgiving. When the report from the doctor stabs through the heart with the dagger of fear. It is not that we are to give thanks *for* the diagnosis, or for a bad or evil report. Rather, we praise God *in* the storm, in the middle of difficulty, because of who He is and what He has promised.

A sacrifice of praise demands of us the greatest humility of all.

It requires abandoning our sense of the way things ought to be. It crucifies the "I have a right" syndrome. Offering genuine praise even when it appears and feels as though everything around us is falling to pieces runs counter to everything in the human part of us. During the battle with cancer; after the funeral flowers are wilted, friends have returned to their lives, and you feel completely abandoned and alone; in the middle of a pandemic, when everyone and no one has an answer...offer a sacrifice of praise to God? Absolutely!

Think of all the businessmen during the 1857 Fulton Street Revival who had lost everything when the stock market collapsed. Call to remembrance the little girl living in the blue-collar, poverty-stricken town of Cardigan when food was scarce who ignited the Welsh awakening by simply saying to her church, "I must say that I love the Lord Jesus Christ with all my heart." Imagine with me what our great God will do if and when we humble ourselves under His mighty and glorious hand, what flood tide of His holy presence may be visited upon us, when through our pain and pressure, our poverty and plight, we give the sacrifice of praise through tear-filled eyes and stammering voice despite the tribulations we are currently standing in and struggling through! I believe we would see that God is faithful to revive our hearts and pour out His Spirit upon us in unprecedented waves of His glory. The heavens will open and give us rain, for it is our season, our time of visitation, our time of unparalleled outpouring that the Lamb of God slain may receive the reward of His suffering! If... Only *if* we will humble ourselves.

Chapter 4

IF MY PEOPLE...
WOULD PRAY

Fᴿᴼᴹ ᴼᵁᴿ ᵀᵂᴱᴺᵀʸ-ᶠᴵᴿˢᵀ-ᶜᴱᴺᵀᵁᴿʸ perspective, the effects of the Welsh Revival on that nation seem almost too fantastic to believe. Profanity was silenced, theater attendance plummeted, bars went out of business, and criminal courts were closed as the crime rate plunged. Even the daily newspaper of Cardiff, the capital and largest city, published what it called "Revival Editions" during that Great Awakening.

Don't forget how the revival began. A little girl in Cardigan openly and with simplicity shared her love for Jesus with her congregation, followed by a zealous young college student who fanned that glowing ember by calling a prayer meeting. That wasn't all; that was enough!

It is difficult to wrap our minds around the possibility that an entire region could be immersed in glorious revival as it was in Wales. I suspect the reason is directly related to the low esteem and light emphasis now given to that which our Bibles declare to be indispensable and imperative—the privilege and practice of prayer. We are in dire deficiency corporately and individually. We have need of that catalyst of desire. Expectation. Simple faith. That assurance that *if* we will ask, it will be given to us (Matt. 7:7). If... Only *if*! Prayerlessness is a sin. We are so informed by the ancient prophet Samuel: "Moreover as for me, God forbid that I should sin against the LORD in ceasing to pray for you. But I will teach you the good and the right way" (1 Sam. 12:23).

The church has not always been prayerless. Previous generations knew how to kneel in the presence of the Lord God Almighty and pray until heaven's answer became the reward of their obedience and persistence. The mighty Pentecostal warriors of old called it "praying through." The rest of the day's assignments and appointments were of no concern. Their aching—and at times bleeding—knees and threadbare trousers were not despised. They were given a mandate from heaven, a kingdom assignment to make their petitions known before the throne of grace and to plead their cause at the seat called mercy. All else faded into insignificance—time stood still, agendas were dismantled, and schedules were shredded. They became the earthen vessels through which the incense of deep intercession ascended to heaven from the altars of their hungry and passionate hearts. Quite unlike today, when if we can't get something downloaded to our smartphone in two seconds or less, it's not worth our time. Our carnality becomes frustrated and impatient, so we just move on to the next shiny and glittery instrument of entertainment. It is no wonder that the modern cold and dry "believer" is impoverished of Holy Ghost–anointed prayer upon bended knees. Through neglect and misuse we have lost our ability to lay hold of the horns of the altar and contend until we've avalanched in victory. This has, not coincidentally, paralleled our loss of heartache and burden for the pitiful plight of hell-bound, lost souls.

Not so with Evan Roberts. I pray and weep hearing his convicting testimony and commitment to prayer:

> For thirteen years I had prayed for the Spirit, and this is the way I was led to pray. William Davies, the deacon, said one night in the society: "Remember to be faithful. What if the Spirit descended and you absent? Remember Thomas! What a loss he had!" [Because Thomas was not with the rest of the disciples in the Upper Room the night Jesus first appeared to them after His resurrection.]

I said then to myself, "I will have the Spirit." And through all weather and in spite of all difficulties I went to the meetings. Many times on seeing other boys with the boats on the tide I was tempted to turn back and join them. But no. Then I said to myself, "Remember your resolve to be faithful," and on I went. Prayer-meeting Monday evening at the chapel, prayer-meeting Tuesday evening at Pisgah (Sunday-school branch); church meeting, Wednesday; Band of Hope, Thursday; class, Friday evening—to these I went faithfully through the years. For ten or eleven years I have prayed for a revival. I could sit up all night to read or talk about revivals. It was the Spirit that moved me to think about this.[1]

"For ten or eleven years I have prayed for revival." When his friends were found fishing and at ease, Evan Roberts was faithfully praying for the Spirit of God to awaken Wales! Do you want to know how a national revival could revolutionize everything from courthouses to horses? Look no further than the thousands of days during which a solitary, devoted young man prayed for God to rend the heavens and send the rain.

Examining the extraordinary moves of God in the Hebrides, Fulton Street, Asbury, and others, it becomes clear that there is no single model nor solitary mold for what a revival should look like. Revival is "of God" and therefore it is as diverse in manifestation as our God is in creativity. Has it a prayer emphasis? Is there prophecy and preaching? Singing and shouting? Are there involuntary outbursts and "jerks"? Is it characterized by worship and mourning or laughing and dancing, or is it typified by holy silence? Does it continue for a weekend? A year? Are there signs, wonders, miracles, and divine healings? Are there manifestations of the gifts of the Holy Ghost and demonstrations of deliverance? Or perhaps there is a brooding presence of the conviction of sin, with deep remorse and repentance. There can be no predicting how God's Spirit will move, nor of any particular form of outpouring which, in His providence, He may choose. He is much too powerful and creative to be pinned down, or hemmed in by human restraint or its prognostication. The Holy Ghost will not be confined to your tidy little box. However, there seems to be a single common denominator in every revival throughout history: they all find their genesis in the foundation of prayer. Of course they do. It is right there in the prescription God Almighty wrote to us in 2 Chronicles 7:14! "If my people...will humble themselves and pray..."

Prior to the outpouring at Cane Ridge, pastors and their flocks became concerned with the growing number of newcomers to the area who were indifferent to faith or even actively opposed to it. With hearts for bringing the gospel to their new neighbors, they determined to set aside time to pray daily. Their earnest plea was for a revival extending salvation to the newcomers and rescuing their community from becoming overrun by ungodliness.

The Fulton Street Revival was wholly centered on prayer. Jeremiah Lanphier was divinely directed to reach the people of New York but was hesitant to go door-to-door with the gospel. After all, he was inexperienced and personally incapable of fulfilling such a task. He received a spark of godly intuition that led him to begin a weekly prayer meeting coinciding with the lunch hour. Perhaps that would open doors for presenting the gospel.

On the Hebridean islands, sisters Peggy and Christine Smith entered a covenant of praying for revival every single night, many times deep into the morning hours. Because of their respective handicaps, they were unable to attend public worship, so their small cottage became their sanctuary of intercession. It was there in their Holy Ghost inundated and saturated home that the promise of Isaiah 44:3 became prophetic inspiration to them: "For I will pour water on him who is thirsty, and floods on the dry ground; I will pour out My Spirit on your descendants, and My blessing on your offspring." They pleaded and confessed, declared and decreed these words of creative power in faith before God's shimmering throne.

If your heart is burdened for true revival, whether individual or corporate, prayer is the key, just as it was for Israel's sweet psalmist. In Psalm 5, King David petitioned, "Give ear to my words, O LORD; consider my meditation. Listen to the voice of my cry, my King and my God, for to You will I pray. O LORD, in the morning You will hear my voice; in the morning I will direct my prayer to You, and I will watch expectantly" (vv. 1–3). In another psalm he sang, "My heart is determined...I will awake at dawn!" (Ps. 108:1–2).

We gaze at the cultural collapse and spiritual drought around us. We proverbially wring our hands in despair witnessing the condition of our nation, our cities, our neighborhoods, our homes. But do we pray? Not much, it seems to me. I wonder, is prayer the subject of our neglect? Is it because somewhere deep in our souls we don't really believe it carries the revolutionary power to effect dynamic, permanent transformation? We must never doubt our living God's integrity and faithfulness to bring to fruition His covenant promise made in His 2 Chronicles 7:14 contract.

The fact is that prayer must become the heartbeat of our lives in Christ. The central theme of our lives. It must become the rhythm in all we do, every day and in every place. We possess no higher calling upon us, no more basic and fundamental, imperative or indispensable ingredient for releasing the rain of revival than that of prayer. As the apostle of prayer E. M. Bounds said:

> The prayers of God's saints are the capital stock in heaven by which Christ carries on His great work upon earth. The great throes and mighty convulsions on earth are the results of these prayers. Earth is changed and revolutionized, angels move on more powerful and rapid wings, and God's policy is shaped as the prayers are more numerous and efficient.[2]

What, therefore, should be the true object of our prayer before the altar of God Almighty? Evan Roberts, along with the Smith sisters, interceded for Holy Ghost rain to fall upon their local communities. The mighty believers of Cane Ridge carried a burden of extraordinary weight for the unreached new arrivals to their region. But what petitions should we offer when our souls ache for personal revival? Our Lord did not leave us without guidance. In fact, Jesus answered this very inquiry without ambiguity: "This is how you should pray..."

Midway through Jesus' longest-recorded sermon, *Sermo in Monte*, the Sermon on the Mount, which covers chapters 5–7 of Matthew's Gospel, the Light of the world illuminated the pathway of prayer:

> When you pray, you shall not be like the hypocrites. For they love to pray standing in the synagogues and on the street corners that they may be seen by men. Truly I say to you, they have their reward. But you, when you pray, enter your closet, and when you have shut your door, pray to your Father who is in secret. And your Father who sees in secret will reward you openly. But when you pray, do not use vain repetitions, as the heathen do. For they think that they will be heard for their much speaking. Do not be like them, for your Father knows what things you have need of before you ask Him.
>
> —Matthew 6:5–8

In my youth, we sang a hymn, "How Long Has It Been?," that asked how long it had been since we spent time with the Lord in prayer.[3]

What a daunting question: How long has it been since you truly engaged the Father in prayer? I'm not inquiring how long since you were obligated to offer a half-hearted, rote blessing before dinner or a low-expectation request over your child's sniffles. Neither am I referring to the self-conscious, performative words you spoke or preached or prayed when called upon to open or close a meeting at church. I am not condemning those moments or any of the other times we lift a few words toward His throne. Certainly, Philippians 4:6 is clear: "In *everything*, by prayer and supplication with gratitude, make your requests known to God" (emphasis added). Rather I am asking, When was the last time you closed yourself away somewhere and lost all track of time as a result of being enveloped in the glory of His holy and consuming presence? How long has it been since you stayed alone in prayer until you were not alone any longer? Have you ever entered His precious presence in the black night and found yourself still there at dawn?

I can recall most vividly a life-changing experience in 1964. I was seven years old, in the second grade. John F. Kennedy had been assassinated only months earlier. My sister was required to stay after school for some reason, so I had to walk a few blocks home alone that day. Upon entering our small two-story frame house, I bounded up the stairs but stood nearly paralyzed halfway up. I heard wailing and groaning, pounding and weeping. As I inched my way up what now seemed a mountain of stairs, I noticed the vacuum cleaner running in the upstairs hallway. There was no one at the controls. The frightening sounds were now much more labored and loud as if someone were in great pain or distress. The ominous noise was coming from the small closet in my sister's room—the door half ajar. I could now recognize the source. It was my mother...praying. Her words are forever etched on the pages of my heart and soul: "God, save my babies—save Debbie, save Rodney. Oh Jesus, please don't let my children end up in hell. Save my babies, God, save them in Jesus' name." I heard that prayer then, and I hear it still.

As I backed my way out of the room, I was surprised—and I'll admit, a bit frightened—to hear my mother praying with such intense fervency. Without a doubt, I was happy that she was praying for me, yet in that very moment I became acutely aware of my need for Christ as Savior and became quite concerned about the reality of a place called hell and me spending eternity there. I certainly didn't want to go there—no one does! But I had heard enough Bible sermons to know that avoiding hell was only possible by being absolutely and positively born again. I resolved then and there to make sure in no uncertain terms that

Jesus Christ was my Savior. It was just a few days after this episode that I made my way to the altar of God (I'm thankful that altars were still an absolute necessity in church décor then) at eight years of age and made my salvation sure by repenting of my sin and making a public proclamation of my faith in Jesus Christ as the Lord and Savior of my life.

In times past, the people of God referred to this compulsion to intercede as a *burden* to pray, so here I call to and plead with every preacher of the gospel and every true believer to become acquainted once again with just such a burden.

Another of my favorite memories of my mother and her impassioned zeal for revival which became a hallmark of my life and ministry is that she kept two volumes on her nightstand. One was her Bible, which she was in the habit of reading every morning and every evening. The other was a copy of Leonard Ravenhill's classic work *Why Revival Tarries*. For many years, it has been my custom to read it several times a year. It encourages me, inspires me, and provokes me to remember that my calling, my ministry, and indeed my life are all about the incessant need of carrying a burden of prayer for "the one."

Which one? The lonely Little Leaguer, the cheerless cheerleader, the woman nursing a bruise from a man who treats her as an object rather than his wife, and the man who is hopeless because he has lost his job and despairs of providing for his family. The one who lives down the street from you, or next door, or down the hall, or even in your own home. That is the one. That one is precious in the sight of God. That is the one for whom Jesus died. That is the one He came to seek and to save, and it is the one for whom your prayer life cannot wane and must never falter.

When was the last time you felt the warmth of your tears streaming down your face and dripping onto your shirt as you communed with the Father? Have you ever fasted by forgetting to eat because you were so enveloped in and overwhelmed by the all-consuming power and presence of the God of glory and His living Christ?

The Lord Jesus modeled such prayer on the occasion of His betrayal by Judas and His subsequent arrest. He then entered into such passionate prayer—His longest recorded prayer—it is commonly referred to as His High Priestly Prayer, preserved for us in John 17. It is upon the wings of such prayer that we ascend to the rarely trodden heights of a personal revival. This is the reason why in Matthew 6, after sharing with the multitude how not to pray, He continued immediately with, "Therefore, pray in this manner" (v. 9). Let's search for deeper understanding from Jesus' familiar yet deeply instructive discourse on the subject of prayer line by line:

> Our Father who is in heaven, hallowed be Your name.
> —MATTHEW 6:9

In its most basic sense, true prayer could be described as worship of the Creator of heaven and earth. Hear the words of the psalmist: "When I consider Your heavens, the work of Your fingers, the moon and the stars, which You have established...O LORD, our Lord, how excellent is Your name in all the earth!" (Ps. 8:3, 9). When we approach our Father—whose name is "hallowed," or holy—we sense the deep urge to bow and humble our hearts before His throne and bestow upon Him unparalleled adoration. You see, "There is none holy as the LORD" (1 Sam. 2:2).

Oh, the unplumbed depths of such a revelation—let us now and forever remember it and never fail, with hearts brimming with faith, to proclaim it. "How excellent is Your name, O Lord! Hallowed be Your name."

Let us not be as the Israelites of old who so often forsook and forgot the very God who had parted and paved the Red Sea and with His own mighty right arm had brought them into a land filled with milk and honey. Mark well the admonition of the Lord God to them from Ezekiel 36.

And wherever they went among the nations they profaned
my holy name, for it was said of them, "These are the
LORD's people, and yet they had to leave his land." I had
concern for my holy name, which the people of Israel profaned among the nations where they had gone.
—EZEKIEL 36:20–21, NIV

Before all else, in approaching the Lord in prayer, the first
words on our hearts and uttered by our tongues must be the
worship of His great name which is holy for He is holy. When
restoring Israel after their captivity, God made glorious promises
to His people, but first He made His priorities clear:

It is not for your sake, people of Israel, that I am going
to do these things, but for the sake of my holy name...I
will show the holiness of my great name, which has been
profaned among the nations, the name you have profaned
among them. Then the nations will know that I am the
LORD, declares the Sovereign LORD, when I am proved
holy through you before their eyes.
—EZEKIEL 36:22–23, NIV

It must also be noted that in the first word of this prayer,
"Our" Father, the living Christ identifies Himself personally with
each of us. He says God is not only His Father but also ours, and
therefore, we are His brothers—heirs of God and joint heirs with
Jesus Christ. (See Romans 8:17.)

Your kingdom come; Your will be done on earth, as it is
in heaven.
—MATTHEW 6:10

In Ezekiel 36 God our Father was clear that His deliverance of
the Israelites had nothing to do with them. Rather, it was entirely
for "the sake of my holy name....Then the nations shall know
that I am the Lord." Jesus was equally clear in Matthew 6:10: We
are to pray for *God's* kingdom to come, not ours. *God's* will be

done on earth, not ours. To rephrase, before we ask God, "Help me to pray," we should plead, "O Lord, help me *desire* to pray." Because when praying, the divine prompting behind our requests must be derived from Him. Our prayers should focus on His will for our lives, not ours.

And what is His will for you? Your reliable guide to His will can be found only within the confines of His Word, your Bible. His Word is a lamp to your feet and a light to your path (Ps. 119:105). Those aren't just red or black ink letters on white paper. They are "alive, and active, and sharper than any two-edged sword, piercing even to the division of soul and spirit, of joints and marrow, and able to judge the thoughts and intents of the heart" (Heb. 4:12).

If that wasn't remarkable enough, every page is filled with great and precious promises (2 Pet. 1:4). Settle this fact; every promise in that holy, living, and life-giving Book is God's absolute will for your life. Those promises reveal without question or apology exactly what Jesus died to make possible for you. Promises of healing, deliverance, provision, and victory. If these weren't the Father's will for you, He would never have promised them. Therefore, if you want to know God's will for your life, then learn God's promises, and allow those promises to become the focus of your prayers. God had made promises concerning the Israelites, and for the glory of His name, He delivered those promises. We must know that His Word is His will, for where the will of God is unknown, faith cannot exist. Faith begins where the will of God is known! Philemon 1:6 says, "That the communication of thy faith [that's prayer] may become effectual [effective] by the acknowledging [referring to] of every good thing which is in you in Christ Jesus" (KJV). The only good thing in you is God's holy Word. So when you pray, you must refer by faith to God's Word, which is His will for you. Pray the Word of God, and your prayer will have great effect!

Refer and rehearse to the Lord the promises the Scriptures make about your situation as you kneel before God's throne. Make this the foundation of your faith, and your will—your desire—will align perfectly with God's plans and purposes. Lay hold of those promises and pray for nothing more and nothing less.

Know that you have yet another ally in your quest to discover and live the will of God. The Holy Spirit is ready and well able to play a powerful role in revealing God's will to you. Remember, John 17:17 says God's Word is (not "contains") truth. In describing the role of the Holy Ghost, Jesus said: "But when the Spirit of truth comes, He will guide you into all truth...and He will tell you things that are to come" (John 16:13).

Receiving and maintaining personal revival means having a clear sense of God's will for your life. We must seek God's face constantly and consistently in prayer so that our minds are renewed and our tongues are set ablaze, preparing us to become vessels of Holy Ghost revival for ourselves and the world!

The previously examined principle of humility means that you joyfully submit to God's will and seek it by faith. But there is still more illumination from the Master to inform our praying.

> Give us this day our daily bread.
>
> —MATTHEW 6:11

On many occasions I have been asked whether or not we should actually ask God for provision. It has become my custom to direct these seekers of truth to Matthew 6:11. Here, directly from the lips of Jesus Himself, we find the answer in the absolute affirmative. It is a direct command in red ink! A command is neither optional nor flexible.

Further into that Ezekiel 36 passage the Lord God adds, in verses 36–37, "I the LORD have spoken it, and I will do it....I will yet for this be enquired of..." (KJV). We must still ask or inquire of the Lord to receive the promise, even when the will of God is directly stated.

God said there were further blessings from His bountiful and benevolent hand in store for them, but they were still required to ask. In Mark 11 the Lord Jesus said, "Whatever things *you ask* when you pray..." (v. 24, emphasis added). In John 16:24 He said, "*Ask*, and you will receive" (emphasis added). The apostle John wrote, "If we *ask anything* according to His will, He hears us" (1 John 5:14, emphasis added). Finally, James put it succinctly: "You do not have, because you do not *ask*" (Jas. 4:2, emphasis added).

Recorded for our understanding of the reason for the divine directive to ask is Genesis 1:26–27. It is there in our created state that the Lord God gave man dominion in the earth and withdrew His right to act independently in our lives. Therefore, our asking is our invitation for God to do that which it is His stated will to do for us.

This is the key to receiving almighty God's provisions and blessings—spirit, soul, and body, and all that pertains to life and godliness. Find His will in His Word and ask Him for it to be done. Jesus Himself was not exempt from this principle. In John 14:16 He asked our Father to send the Holy Spirit. If asking was required of Jesus, how much more so for you and me? The Son of God would never have commanded us to ask if it were unnecessary, nor if He would refuse to bring about what He commanded us to ask Him for.

> And forgive us our debts, as we forgive our debtors.
> —MATTHEW 6:12

It was in Psalm 24 that King David asked and answered what might well be the most urgent question of our hearts:

> Who may ascend the hill of the LORD? Who may stand in His holy place? He who has clean hands and a pure heart; who has not lifted up his soul unto vanity, nor sworn deceitfully. He will receive the blessing from the LORD, and righteousness from the God of his salvation.
> —PSALM 24:3–5

Oh, the grandeur that accompanies that prospect that we might ascend the hill of the Lord and stand in His holy place! If... Only *if*! This is the zenith of hope for our ultimate end, which is no actual end at all but rather continues in God's glorious presence for eternity. The revived life surely begins here on earth, but the ultimate revival of our lives—our becoming truly revenant—still awaits us on the other side of the grave. That's when "'God shall wipe away all tears from their eyes. There shall be no more death.' Neither shall there be any more sorrow nor crying nor pain, for the former things have passed away" (Rev. 21:4).

Yet in a sense, it is possible to enter God's presence now, in this life. Jesus' life, death, and resurrection are the sole reasons that it is possible for us to "ascend the hill of the Lord." However, to do so requires what is repulsive to the recoiling modern, nominal Christian—namely "holiness." "Clean hands and a pure heart," made possible only by appropriating Jesus' cleansing blood through sincere Bible repentance and by asking in the greatest humility for God's forgiveness. There, at the base of Calvary, the exchange is made and we become "clothed" in His righteousness. (See Romans 13:14; 2 Corinthians 5:21; Galatians 3:27; and Philippians 3:9.)

The prayer Jesus gave us reveals that, having received God's forgiveness which we do not deserve, we are expected to forgive those who trespass against us. For those of us who have been forgiven an unpayable, egregious debt, the crimson King of Calvary issues a stern warning against any reluctance we may have to forgive others. In His parable of the unforgiving servant, He admonished the servant who refused to forgive an infinitesimal debt when compared to the enormous debt that he had just been forgiven:

> "O you wicked servant! I forgave you all that debt because you pleaded with me. Should you not also have had compassion on your fellow servant, even as I had pity on you?"

His master was angry and delivered him to the jailers until he should pay all his debt. So also My heavenly Father will do to each of you, if from your heart you do not forgive your brother for his trespasses.

—Matthew 18:32–35

Jesus' paramount twin statements on the subject of forgiveness given in the Lord's Prayer are prophetically connected. Revival comes to individual believers who have been cleansed of sin and clothed in His righteousness *and* thereby are always eager to forgive others, as they have been forgiven. The Lord then adds one more request to His overtly instructive prayer. In it He gives us a model for inviting and igniting Holy Ghost revival:

And lead us not into temptation, but deliver us from evil.

—Matthew 6:13

In Gethsemane, under the illumination of the Passover moon, Jesus directed His disciples, "Watch and pray that you enter not into temptation. The spirit indeed is willing, but the flesh is weak" (Matt. 26:41). Truer words were never uttered and heard by mortal men. Our good intentions, emotional whims, and our unwise, immature zeal will cause us to write checks that our frail, fallible flesh just can't cash. This is precisely what Peter exhibited when he told Jesus he was prepared to fight and die for Him, and then less than twenty-four hours later he was swearing that he didn't even know Him.

Jesus was clear: our struggles do not come from our born-again spirits, because they have been breathed upon by the Almighty. Our spirit is always willing to do that which God desires. The problem arises from our flesh and the temptations by which we allow ourselves to be influenced. This is the necessity for this particular clause in Jesus' mighty model of prayer. He's asking us to pray daily that we would be led by His Spirit rather than by our flesh. Perhaps it would be advantageous to put voice to it and declare, "Flesh, you are my servant. My born-again spirit, animated by and submitted to the Holy Spirit of the living God, is dominant in my life!" The point is, we must follow the Holy Ghost, not the dictates of our flesh. Paul shouts it in the iconic eighth chapter of Romans:

> There is therefore now no condemnation for those who are in Christ Jesus, who walk not according to the flesh, but according to the Spirit....For those who live according to the flesh set their minds on the things of the flesh, but those who live according to the Spirit, the things of the Spirit. To be carnally minded is death, but to be spiritually minded is life and peace.
> —ROMANS 8:1, 5–6

Notice that our Lord did not say, "Lead us out of temptation," but rather, "Lead us not into temptation." Resistance against the flesh must never begin when the adversary of our souls shows up in the heat of temptation, with his fiery darts flying. Resistance begins every morning we awaken in our flesh. We must launch an offensive of prayer then and there for the Holy Spirit to lead us in the complete opposite direction of all temptation.

> For Yours is the kingdom and the power and the glory forever. Amen.
> —MATTHEW 6:13

Jesus closes His model prayer for us with a powerful reminder that our great God is ultimately and absolutely in control and has all power and authority in every situation. Everything we just prayed is valid and appropriate and endorsed by heaven because the One to whom we pray is the one true King. Our Holy Ghost–empowered breakthroughs and victories glorify the One to whom all glory belongs.

ෂ

The foundation and fuel of every massive and mighty revival throughout history has been prayer. It seems that God will not move in that way unless His people fervently ask for it. And what is true for churches and cities and nations is true for you and me. The promise of 2 Chronicles 7:14 has never been repealed or withdrawn. If you deeply desire personal, ongoing, life-renewing revival, you know the way. We begin by humbling ourselves. Then we pray. If... Only *if*! But the journey certainly does not end there.

Chapter 5

IF MY PEOPLE...
WOULD SEEK MY FACE

"**T**HE FACE OF the king." In biblical language, indeed in the language of all ancient cultures, the king's "face" was a symbol and metaphor for royal access. Only the supremely most privileged were ever afforded the honor to behold the face of the king. The preponderance of any king's subjects would live and die without ever once glimpsing the visage of their monarch. If they were among the uncommon few, it was usually little more than a hurried glimpse from the side of the road as the tightly guarded caravan of the sovereign passed swiftly by.

In a monarchy, those with access to the king's face had an enormous advantage over the beneficiaries possessing no such access. They had opportunity to petition for favors and advocate for causes. They could discern what pleased their king, as well as observe what angered him and tilted his crown. They might even become privy to his thoughts or plans.

Pharaoh Ramses II understood what it meant to have access to his face. He had this in mind when, in anger and exasperation after ten plagues had ravaged and tormented his kingdom, he barked his response to Moses: "Get away from me! Watch yourself, do not see my face anymore; for in the day you see my face you shall die" (Exod. 10:28).

As David was ascending to the throne of Israel, Abner, the mighty military general, sought to enter into a covenant of loyalty with the emerging king. David's response was, "Very well, I will make a covenant with you, but I require one thing from you: you will not see my face unless you bring Michal the daughter of Saul with you when you come to see me" (2 Sam. 3:13). In the Book of Proverbs, David's son, King Solomon, advised his own son, "In the light of the king's countenance is life, and his favor is as a cloud of the latter rain" (Prov. 16:15). In numerous psalms David implores God, in various ways, "Please don't hide Your face from me." And in Psalm 4:6 he writes, "Many are saying, 'Who will show us any good?' Lift up the light of Your face over us."

With this in view, we can see that God has something very specific and important in mind when in 2 Chronicles 7:14 He prescribes that His people "seek His face." God is asking us to deeply desire access to His royal throne with eager anticipation. We are to aspire to, above all else, be granted the privilege of His presence.

What does it look like, in practical terms, to seek the King's face? To answer the *what*, we must execute an examination of the *who*, *why*, *when*, and *how*.

Firstly, one must inquire, "Whom am I seeking?" Or to restate, I must ascertain the true and actual identity of that God who so loved the world and me. Are you wholeheartedly seeking out the omnipresent, omniscient, and omnipotent God of the Bible, or have you forgotten who He rightly is and all of His glorious deeds? Has the Mighty One become small and diminished in your eyes?

What an incomprehensible tragedy! The oldest book in the sixty-six volumes of our Bible is Job. Its forty-two chapters were written during the second millennium BC. In chapter 26 verse 7, Job illuminates some slight understanding of the infinite power and creative capacity of our God with these words: "He stretches out the north over empty space, He hangs the earth upon nothing." Then in verse 14 we find this revelation: "Indeed, these are but a part of His ways, and how small a whisper we hear of Him! But the thunder of His power who can understand?"

As I alluded to in my book *Gone: One Man...One Tomb...One Sunday*, astronomers tell us that thirteen hundred light-years from earth in the northernmost part of the intergalactic nebulae, at the heart of the constellation Orion, is a gaping black hole with a mass two hundred times that of the sun. The psalmist said, "Beautiful in elevation, the joy of the whole earth, is Mount Zion, on the sides of the north, the city of the great King" (Ps. 48:2). Our God fills all in all. The notion that God is omnipotent, omniscient, and omnipresent has fallen out of favor in our enlightened age. In the 1960s, so-called educated men sat behind mahogany desks in the ivory towers of academia, stroked their goatees as a wreath of pipe smoke encircled their brows, and with dogmatic certainty declared with solemnity that God was dead.

Allow me to pose a few questions: If God is dead, who was His assassin? Where is the cemetery plot that contains His remains? Where was the tombstone created, and who etched His name upon it? If God is dead, what exactly were the dates of His birth and death? How many men were needed to produce the strength required to carry His coffin? Where is the funeral home that handled His arrangements? And if God is dead, why weren't all the members of His family notified? The ever-living God cannot die by assassination or accident, nor by the proclamation of fools. He will never die—He is eternal. He will never grow weary. He will outlast all of His deniers and skeptics. He will not cease to exist because of backslidden church boards and lazy, lustful preachers. He will not be affected by the leaven of the modern Pharisees who pile on their religious rules and rudiments, nor will He be diminished by the modern Sadducees with their weighty volumes declaring the death of the supernatural.

How great is our God? He'll provide for us as He did for Peter when He told him to go fishing. The result? A fish with a coin in its mouth. He heals today, just as He healed blind Bartimaeus begging by the roadside. He delivers today, just as He set the man of Gadara free who was possessed by a legion of demons. He ever remains the same yesterday, today, and forever!

Since their declaration that God was dead didn't gain much traction, the erudite and elite changed the conversation and said, "If God is not dead, where did He come from?" Their purpose, of course, was not to engage in a legitimate discussion but to ensnare believers just as the Pharisees sought to entrap Jesus into saying something about which they could accuse Him to the authorities.

As I discussed in my book *Gone: One Man. One Tomb. One Sunday*, their logic went like this: If God had a beginning, then we can argue that He also has an ending. Wrong again. I have more good news for you—God came from nowhere because there was nowhere for Him to come from. Then He reached out into nothing, since there was nothing to reach for. He then took hold of nothing, called it something, pulled it out of nowhere, and hung it on nothing. He pointed His finger at it and told it to stay where He put it. And no one disagreed with Him because there was no one there except Him. He grinned, folded His arms, tilted His head, and said, "It is good."[1] It would be irrational and futile to petition a small and weak god for a mighty revival. But our God is the mighty God—how great is our God!

The Lord God, through the prophet Isaiah, once actually posed that very question to a group of people:

> Certainly, the hand of the LORD is not so short that it cannot save, nor is His ear so dull that it cannot hear. But your iniquities have made a separation between you and your God, and your sins have hidden His face from you so that He will not hear.
>
> —ISAIAH 59:1–2

Notice another reference there to the face of the King? Come once again to the altar of remembrance and there be reminded of the greatness of our God. Oh that we, in deep humility, might revive the undeserved honor and privilege we have been granted to seek His face. If... Only *if*!

So that this will be a sign among you. When your children ask, "What do these stones mean to you?" you will answer them that the waters of the Jordan were cut off before the ark of the covenant of the LORD. When it crossed the Jordan, the waters of the Jordan were cut off. These stones will be a memorial for the children of Israel continually.

—JOSHUA 4:6–7

Why was it indispensable to God that His people remember Him and His deeds in such a way? Lasting legacy. A stone altar lasted for many generations. Some constructed three thousand years ago still stand today. And God knew how quickly faith by remembrance can be lost from one generation to another. One generation's miracle and deliverance is the next generation's interesting story. For the subsequent generation it becomes a tall tale their grandparents used to tell. And then in the next, it's forgotten or even mocked. A stone altar was a witness. It spoke. It testified. It provoked curiosity; it prompted questions, questions that kept alive the greatness of our never-changing God. The fire of faith and revival were kept ablaze.

Yet even a stone altar of remembrance can fail to overcome our human proclivity to forget. From the Israelites who had walked across a divided and dry Red Sea to the disciples who had lost all hope after the crucifixion, far too many fail to stop and ponder at the altar of remembrance. If we have forgotten the grandeur of past experiences, how shall we sacrifice and hunger for an outpouring again?

When the doctor says the words "stage 4 cancer" to you or someone you love, the memory of past victory is easily eclipsed by that moment of present pain. The tendency is to forget that we serve the God who extended Hezekiah's life by fifteen years. When our bank statement makes tithing seem ill-advised, have we forgotten that our God owns the cattle on a thousand hills? Even Jesus' disciples seemed to suffer from severe short-term memory loss and lack of faith. Mark the Gospel writer describes the terrifying storm that had the disciples convinced they would all soon drown. After they rudely interrupted a sleeping Jesus, He immediately rebuked the wind and calmed the sea, asking His disciples, "Why are you so fearful? How is it that you have no faith?" (Mark 4:40). They had failed to visit the altar of remembrance. They had forgotten who was with them on that boat. Have you? Perilous times are but dangerous opportunities.

Hear the words of young David and allow them to strengthen your halting heart for the battles and victories of the next great move of the Holy Ghost! In 1 Samuel 17:37, "David said, 'The LORD who delivered me out of the paw of the lion and out of the paw of the bear, He will deliver me out of the hand of this Philistine.' And Saul said to David, 'Go, and the LORD be with you.'" That's future faith from past experience!

Build for yourself an altar of remembrance. Erect it in your home, in your prayer closet, in a secret place. Place in your mind and heart spiritual "forget me nots" of your breakthroughs, victories, healings, deliverances, and miracles. Allow them to quicken your memory. Shout over them; testify of them. They are the fuel of revival! If... Only *if*!

ॐ

Seek the face of God. There you will discover the voice of His Word, the breath of His Holy Spirit, and the smile of His favor. Seek those things—not prestige; not wealth; not the gratification of sensual desires; not friends, food, or fun. Second Chronicles 7:14 doesn't mean to amalgamate occasionally seeking His face with our crowded agendas or fleshly pursuits. Placing God on a crowded, rotating carousel of priorities and activities will never rend heaven and produce a deluge of vitality and spiritual awaking. Jeremiah 29:13 is clarifying: "You shall seek Me and find Me, *when you shall search for Me with all your heart*" (emphasis added).

That seeking which sparks revival is an all-consuming, passionate hunger. It speaks of a desperation that makes His "face" the priority that dwarfs every other desire. The psalmist captured this passion and urgency when he wrote:

> As the deer pants after the water brooks, so my soul pants after You, O God. My soul thirsts for God, for the living God. When will I come and appear before God? My tears have been my food day and night.
>
> —PSALM 42:1–3

There's an exclusivity to it, an outright abandonment—a desire experienced by a drowning man for a breath of air. It's knowing that if we don't receive the fresh wind, the holy air, or the sacred breath of an outpouring, we will die.

Nevertheless, in the current state of church normalcy in our fallen, broken world there is the ever-present danger of being seduced by three things that drew Solomon, the wisest man who ever lived, off the course: money, sex, and power. In the end he found it all empty and meaningless. "I have seen everything that is done under the sun, and indeed, all is vanity and like chasing the wind" (Eccles. 1:14). "Everything under the sun" covers a lot of ground. Solomon had vast wealth, unrivaled power, authority, and a thousand wives. "All is vanity and like chasing the wind," said he. Those slithery seductions remain today. They are deadly roadblocks to revival. God has so blessed our nation that what once only kings enjoyed is now available to every working-class American. These counterfeit pleasures and false gods are clogging the spiritual arteries by occupying the thoughts, dreams, goals, and energies of God's people. Solomon would warn, "All is vanity and like chasing the wind." Indeed, he could speak to them, but Ecclesiastes is right there in the heart of their dusty, neglected Bibles!

How do you seek God's face? By thirsting for it like a parched deer in the desert. By creating spiritual hunger because we are no longer full of the husks that the swine eat. By Him becoming everything we want, need, and hope for. But this leads us to another question.

☙

When? When do we seek Him?

In one sense the answer is an obvious one...always. David sang, "Morning, noon, and night I cry out in my distress, and the LORD hears my voice" (Ps. 55:17, NLT). The God who never sleeps nor slumbers commands us to "seek His face continually" (1 Chron. 16:11). True, but not actually what I am getting at when I question, "When?"

Another accurate answer would be at the prompting of the Holy Ghost. Certainly there is no dissatisfactory moment in time to pursue God's presence, but not all times of day are as productive as others. Very often one particular time of day appears in God's Word as exceptionally powerful and fruitful for divine encounters: it is the morning. This could be because we have been still and quiet, or because it is the offering of the firstfruits of a new day. It's morning.

> O LORD, in the morning You will hear my voice; in the morning I will direct my prayer to You, and I will watch expectantly.
>
> —PSALM 5:3

> Awake, my glory! Awake, psaltery and harp! I will awake the dawn.
>
> —PSALM 57:8

> O God, You are my God; early will I seek You.
>
> —PSALM 63:1

> I arose before the dawn of the morning and cried for help.
>
> —PSALM 119:147

> Cause me to hear Your lovingkindness in the morning; for in You I have my trust; cause me to know the way I should walk, for I lift up my soul unto You.
>
> —PSALM 143:8

Clearly, at least for David and the other psalmists, morning was the prime time for encounters with the King of glory. Consider as well the example of the Lord Jesus. Mark 1:35 is revealing: "In the morning, rising up a great while before sunrise, He went out and departed to a solitary place. And there He prayed."

Need we any greater example? Do we often or ever follow the footsteps of the Master? Do our eyes view the vast horizon as the black sky mixes with the radiance of first light and the kaleidoscope of color announces that we are greeted with a new day? In those first moments do our spirits and our souls find themselves longing, aching for Him before all else? Do we reach first for the cell phone or remote control? Are we thirsty after the long night for living water or Starbucks? Are we hungry for the bread of heaven or breakfast? Do we seek first our reflection in the mirror or the looking glass of His Word?

It was Socrates who offered this enlightenment: "The unexamined life is not worth living."[2]

Deeply embedded in the Levitical law was the principle of "firstfruits" offerings. (See Leviticus 23:10; Proverbs 3:9; and Ezekiel 44:30.) The Israelites were to sanctify and present the first of all their increase so that what remained would be blessed. Those desperate for revival would do well to offer the "first" of every day to seek the face of God. Romans 11:16 establishes the principle of firstfruits as solid New Covenant theology: "If the first portion of the dough is holy, the batch is also holy. And if the root is holy, so are the branches."

For the sake of this dying world, let us arise not simply from the ease of spiritual slumber but from the comfort of natural rest. Let us meet the dawn of every new day with the strength of spirit and the heart of the Lion of Judah. Let us charge the light to find the place of His holy presence, there to offer Him ourselves as firstfruits sacrifices for His delight and the increase of His kingdom and the glory of His Christ.

May we, for the sake of revival, rise early and give our first moments, our initial thoughts to Him. May our first vocalizations be praises of adoration to the magnificent and glorious God! Imagine how transformed our first outlook on each day would be. Offer Him the morning, that pristine time of expectancy and opportunity. He who never slumbers is there waiting for us in the morning. If... Only *if*!

ॐ

"Come near to me," Elijah instructed the Israelites after the prophets of Baal had embarrassed themselves for hours in their failed attempts to get their false god to accept their sacrifice. His order was announced in the hope of giving that backslidden crowd a front-row seat for witnessing the mighty hand of God manifest a miracle. Elijah not only wanted them to "see" the God of heaven rain down fire upon the altar he was about to construct; he wanted them to feel the heat on their faces. Even better if their eyebrows got singed.

The prophet then assembled twelve stones to build an altar to the Lord. He carefully arranged the wood and crowned it with the sacrificial bull, then made every attempt to make it all but impossible for the wood to catch fire. He took twelve barrels of water and completely drenched the bull and the wood, even filling up the surrounding trench with water. The atmosphere was inundated with tension, and the stage was set.

The miraculous display of Jehovah's unrivaled power was about to unfold as the curtain rose. The Scriptures report the scene as follows:

> At the time of the offering of the evening sacrifice, Elijah the prophet came near and said, "The Lord, God of Abraham, Isaac, and of Israel, let it be known this day that You are God in Israel and that I am Your servant and that I have done all these things at Your word. Hear me, O Lord, hear me, so that this people may know that You are the Lord God and that You have turned their hearts back again." Then the fire of the Lord fell and consumed the

burnt sacrifice and the wood and the stones and the dust
and licked up the water that was in the trench. When all
the people saw it, they fell on their faces and said, "The
LORD, He is God! The LORD, He is God!"

—1 KINGS 18:36–39

As it was then with Elijah, so it is now with our King. He's
saying, "Come near to Me!" He is fully aware that if we catch
just a glimpse of His glory and goodness; His majesty and
might; His power and glory; His unfailing love for broken,
fallen, rebellious humanity, we, like those Israelites, will fall
upon our faces crying out, "The Lord, He is God!" It is no accident that one of the key waypoints on God's prescribed path
for an unprecedented outpouring of revival is "Seek My face!"
This is more than a command; it's also a royal invitation. Indeed,
it's the invitation of the ages. Remember where we began this
chapter—with the revelation that the king's "face" represented
access to his imperial throne along with all of the privileges that
are afforded by such access.

Now ponder this reality: God, the ruling Monarch of heaven
and earth, is requesting by royal decree for you and me to seek
access to His face, while signaling His merciful, gracious willingness to grant it! Accepting that invitation requires faith. As
the writer of Hebrews put it, "Without faith it is impossible to
please God, for he who comes to God must believe that He exists
and that He is a rewarder of those *who diligently seek Him*" (Heb.
11:6, emphasis added).

Massive, earth-shaking moves of the Holy Ghost of God are
life-altering, destiny-changing, and history-making. Revivals
that sweep through churches and entire cities and even nations
are glorious indeed. But equally glorious is that personal revival
of a solitary, parched soul. Why not you? Why not now? History
reveals that the fire of your very own personal outpouring might
very well be the spark that ignites a nation-shaking conflagration
of glory. If... Only *if*!

My solemn prayer is that a fire of desire for your personal

revival is being set ablaze. If so, then there is one additional item in God's 2 Chronicles 7:14 blueprint that we have yet to examine. Let's get to it.

Chapter 6

IF MY PEOPLE... WOULD TURN FROM THEIR WICKED WAYS

PREVIOUSLY MENTIONED THE indelible impact the late Leonard Ravenhill had on me as a young man. That influence has not diminished in the swiftly passing years. Even though he received his eternal reward in 1994, I still hear his voice, thundering with prophetic authority and palpable anointing. One specific quote of his resonates deeply within my spirit: "There's one thing we need above everything else; it's something we don't talk about these days. We need a mighty avalanche of conviction of sin."[1]

Both of those sentences are unequivocally true, by the way. There is no doubt that we desperately need an "avalanche of conviction of sin." But it's paramount to understand the weighty subject of sin and its damning effects on our lives. So also, we must understand its ability to separate us from the holy presence of God for eternity. Notwithstanding, the subject of sin is rarely, if ever, discussed among God's people—much less taught or preached from our pulpits. But God didn't bring me back victorious from a battle with vocal cord cancer to remain silent on important topics like this that have eternal consequences! Let's delve into God's 2 Chronicles 7:14 strategy for revival in the context of seeking personal, individual revival. Let's pursue the kind of revival that causes the effervescent life of God to radiate from every part of our being to draw lost and hurting souls to the "old rugged cross." As we've reached the final of four waypoints on that pathway, let's view that deeply revelatory verse in its entirety again:

> If My people, who are called by My name, will humble themselves and pray, and seek My face and turn from their wicked ways, then I will hear from heaven, and will forgive their sin and will heal their land.
>
> —2 CHRONICLES 7:14

As I so often say, we can't just read the Bible; we have to *read* the Bible. So let's reset and reorient ourselves by revisiting the individual factors of this divine equation—an equation that culminates in a supernatural outpouring of Holy Ghost power and a harvest of born-again, revived, and revenant souls being ushered into the kingdom of God and of His Christ. Again, note the first three words:

"If My people..."

Jehovah is addressing His own people here. At the time, He was referring to the Israelites, the children of Abraham living under the old covenant. He wasn't speaking to the Moabites, Philistines, or the Babylonians; rather the Holy One of Israel was conveying explicit instructions solely to His chosen people. Today, when the Lord God speaks of "My people," He is including all those saved by the redeeming blood of Christ whose sins have been washed white as snow and are living under the new covenant. Both Jews and Gentiles.

You may be curious as to why I am forcefully reiterating this point now, as we have already deliberated the first three spiritual requisites on God's roadmap to revival. But let's think of this as an opportunity for self-examination and take a personal, spiritual inventory as you ponder these questions. To what degree have you intentionally been

1. humbling yourself before God;

2. praying consistently and fervently, giving God the firstfruits of those early hours of your days; and

3. seeking His face in passionate pursuit of His presence?

But what about this fourth and final piece of the prescription? "…turn from their wicked ways…"? *Whoa now, Pastor. Wait just a second. Me? I'm far from perfect, but "wicked ways" seems a little extreme.*

That language should never bewilder us. We're all familiar with the words of the "weeping prophet" Jeremiah. Hear him in chapter 17, verse 9 from the book that bears his name: "The heart is more deceitful than all things and desperately wicked; who can understand it?"

Again, we must *read* the Bible! Second Chronicles 7:14 confirms that it is God's own people who are still languishing and wallowing in their "wicked ways." And it's not just the Modern English Version we've been quoting that illuminates this biblical reality. Cross-reference the verse in any other translation and you'll only find "wicked ways," "evil ways," or "evil practices" to communicate God's intent. When we *read* the Scriptures, it's inescapably clear—God is not addressing those outside the church in 2 Chronicles 7:14, but rather those of us who claim the name of His Son. According to our omniscient, sovereign Creator, there is wickedness from which we have yet to turn. When we do, we turn—or repent—and "set [our] affections on things above" (Col. 3:2).

As I addressed earlier, the incomparable Leonard Ravenhill spoke the dreadfully grievous and tragic truth when he declared that we don't talk about sin in the church much anymore.

Far too often and increasingly more as time progresses, I have witnessed a prominent Christian leader or two—or twenty—for whom Ravenhill would have had some stern words of admonition.

He would have unambiguously and unequivocally pointed them toward the Bible and its thousands of words on subjects like holiness, sin, and most certainly, on hell.

It seems that every few months lately some new pastor, Christian writer, or singer who made a name for themselves in some form of "Christian media" is undergoing a "crisis of faith." They suddenly no longer believe in a God who punishes rebellion and judges sin. They no longer accept the fact that eternity without God awaits those who recoil at the very mention of such crude and outdated notions. A few have even deceived themselves and others into believing that hell itself is a fiction.

This is an epidemic of spiritual treachery spawned amid the current wash of cultural demise, secular humanism, the gay agenda, racial division, a collapsed education system, failed government policies, political correctness, and spiritual drought. Silent or backslidden, pandering, pampering pulpits and barren altars are producing barren "believers." It has all generated a wave of "theologians" and "teachers" who are reverse engineering their faith and doctrinal truth. By that I mean they take that demonic, grotesque form of theologically humanistic idolatry which begins with what they prefer God to be like and work backward from there. They begin with how they wish God ran the universe and then cherry-pick a few Bible verses that out of context seem on the surface to support their profane preference. They then dismiss, discard, or disregard those that don't fit their new and improved "reimagined" model. The result is a custom-crafted feel-good-about-yourself brand of positive thinking or soulish spirituality that bears no more resemblance to the unadulterated gospel of Christ than a kitten resembles a lion. May God help us.

The Romans Road of true salvation still begins with "For all have sinned and come short of the glory of God" (Rom. 3:23) and then leads directly to "The wages of sin is death" (Rom. 6:23). Ezekiel rises to testify of this blatant warning: "The soul who sins shall die....The righteousness of the righteous shall be upon himself, and the wickedness of the wicked shall be upon himself"

(Ezek. 18:20). The living Christ of Calvary Himself graphically illustrated the fact: "And if your eye causes you to sin, pluck it out and throw it away. It is better for you to enter life with one eye than having two eyes to be thrown into the fire of hell" (Matt. 18:9)? The Holy Ghost–inspired writer of Hebrews put it in terms even a child can understand:

> As it is appointed for men to die once, but after this comes the judgment.
> —HEBREWS 9:27

Indeed, the Revelation of Jesus Christ, John's apocalypse, gives us a sobering, cinematic, panoramic view of where that "judgment" after death will take place:

> Then I saw a great white throne and Him who was seated on it. From His face the earth and the heavens fled away, and no place was found for them. And I saw the dead, small and great, standing before God. Books were opened. Then another book was opened, which is the Book of Life. The dead were judged according to their works as recorded in the books. The sea gave up the dead who were in it, and Death and Hades delivered up the dead who were in them. And they were judged, each one by his works. Then Death and Hades were cast into the lake of fire. This is the second death. Anyone whose name was not found written in the Book of Life was cast into the lake of fire.
> —REVELATION 20:11–15

It grieves me to contemplate that as I walk the dangerous streets of American cities, I am surrounded by people who have been in church all of their lives and yet never once heard a sermon expounding upon the passage above. Or any message of warning, for that matter. If your pastor, TV preacher, blogger, vlogger, or social media "influencer" would never minister from portions of the Word of God such as Ezekiel 33:8–9, please don't walk away…

run! Your soul is in jeopardy. And I don't speak of the game show. I present it here for your review:

> When I say to the wicked, "O wicked man, you shall surely die," and you do not speak to warn the wicked from his way, that wicked man shall die in his·iniquity. But his blood I will require from your hand. Nevertheless, if you on your part warn the wicked to turn from his way and he does not turn from his way, he shall die in his iniquity. But you have delivered your soul.

Here's another text you won't hear preached on a Sunday morning in today's patty-cake churches with these placating, faux preachers: "You adulterers and adulteresses, do you not know that the friendship with the world is enmity with God? Whoever therefore will be a friend of the world is the enemy of God" (Jas. 4:4). A social media advertisement of that text will pack out the building next week! Enmity is hatred, warfare against God Himself. While you're enjoying the light show and twenty-minute motivational talk from Pastor "Life Coach" next Sunday, quietly read that verse to yourself. Gulp!

Scripture could not be more clear or direct. *Sin is real. Hell is real. God hates sin.* Oh, there's another "canceled" verse— Psalm 7:11, "God judgeth the righteous, and God is angry with the wicked every day" (KJV). Nope, sorry, that one simply will not work for next month's sermon series from Pastor "Twenty Minutes or Less." It just isn't "marketable." Our chromium-plated, over-organized, streamlined, social media–devised, streaming-synthesized form of Christianity is impotent to produce any form of true revival, and it always will be.

Sin has consequences—now and throughout eternity. To say there's no sin, though, is to also say there's no forgiveness, because what do we need to be forgiven of? If there's no forgiveness needed, why did Jesus suffer, sigh, cry out, and die on that angry, mean, biting beam? I pray that at least some can track with that logic, but then many others have an issue even hearing about anything on the subject of sin. One young lady who had begun regularly sipping on the syrupy-sweet false doctrine she was hearing elsewhere told me, "I can't take hearing about sin, hell, and the great white throne judgment seat of Christ anymore. It's time I find another church."

What she meant was that she didn't like hearing about *her* sin. *Her* wickedness. *Her* unavoidable date before the judgment seat. Honestly, she represents most who have abandoned their Bible-teaching church for another whose pastor panders to a culture looking only for a spiritual New Age guru who agrees with their idolatrous, conscience-soothing drivel, while true awakening produces those full of Holy Ghost power who understand that a genuine move of God's Spirit is dependent upon moral virtue. It becomes necessary when the virtue and intelligence or vice and ignorance of the people demand it. At that point, compromise and negotiation become void and an outpouring becomes inevitable. These understand that the only way for evil to excel is for good people to do nothing. And any church that professes to uphold the cause of Christ yet condemns cultural confrontation is no more than a social club desiring rain with no thunder and lightning. They long only to avoid confrontation by dwelling in the devil's demilitarized zones of apathy in a vain attempt to preserve their façade of peace.

Those touched by the spirit of revival know that power concedes nothing without a demand, and that brave men negligent to their office are of little more value than the coward who deserts in times of grave danger. We have now reached the boiling point. Our churches and culture are in chaos. The moral foundations once constructed by the tenets of our faith are quickly crumbling around us, and true repentance, leading to revival, is the only cure. We are at a crossroads, a strategic inflection point. We are faced with a choice. When complacency exceeds our personal and spiritual desire for change, the consequence becomes concession, which breeds chaos. But when comfort and contentment no longer pacify the people of God, negotiation is no longer tolerated and prayer becomes the catalyst that produces confrontation and permanent change. I sense a stirring as this collapsing culture is beginning to groan under the pressure of giving birth to a heaven-sent revival and earth-shaking outpouring of God. The very moral climate of our churches and cities is beginning to change, and the effect will be felt like shockwaves across the nation.

At the birth of the infant church, such a culture-shaking revival was apparent. Men and women became martyrs and misfits. They were mocked, tormented, and even tortured by the religious, political, and academic elites. They became ostracized. But, like Shadrach, Meshach, and Abednego, they refused to bow and they could not burn. I pray to see that same fire burning and a glorious church rising from obscurity. I pray for a remnant that will gladly exchange their comfort for a cause much greater than themselves.

There is no greater drama than the sight of revenant believers scorned by a succession of adversaries, yet bearing trials with tenacity, multiplying miraculously, building order in chaos, fighting the sword with the Word, displacing lying hypocrisies with truth, and defeating the strongest of adversaries. All this they do while rescuing the despondent, restoring the downtrodden, and reviving the life of Christ in the hearts of their fellows.

These may at times appear beaten and battered, but never are they bowed. They are propelled by a power greater than themselves. They are compelled by an inward desire to serve an infallible leader with irresistible power based upon absolute truth. Men and women of such spiritual DNA will never cave in to the pressure of popularity. God, give us such a revenant remnant who, like David in the face of Goliath and the Philistine armies, cry out, "Is there not a cause?" Who, like Moses in Pharaoh's court, declare and decree, "Let my people go!" (See Exodus 5:1.) Give us world changers who, like Dr. Martin Luther King, Jr., preached in the face of racial segregation and bigotry:

When we allow freedom to ring, when we let it ring from every village and hamlet, from every state and city, we will be able to speed up that day when all of God's children—black men and white men, Jews and Gentiles, Catholics and Protestants—will be able to join hands and to sing in the words of the old Negro spiritual, "Free at last! Free at last; thank God Almighty, we are free at last!"[2]

Give us those mighty men and women of valor who, like Patrick Henry at the birth of the American Revolution, wail, "Is life so dear, or peace so sweet, as to be purchased at the price of chains and slavery? Forbid it, Almighty God! I know not what course others may take; but as for me, give me liberty or give me death!"

This revival is not for the timid and the weak but for the strong and the brave who have stepped over the line and out of their comfort zones—those who have truly decided to become disciples of the living Christ. These no longer seek preeminence, a position, popularity, nor a pat on the back. These enlist to following orders.

So let me encourage all who will listen. Take up your spiritual weapons. We must invade the corridors of the doomed and the damned. We must engage our archenemy, Satan, and set this hell-bound generation free. It is our lot to thrust in the sickle and reap, for the harvest truly is ripe. The apex of all Christian endeavor must become to place the jewel of a soul in the crown of our Savior that the Lamb of God slain may receive the reward of His suffering.

In this moment, the eyes of the Lord are running to and fro. He is seeking that remnant who will stand in the gap and make up the hedge for humanity. He is looking for warriors who don't have to be right, recognized, rewarded, nor regarded, for these and these alone will reap that great end-time harvest of souls. They will receive His eternal reward. They will hear His righteous commendation. I pray that the living God will rise up within your heart. I call on you to sound the alarm and proclaim with me, "Let the Holy Ghost awakening begin!"

Of course, modern churchgoers can't abide hearing about sin, hell, and judgment. However, while their flesh protests, "Don't you dare put condemnation on me, p

reacher," our merciful God purposes for them to experience conviction. Condemnation leads to avoidance; conviction leads to repentance. The difference between the two is literally life and death.

Again, conviction is to your soul what pain is to your body. Pain is not your enemy; rather, it is an indication that an enemy has invaded your life. Without the convicting power of the Holy Ghost, I could live each day stained and stunted by the scourge of sin. I would be completely unaware of how my spiritual growth was being hindered, not to mention the horrific consequences of eternal damnation that would await me as a result of my sin.

The young lady who left our church because she didn't want to hear any more about the convicting power of sin and the impending judgment is comparable to someone suffering from severe abdominal pain who doesn't want to hear about needing her appendix removed. So, instead, the person finds a doctor who will continue to prescribe ever-more-powerful painkillers, only camouflaging the true issue. That, of course, will not end well. The pain, the conviction is often God's signal that something is terribly wrong, and if left unattended, it will lead to death.

The conviction of the Lord is actually a gift to us. We should never run away from the conviction of God; rather we must confront it. In his classic devotional, *My Utmost for His Highest*, Oswald Chambers writes, "Conviction of sin is one of the rarest things that ever strikes a man. It is the threshold of an understanding of God....Strictly speaking, a man cannot repent when he chooses; repentance is a gift of God."[3]

If as God's people we are to turn from our wicked ways and our sin and be revived, then the convicting grace of the Holy Spirit in response to our sin is absolutely indispensable. The modernistic preachers of this hour who have claimed conviction as contraband are but deceiving charlatans from whom we must cleanse ourselves or fall by our own weight. The great nineteenth-century voice of Charles Finney echoes a thunderous amen: "Revival is a renewed conviction of sin and repentance, followed by an intense desire to live in obedience to God. It is giving up one's will to God in complete humility."[4] If I were preaching, I'd repeat that three times.

What is meant by a "renewed conviction of sin"? Are there any specific sins of which we may especially need a renewed conviction? And how "intense" does one's desire to obey God really need to be? These are important questions. Let's find some answers.

๛

Prior to the revival at Cane Ridge in 1800, many of God's people noted with alarm an unmistakable combination of moral decline and anti-God sentiment in their community. They refused to accept such a decadent decline, and took action. They did *not* form a committee. They did *not* circulate a petition. They got on their knees and bombarded the throne of God Almighty, asking Him to send revival. They knew that a pacifist approach could not be afforded, nor would complacency succeed in reversing the downward spiraling in the spiritual climate of their community. They had Bibles; they had read and taken seriously the warning given in Ephesians 4:27 about never allowing the devil a "foothold" (NIV).

As we discussed in chapter 1, soon after the completion and dedication of God's temple, Solomon granted Satan just such a "foothold" by willfully disobeying God's direct command against intermarriage with foreign women. "You shall not go in to them," Jehovah had decreed, "nor shall they come in to you, for they will surely turn your heart away toward their gods" (1 Kings 11:2). A thousand wives later, many of whom worshipped false gods, that's precisely what transpired. To the peril of all Israel, "Solomon did what was evil in the sight of the LORD and did not fully follow the LORD as his father David had done. Then Solomon built a high place for Chemosh, the abomination [idol] of Moab, in the hill that is close to Jerusalem, and for Molek, the abomination [idol] of the children of Ammon. He did the same for all his foreign wives, who burned incense and sacrificed to their gods" (1 Kings 11:6–8).

From Solomon's later writing of Ecclesiastes, it is possible to deduce that the backslidden king eventually experienced a renewed conviction of his sins. As he writes, "I set my heart to know wisdom and to know the folly of ideas and to know foolish behavior, and I know that this as well is like chasing the wind" (Eccles. 1:17). However, the devastating damage to the spiritual health of Israel had long been done. Israel would never fully recover from the abominations that Solomon unleashed upon the land through rebellion with his foreign wives. Where had that conviction of sin been decades earlier? There is always a severe price to be paid when one travels the prodigal's hogpen trail. Something is always lost that can never be recovered. How much better would it be to stay at home in our Father's house (Luke 15:11–17)?

Like the godly people of Cane Ridge, we too must be cognizant of the dangers of giving the enemy of our souls a foothold in our lives. In my book *Could It Be?* I wrote:

> As God's redemptive souls, we have an obligation to live
> above the blight of sin that plagues us. We have profaned
> the living temple with dead idols for which there can be
> no agreement. The holy cannot make the unholy like itself,
> but the unholy can profane the holy. Like the Pharisees, we
> have been more concerned with cleaning the outside of the
> bowl while leaving the inside unwashed.[5]

You'll win no popularity contests nor will you receive a glitter-encrusted invitation to party with the pop stars by speaking the truth about sin. Just when did we, like Peter, warm ourselves by the fires of worldliness that such fleshly ridiculousness became the goal? But God's truth will make us free. The heart of man's problems is the problem of the human heart. Man has a sin problem, which Romans 6:23 reveals creates a death problem. The death rate among humans remains stubbornly at 100 percent. The penalty for sin is death. All men die; therefore, all have sinned.

A juvenile once asked me a question: "When can I stop repenting?" The answer came easily enough: "When you stop sinning." To His eternal glory and our eternal gratitude, the Lord Jesus Christ died that death for us. Yet appropriating His sacrificial, atoning death requires repentance and the humility to accept it. The subject of sin has been successfully sequestered from most churches. To our eternal peril, sin and its devastating consequences are no longer taken seriously. This is the result of men pleasing men with seared consciences, whose preachers have convinced churchgoers that as long as they appear morally acceptable on the outside, they can harbor corruption, uncleanness, and death on the inside. God gives some revivalists the moral fortitude and Holy Ghost power as our Savior had when He thundered judgment at the pseudo-religious and called them "whitewashed tombs" (Matt. 23:27). Presentable on the outside. Filled with devils and death on the inside.

In the 1880s John George Govan and the Faith Mission organization he founded were gloriously used in a mighty outpouring throughout Scotland. During these Holy Ghost–orchestrated meetings, people were actively instructed that they would not be prayed for to receive salvation until they had been directly under conviction of the Holy Spirit for at least six weeks' time. Can you imagine walking down the aisle and being told, "No, you're not ready"? No little "Now I lay me down to sleep" prayer or thirty-second confession was permitted. Complete repentance and surrender to the lordship of Christ is not simply about asking Him to come into your heart and add your name to the Book of Life. Seekers must understand their "lost-ness," their depravity, and the profound extremity, poverty, and burden of sin to actually feel the full weight of their sins.

Has the heaviness of your sin and the convicting power of the Holy Spirit ever weighed upon your heart to the point that you had to choose between surrendering it all to Christ or dying? That was the point the Lord God as well as Govan and the Faith Mission were making, and it is of absolute importance for us to recognize in this hour if we are ever to fulfill the 2 Chronicles 7:14 requirement of turning from our wicked ways.

Wicked ways about me?! Even you, my dear reader, may at this very moment be recoiling at the suggestion of there being any wicked ways about you. Admittedly, the term *wickedness* conjures a number of difficult images in people's minds, usually involving blatant sexual immorality, decadence, and debauchery. However, God and His Word disclose a multitude of devices He considers wicked that may not occur to many modern "Christians" or unbelievers.

There is logic and divine purpose revealed in the order of the four steps outlined in 2 Chronicles 7:14. There is a reason why "turning from our wicked ways" appears last in the sequence. For it is only in humbling ourselves, then pausing to quiet our frantic souls and overly busy lives long enough to pray, that we are in a proper position to seek the face of God. And it is only in seeking God's face, His holy presence, that we begin to understand the depth and nature of our sinfulness. There, in the beaming light of His glory, much is exposed and realized. Light exposes things, illuminates dark corners of our lives and thoughts.

Isaiah, in his iconic sixth chapter, reports that "in the year that King Uzziah died" (Isa. 6:1) he was transported to the pavilions of heaven. Isaiah was granted a glimpse of God's holy throne room. Jehovah Himself appeared, seated with winged creatures above Him. The seraphim cry out in peals of thunder, "Holy! Holy! Holy!" Beholding such purity and majesty provoked this response:

> And I said: "Woe is me! For I am undone because I am a man of unclean lips, and I dwell in the midst of a people of unclean lips. For my eyes have seen the King, the LORD of Hosts."
>
> —ISAIAH 6:5

Witnessing the face of God evokes in us an acute awareness of our uncleanness, and that is a very good thing. According to Romans 2:4, "the goodness of God leads you to repentance." What a thought, that we can come from the cross with a right heart and a clear conscience (Heb. 9:13–14).

If given the opportunity, what might the light and holiness of God's presence reveal in our hearts? It would be difficult to create a comprehensive list of all the wickedness that afflicts men. The apostle Paul made an attempt in Galatians 5:

> Now the works of the flesh are revealed, which are these: adultery, sexual immorality, impurity, lewdness, idolatry, sorcery, hatred, strife, jealousy, rage, selfishness, dissensions, heresies, envy, murders, drunkenness, carousing, and the like. I warn you, as I previously warned you, that those who do such things shall not inherit the kingdom of God.
>
> —GALATIANS 5:19–21

(By the way, when is the last time you saw those verses "tweeted" or preached from?)

It's quite enlightening to see sins such as strife and envy listed alongside "biggies" like adultery and sorcery—yet there they are. Selfishness is in the same list as murder. We must recalibrate our sensitivities and rankings on all of those things that offend God and grieve His Holy Spirit. Here are a few satanic strongholds that only become illuminated in the hearts of believers after they walk the 2 Chronicles 7:14 path to presence.

Anger. James 1:19–20 brings clarity: "Therefore, my beloved brothers, let every man be swift to hear, slow to speak, and slow to anger, for the anger of man does not work the righteousness of

147

God." The Lord Jesus raised anger to an even more serious level: "You have heard that it was said by the ancients, 'You shall not murder,' and 'Whoever murders shall be in danger of the judgment.' But I say to you that whoever is angry with his brother without a cause shall be in danger of the judgment" (Matt. 5:21–22).

The apostle James lends his agreement: "...for the anger of man does not work the righteousness of God" (Jas. 1:20). Away with the wickedness of anger.

Rebelliousness. The government-imposed lockdowns that restricted millions of Americans during the COVID-19 pandemic exposed that wickedness at work in the hearts of many "believers." Yet Isaiah 30:1 warns, "Woe to the rebellious children, says the Lord, who take counsel, but not from Me, and make an alliance, but not of My Spirit, in order to add sin to sin." Any form of rebellion against God-ordained authority is rebellion against God Himself. Paul the apostle did not stutter when he said we are to serve under all authority figures in our lives "with good will doing service, as to the Lord, and not to men" (Eph. 6:7).

God, send a flood of repentance against every rebellious spirit. Unless an authority is directing us to violate the commands of God, to commit sin, we are to be obedient, "knowing that whatever good thing any man does, he will receive the same from the Lord, whether he is enslaved or free" (Eph. 6:8).

The Love of Money. We know Jesus declared one cannot serve both God and money. Paul also wrote:

> For the love of money is the root of all evil. While coveting after money, some have strayed from the faith and pierced themselves through with many sorrows.
> —1 Timothy 6:10

As I have preached, show me your checkbook, and I'll tell you who is your true God. Money is inanimate and therefore cannot be evil. In fact, it is quite necessary; however, it can become very seductive. In Jesus' parable of the soils He added "the deceitfulness of riches" to those things which tend to "choke" the life out of the Word of God sown in your heart (Matt. 13:22). The abundant scriptural warnings about it testify to the temptation of making wealth an idol to be served rather than a tool to be used. Oh, the terrible sin of "serving" money! And the transgression of slaving away to earn as much as possible in order to increase your personal wealth, hoarding it for your own selfish pleasure. Solomon was the richest man that ever lived. Jeff Bezos, Bill Gates, and Elon Musk would have to combine their wealth to even come close to that of the last king of united Israel. Yet Solomon lamented, "All of it was vanity and chasing the wind. And there was no benefit under the sun" (Eccles. 2:11).

If approaching the face of our holy God and righteous Judge reveals your love of wealth and status above your love for the Master, you know what to do. Confess. Repent. Apply the blood of the Lamb. And receive supernatural help in changing your deceived heart.

Lack of Empathy for the Poor. We find a stinging indictment in James 2:5–6: "Has God not chosen the poor of this world to be rich in faith and heirs of the kingdom which He has promised to those who love Him? But you have despised the poor." Remember, Jesus' brother was writing to the church. These are Christians who "have despised the poor." It has probably never crossed your mind that you might be guilty before God of that charge. *Only a truly terrible person would do so,* the religious respond. I suspect the recipients of James' letter had convinced themselves in a similar fashion of deceit. May I inquire regarding your generosity toward those who possess less than you? Do you regularly look for ways to serve and provide for those in need? How would your bank account spending register testify if called as a witness? There is a reckoning, you understand. While many are busy needing the newest electronic gadget, others have their electricity turned off. Help us, Lord! If the light of God's Word or His Spirit puts a spotlight on a stain in your heart regarding this, you know what to do—as is the case with this next common area of rebellion and sin.

Hardness of Heart. Would others describe you as tender-hearted? If not, why? Romans 5:5 reveals that "the love of God has been shed abroad in our hearts by the Holy Spirit." If that love is not flowing through you to those around you, especially those in obvious need or pain, perhaps you have succumbed to the sin of hard-heartedness. Perhaps you need a fresh filling of the Spirit, who distributes that love.

Life in the broken, twisted world can make us cynical. Calloused. Blind to real need and deaf to cries for help. We must lay our hardened hearts at the altar and pray that God would use us as instruments of healing and restoration throughout the earth.

Paul exhorted the Ephesian church:

> From now on you walk not as other Gentiles walk, in the vanity of their minds, having their understanding darkened, excluded from the life of God through the ignorance that is within them, due to the hardness of their hearts. Being calloused they have given themselves over to sensuality for the practice of every kind of impurity with greediness.
> —EPHESIANS 4:17–19

We Pentecostals are quick to quote the beginning of Luke 4:18, "The Spirit of the Lord is upon Me," but much slower to understand and do its first purpose, because "He has anointed Me to preach the gospel to the poor." I grow increasingly weary and, at times, distraught with church planters and their desire to search out the highest-income portions of a city to place a new church. That is so very self-serving. You could build a church next door to hell if you are called of God. Wouldn't it be better for the Holy Spirit to direct you? But then that would require prayer and faith.

Clearly there are a great number of sins that plague the modern churchgoer. I have mentioned these few to encourage you to begin the process of self-examination in the light of God's holiness and His Word. The key is to pray, as David did, "Search me, O God, and know my heart" (Ps. 139:23), and ask that He would reveal to us those areas of wickedness in which we violate His commands or offend His Spirit...sin.

Solomon's temple was meticulously designed and maintained to the highest of standards. The utmost reverence was shown to the house of God. According to the New Covenant, we are the dwelling places of the living God, the temple of the Holy Spirit. We must afford no mixture, no amalgamation, no hybrid, no blending of the holy and the profane, the godly and the ungodly, light and darkness. Winston Churchill astutely said, "When the eagles are silent, the parrots begin to jabber."[6] For those who parrot "we have to join them to win them," I offer this rebuke: Jesus ate with sinners; He did not sin with them. To become the true dwelling place of God, each of us must repent of all wickedness and become a continual living sacrifice before the Lord. If... Only *if*!

Paul said it: "I urge you therefore, brothers, by the mercies of God, that you present your bodies as a living sacrifice, holy, and acceptable to God, which is your reasonable service of worship. Do not be conformed to this world, but be transformed by the renewing of your mind, that you may prove what is the good and acceptable and perfect will of God" (Rom. 12:1–2). We have been called and therefore are expected to rise far above the morally bankrupt and demonized culture of our day. May God search our hearts and reveal to us the sin in our lives of which we are unaware, lest we perish. May our heartrending cry become "Holiness unto the Lord now and forever!"

This is no one-and-done proposition. It is a lifestyle of seeking, surrender, and sacrifice. Nevertheless, it is also the vital fourth and final requirement the Lord God established for the fulfillment of His promise to release the floodgates of heaven and send the rain of Holy Ghost revival. Open your heart, bare your soul before Him, and passionately pursue just such an awakening for yourself, your family, the church, the nation, and the world. If it were easy, everyone would be doing it. But I can bear enthusiastic witness to the fact that it is beyond worth it all. Experiencing personal revival means righteousness, peace, and joy in the Holy Ghost. It means seeing your family born again and filled with the fire of the Holy Ghost. It means seeing miracles manifested all around you. It means living with maximum influence and fruitfulness for your merciful, suffering Savior who became the ultimate sacrifice for your sin and iniquity. There is no better way to live than in the river of revival.

Our brief review of history affirmed that revival is contagious. Let's let it spread. If... Only *if*!

PART THREE

જી

HE WANTS TO REVIVE HIS CHURCH

A revival does two things. First, it returns the Church from her backsliding and second, it causes the conversion of men and women; and it always includes the conviction of sin on the part of the Church. What a spell the devil seems to cast over the Church today!

—Billy Sunday

Chapter 7

IF MY CHURCH...
WOULD HUMBLE ITSELF

IT IS THE final decade of the first century, and in most places throughout the Roman Empire it is extraordinarily dangerous and onerous to be recognized as a Christian. In the subsequent decades since the mighty outpouring of the Holy Spirit in downtown Jerusalem on the day of Pentecost, persecution from the unscrupulous Jewish establishment has given way to even more brutal and intense persecution by the Roman authorities. Wherever people call upon the name of Jesus Christ, they face ostracism, sanction, imprisonment, and frequently death.

As early as the AD 60s, the author of Hebrews would write to commend believers for their steadfast endurance to the tenets of their most holy faith through unimaginably perilous seasons...

> in which you endured a great struggle of afflictions. In part you were made a spectacle both by reproaches and afflictions. And in part you became companions of those who were so abused. For you had compassion on me in my chains and joyfully endured the confiscation of your property, knowing that you have in heaven a better and an enduring possession for yourselves.
>
> —HEBREWS 10:32–34

In the decades that followed, Christian persecution intensified exponentially as Roman emperors—indulging in demonic delusions of divinity—demanded worship and veneration from all their subjects. Yes, for the Christian congregations of the Roman Empire here in the waning years of the first century, identifying with and claiming the name of Jesus Christ means embracing a life of intense hardship, severe suffering, and unimaginable state-sponsored cruelty and oppression.

How far we have fallen from the faith that was once delivered to the saints! According to Christian researcher George Barna, one in three practicing Christians has stopped attending church services in person during the COVID-19 pandemic. Many of those who have stopped have no intention of ever going back again. The average churchgoing person is not challenged to change anything about their religious routine. They are comforted and cosseted, pampered and placated by the cappuccino machines in the foyers, the carefully choreographed light shows on the platform, and the nonconfrontational pastor in the pulpit. When they come to church at all, they arrive late, leave early, and get nervous if the service approaches one hour in length. For them, soft-serve Christianity is not the exception but the rule. They would have sworn allegiance to Caesar in a heartbeat. Who knows what kinds of abominations they are bowing down to now?

Yet the believers of Laodicea in the Roman province of Asia aren't experiencing the same plight of oppression. For them life is pretty good compared to their counterparts in other provinces. It's true that the main streets are adorned with temples to the pagan gods of Rome and other peoples. The city shines with beautiful and decadent marble temples dedicated to the worship of Jupiter, Apollo, Artemis, Aphrodite, dozens of other deities, and of course, the shrine of the cult of the emperor.

The fact is, Roman citizens enjoy an unusual form of "religious freedom." They are at liberty to worship any god they choose, on one condition: they must periodically also amalgamate offering sacrifices or burning incense at the shrine of the emperor cult in support of his well-being and success. In the mind of the

Romans, if the emperor prospers and thrives, the empire does too. This mere acknowledgement of the king's "divinity" is, in effect, a license to worship whatever god or gods one prefers. Across the empire, the refusal of followers of Jesus to engage in this affirmation of the emperor's sovereignty has come at an enormous cost. In Laodicea the situation is different.

Laodicea is situated on the bustling river Lycus in what will eventually become modern-day Turkey, and in a fertile, well-watered valley that makes it not only a center for agriculture but also an indispensable crossroads for traders moving goods both east-west and north-south. Add to these economic advantages abundant local deposits of fine marble and the production of rare black wool in the area and you have a formula for elevated levels of wealth, prosperity, and prestige in this metropolis. The rising tide of a booming and profitable economy in Laodicea has caused all boats to rise—including the boats of the Jesus followers there.

What's more, Laodicea is enjoying a degree of independence from Rome (eleven hundred miles away) that few cities in the vast empire are granted. This means the malicious and brutal persecutions that Christians across the rest of the empire currently encounter under the edicts of emperor Domitian aren't being imposed here. What a tremendously fortunate and opportune yet tempting situation the believers of Laodicea find themselves in. To turn a phrase, they're blessed and highly favored by Jehovah God. "We must be doing something right!" they constantly reassure themselves. But in reality, they have become comfortable, complacent, cocky, and therefore, increasingly compromised in their faith. Then a letter arrives.

The courier delivers compelling correspondence from the only living original disciple of the Lord Jesus Christ—His beloved disciple, John. Now in his nineties, John is leading a markedly different and certainly more difficult life than those fortuitous folks in Laodicea. He has been exiled to an existence of slave labor in the marble mines of Patmos Island. The truly startling thing about this letter is that it carries the words of the risen King Jesus himself. The Lord of glory has appeared to the apostle in a supernatural and apocalyptic vision and has directly dictated a message specifically for *this* congregation, addressed to the "angel," that is, the head overseeing pastor, of God's church in Laodicea. Perhaps upon hearing about the letter the members speculate that the Lord will commend them for achieving such a comfortable, gratuitous lifestyle in a world filled with so much misery, especially for their brethren spread far and wide in other provinces. If so, they are gravely mistaken.

> To the angel of the church of the Laodiceans write: "The Amen, the Faithful and True Witness, the Beginning of the creation of God, says these things: I know your works, that you are neither cold nor hot. I wish you were cold or hot. So then, because you are lukewarm, and neither cold nor hot, I will spit you out of My mouth. For you say, 'I am rich, and have stored up goods, and have need of nothing,' yet do not realize that you are wretched, miserable, poor, blind, and naked. I counsel you to buy from Me gold refined by fire, that you may be rich, and white garments, that you may be dressed, that the shame of your nakedness may not appear, and anoint your eyes with eye salve, that you may see. Those whom I love, I rebuke and discipline. Therefore be zealous and repent."
> —REVELATION 3:14–19

When the reigning King of glory and your Commander in Chief personally composes and dictates a correspondence from the realm of eternity to you and your fellow believers, it should take priority and preeminence over anything and everything. But I submit to you that this letter has a shelf life that extends far beyond the lives of those first-century Christians. Indeed, it extends powerfully and prophetically to our time and to this place—to you and me, and to those who gather with us on Sunday mornings across this extraordinarily prosperous continent.

As with the Laodiceans, the personal cost is virtually nothing for the vast majority of those who claim to follow the gospel of Christ. They seem to, on the whole, mirror the lazy, lackluster, self-indulgent, self-absorbed and selfish, comfortable, complacent but increasingly compromised comfort-zone dwellers of Laodicea. They lounge in apathetic ignorance as our Christian brothers and sisters around the world suffer blatant, brutal persecution for simply loving and following the commands of Christ.

In the war-ravaged nation of South Sudan, our Bridge of Hope ministry has freed more than forty thousand human slaves over the course of several years, some whose bodies have been maimed and mutilated for simply being Christians. Born-again Christians in other places such as China, Nigeria, the Middle East, and countless other points across the globe also face starvation, deprivation, and grave dangers with tenacious courage and resolute faith. Here, we have a fainting spell or an all-out fit of rage if someone calls us a name on social media or simply unfollows or unfriends us! To put it in modest terms, are we not exceedingly rich in global terms? And to our deep shame, are we not lukewarm?

Since the term *lukewarm* has been introduced, let me include an illustration that may help you understand why these words of rebuke are so sharp. Those who are involved in the food safety business repeat this saying continuously: Keep hot things hot and cold things cold. If it's cold, keep it at 40 degrees or below. If it's hot, keep it at 140 degrees or above. They are warning us about the dangers of food poisoning, which happens more often than you realize. Bacteria multiply exponentially in this danger zone between cold and hot. There are enough hazards in the world without introducing more of them with every bite of lukewarm food. Think about that the next time you see potato salad sitting in the sun all afternoon at the family picnic.

What Jesus was saying to the lukewarm Laodiceans (and to all who have ears to hear) was this: a lukewarm condition, whether natural or spiritual, is not just laziness; it is dangerous, and potentially deadly. No wonder He said He would spit them out!

The Lord Jesus' letter to the church in Laodicea seems custom-tailored to much of the American church in this critical moment in human history. They are at ease in Zion—complacent, self-sufficient, having need of nothing; outwardly professing the name of the risen Christ yet displaying none of His internal presence or outward expression or manifestation of His mighty Holy Spirit. Although stern in its warning, it is in actuality a genuine letter of love. Jesus closed this imperious epistle with an admonition. The very fact that He had written such a charge against them, both rebuking and disciplining them, indicates His great love for them. This love and letter are proof of His infectious passion to promote His kingdom on the earth and to secure their eternal reward in heaven. Jesus' final words to the Laodicean believers are a five-word requisite for revival—if, only if, they'll...

Therefore be zealous and repent.

Is this not merely a brilliant condensation of the 2 Chronicles 7:14 outline for revival? And as with those He originally addressed by letter in Laodicea, it is not our Elder Brother in the faith's greatest desire for each of us to be set ablaze in the Holy Ghost and to carry the flaming embers of revival and awakening to this nation and the world?

I believe that's why God supernaturally deposited in my spirit the concept for this book. It is my earnest prayer that it will serve as just one of many ways our mighty and holy God pleadingly entreats us in this late hour of church history, that the church might rouse itself from its backsliding and destitute lives of comfort, carnality, and convenience, yet destitute of conviction. That Jehovah would bear His mighty hand and deliver us from the deceitful preaching of placating people-pleasing from the prideful pulpits of our churches. He counsels: "Buy from Me gold refined by fire, that you may be rich, and white garments, that you may be dressed, that the shame of your nakedness may not appear, and anoint your eyes with eye salve, that you may see" (v. 18)

We have desperate need of the anointing, the eye salve of God's righteousness, as we've become blinded by our own self-absorption, contented with our shallow, half-hearted relationship with God. We have committed spiritual adultery. Multitudes serve God to serve themselves, soothe their seared consciences, and increase their social media status. Now we must repent and discover how to "buy" this "gold refined by fire." There is but one currency accepted. *Humility.*

Allow me to remind you that this prophetic proclamation from the Lord Jesus Christ was not addressed to an individual but to the entire congregation at Laodicea. In the same way that God's promise to King Solomon, "If My people, who are called by My name, will *humble themselves*," was also directed to a group. And likewise, this arduous but rewarding process begins with heads hung down in the shame of heartfelt humility in the presence of His holiness.

It is this same pathway of humility that we must trod and upon this path alone where we will receive the drenching deluge of a heaven-sent rain upon us as individuals prostrate over our closet of prayer. And from thence, spread upon any group of believers who collectively have tread the highway of humility and repentance. If… Only *if*!

All must be willing to lay aside the demon of pride and every other sin that so easily besets them, and fully affirm and recognize that they are "wretched, miserable, poor, blind, and naked" in the lukewarm morals of spiritually contented mediocrity. The desire to reignite the flames of revival in one's own personal life must become a passion and priority as he or she abandons self on the altar of sacrifice. Though multiple factors seem to indicate that we are living in a Laodicean age, we are confident that our gracious God will not abandon us there *if* we pour out our souls to Him in consecration and have a deep desire to change.

Oh, that we might sing again on Sunday morning the great Cindy Walker song "Child of the King," which proclaims that through Christ's blood the wretched and poor are now God's children.[1]

ಹಿ

The verb form of the word *humble* means "to destroy the power, independence, or prestige of" a thing.[2] America's great cities are filled with enormous churches that are convinced they have "prestige." And they are not necessarily wrong. In many cases, these churches are admired, even envied, for their apparent success. Many of their members take great pride in their affiliation. This shouldn't surprise us. There is something deeply embedded in American DNA that celebrates success and growth. This is a key element of America's entrepreneurial spirit. We're challenged, even gratified, observing small start-ups swell into mammoth enterprises. Multitudes of modern ministry leaders today view themselves as much or more as founders of a kingdom business as they do God-called and anointed shepherds.

Don't misunderstand. There is nothing inherently suspect about growth in a congregation. On the contrary, as we've seen in our review of great revivals, a move of the Spirit often produces rapid kingdom expansion. Growth is a sign of life. Anything alive should be in a continuous state of growth. However, it is entirely possible in revival to decrease in numbers and increase in anointing. Stature and prestige can actually hinder a church from having an impact for the gospel. *How can that be?* you may be wondering. *If a church is large, then it must be doing something right that God is blessing with numbers, right?* That makes sense to the carnal mind, but in God's paradoxical economy, less is frequently more. I'd prefer to follow a cloud rather than a crowd. After all, it was popular opinion that led to the savage crucifixion of our Savior. Matthew 7:13–14 arrests modern church growth experts: "Enter at the narrow gate, for wide is the gate and broad is the way that leads to destruction, and there are many who are going through it, because small is the gate and narrow is the way which leads to life, and there are few who find it."

Judges 7 is a text rarely taken at any pastors' conferences these days. It would seem counterintuitive to the "bigger is always better" crowd. It's there we discover the chronicle of Gideon, a military commander about to lead 32,000 Israelite soldiers against a Midianite army of approximately 130,000. Still, Jehovah counseled him, "You have too many people with you...lest Israel glorify themselves over Me, saying, 'Our own power saved us'" (Judg. 7:2). Through what seemed to Gideon a strange elimination process, the Lord God whittled his army down from 32,000 to 10,000. And then further still, down to 300! Now with less than 1 percent of the army with which Israel had begun the day, God looked down and essentially said, "Now we're talking. This is an army I can bless!" The Lord assured Gideon, "With three hundred men...I will save you and give the Midianites into your hands" (Judg. 7:7).

Can you imagine the church board meeting when, under a pastor's leadership, a congregation decreased from 32,000 to 300? I'd love to be a fly on that wall. I've so often heard pastors inquiring of others, "How many do you have coming?" A valid response should be, "How many do you have going...into all the world?"

Survey the Scriptures and you will discover that God often employs a strategy of decreasing the crowd. Both trees and vines require being culled or pruned often to become fruitful. The Lord Jesus drew enormous crowds but chose only twelve men to follow Him. And among the twelve, He selected only three as unique recipients of the most significant revelation and insight. From the billowing multitudes that heard the Savior speak, He sifted only seventy as His emissaries to cities where He would manifest His mastery. The risen Christ appeared to more than 500 people, yet Acts 1:15 astonishingly reveals that a mere 120 were gathered in the Upper Room chamber when the church of the living God was about to be birthed. This is multiplication by subtraction.

People are drawn to a church for a variety of reasons—certainly not all of them righteous. The rich young ruler of Matthew 19 would be a prized prospect for membership in most American churches. Why, he would be recruited and courted and given access to the "close friends only" section of the pastor's Instagram. Yet Jesus confronted the man's idolatry and then watched him walk away. What percentage of preaching (supposing there is preaching) from our celebrity pulpits today ever confronts the idolatries of the typical person in the pew or theater seat? How many wealthy attenders is the typical pastor willing to risk offending? God, give us clergy willing to speak the truth in love. Give us those willing to offend people and please God rather than offend God and please people.

In America's media-saturated, entertainment-rich culture, the things that draw a crowd are rarely holy or wholly biblical. In fact, as with the rich young ruler, what is holy and wholly biblical frequently drives such people away.

America is an entrepreneurial culture. We glorify and admire the men and women who open a business in their garage and grow it into a giant enterprise. And rightly so. But far too many church founders approach pastoring as if they have just launched a business start-up. Many study the methods and strategies of successful business start-ups in search of keys to "scaling up" their business (the church) as large in numbers as possible as fast as possible at the expense of the spiritual growth and discipleship of the people. Away with those who love the crowd and behind closed doors speak disparagingly of the people. They are so quick to count. Those hirelings adore the crowd and despise the sheep.

God, deliver us from those with an entrepreneurial mindset and no intercessory heart, from those who worship at the shrine of numbers. From the Sunday morning attendance totals, to the number of services conducted at what number of satellite campus locations, to the number of live stream viewers and downloads of the church's online content—far too many church leaders define success wholly in terms of numbers. Where are those who cry, "Lord, give us souls lest we die?" as opposed to, "Lord, give us another attender we can count!" In the light of eternity, the only yardstick by which the Eternal One will measure will be, Did we build our kingdom or His? And how many will be in heaven as a result of our obedience? None of Jesus' letters to the seven churches recorded in the Book of Revelation commended them for their size. In none of them does Jesus say, "But I have this against you: You only have one service on the weekend and your live-streaming numbers are anemic."

There is an award-winning church growth formula found in the Book of Acts. However, in an hour when the Holy Ghost is more ignored than denied; when a powerless Pentecost is the norm and its manifestations are forbidden; when speaking in tongues is relegated to a home group (if tolerated at all), the Book of Acts' formula won't work—how do we expect to build His church without His Spirit? Utterly impossible. Here's the Acts formula: Preach the born-again experience, minister the baptism of the Holy Ghost, train disciples, and send these disciples out to win others. Hey, that brought increase to the church daily (Acts 2:47). Peter preached it and saw three thousand answer the altar call—but then, he actually gave an altar call. Does your pastor?

The Son of God, who oftentimes attempted to escape the crowds, is not nearly as excited as we are about our packed sanctuaries. So why would we think these serve as precursors of revival? Over 100,000 attend The Ohio State University football games at the Horseshoe in Columbus. I love the atmosphere. But I've never sensed the anointing or seen anyone healed or delivered there. If God is going to revive His church, He will do so when we become more concerned with quality than quantity; more excited over souls than the show.

Adopting the biblical quality-over-quantity mindset and heart reset requires a level of humility not often seen among church leaders today. It means moving from asking, "How can we best get the word out about our church and increase our numbers?" to "How can we elevate the name of Jesus even if it results in thinning the crowd?" The church must begin thinking along the lines of John the Baptist, who said, "[Jesus] must increase, but I must decrease" (John 3:30).

This is almost heretical to say in some church circles today, but as with Gideon's shrinking army, a decline in church attendance could very well be a sign that the pastor is doing something right, not wrong. It could be indicative not of sickness but rather of health, due to an infusion of the presence of God and the bold, unapologetic proclamation of holy, biblical standards. Unfortunately, we have lowered our expectations so far that what many are now aiming at was once beneath our feet. A church can cut programs while increasing impact. The gospel can spread even after a staff trims its fat and refocuses its priorities.

To be clear, I am not advocating slashing budgets, dropping programs, and pruning the church rolls solely for the sake of shrinking. Nor am I implying that your city's megachurches with eighty-acre campuses are not Christ-centered, Bible-teaching bodies ripe for revival. What I *am* saying is that when a church humbles itself by focusing not on the number of people in front of the pulpit but on the power of the cross behind it, and returns to the purity of gospel preaching, it may indeed result in a Gideon-like decrease in numbers. There will always be members and attenders who flock to whichever pastor is making them feel the best about their lifestyles. There will always be those chasing the popular new "flavor of the month." However, if the Bible is an accurate indication of what follows when Jesus decreases the numbers, then perhaps it is time to prune by seeing how many in the pews will remain and embrace a call to humility and godliness through repentance and sacrifice.

If God could use 300 soldiers who lapped up water like dogs to defeat an army that was 135,000 strong, how concerned should we be when anyone—let alone fair-weather trend chasers—decides our church is no longer for them? Instead, our focus should be on returning to the core elements of church life and practice: pure worship and selfless service. Why these two elements? Because the former produces humility, and the latter requires it. And as we've seen, authentic humility is vital if we are to please the God who rewards the humble with revival.

ॐ

From those browsing their local church options like bargain hunters rummaging through the racks in the sale section of a clothing store, you'll often hear something along the lines of, "I'm looking for a church that has great worship." Of course, in actuality, the window-shopper is evaluating each church's style, presentation, and excellence (or lack thereof) in performing music. The operative word in the previous sentence is *performing*. Is that a biblical view of what the Bible would identify as worship?

Genuine biblical worship often involves music, utilizing both instruments and the lifting of human voices in unified agreement before the throne of God. The witness of Scripture is clear on this. In fact, the Book of Psalms is made up entirely of worship songs—150 of them! The final psalm captures the essence:

> Praise the LORD! Praise God in His sanctuary; praise Him in the firmament of His power! Praise Him for His mighty acts; praise Him according to His excellent greatness! Praise Him with the sound of the trumpet; praise Him with the lyre and harp! Praise Him with the tambourine and dancing; praise Him with stringed instruments and flute! Praise Him with loud cymbals; praise Him with the clanging cymbals! Let everything that has breath praise the LORD. Praise the LORD!
>
> —PSALM 150:1–6

That is God's Word on the subject. With every instrument available and with our every breath, true believers possess an inward unction of the Holy Ghost to praise and worship our great God even as a newborn child cannot help but cry out. It seems the vast majority of churches are overflowing with talented musicians leading their congregations in everything from modern praise and worship to classic hymns. The people are undoubtedly being entertained by these gifted servants, and musical entertainment has its role in the Christian life. But worship through music was never meant to be about entertaining God's people. It was solely about leading us into the presence of and into communion with the Creator of heaven and earth, our glorious Savior.

Authentic worship will draw the redeemed of the Lord so deeply into His holy habitation that their faces will shine as that of Moses in Exodus 34:35. Away with frivolous music and lyrics. Bring us that which humbles us and exalts the Excellent One. Let us worship again in the adoration of His holiness. Let us sing with uplifted voices with the strength of doctrinal accuracy. May our admiration and celebration belong to and center upon the only One worthy to receive it. May our every voice, shout, clap, dance, and instrument be touched by the Holy Ghost and break forth with effervescent sounds that cannot be silenced. May we fall prostrate upon tear-stained faces. May we run and leap in unrestrained and unashamed joy and freedom for He has made us glad.

True worship compels us to place our entire lives upon the altar of self-abandonment afresh. The Lord Jesus Himself spoke of true worship in His conversation with a Samaritan woman over a drink of water. "True worshippers," He explained, "will worship the Father in spirit and truth. For the Father seeks such to worship Him. God is Spirit, and those who worship Him must worship Him in spirit and truth" (John 4:23–24). Worshipping "in spirit" is impossible unless and until the whole heart becomes engaged. All else is the folly of emotionalism, falling far short of the throne and void of all but surface relationship, fellowship, and communion. Without the human spirit involved, the offering of worship becomes polluted and an unholy union of the secular and divine.

That means not all Christian singing constitutes authentic worship. At the same time, not all true worship requires music or singing. Moments or hours spent lost in the depths of the living Word of God is worship. A walk in the woods can become a time sanctified away from the trappings of this world and unto God is worship. Silence itself in waiting upon Him is worship. Anything that ushers you into the holy presence of the living

Christ and compels you to an acute awareness of your heart—
your very being alive, and with awe, gratitude, and wonder as you
but glimpse His beauty, holiness, otherness, and majesty—is an
open doorway to true worship.

There is an additional experience awaiting a heart hungry for
a glimpse of such glory: Holy Ghost–inspired humility and conviction. Isaiah testifies of that truth. In chapter 6 of the book
that bears his name, he reveals his extraordinary encounter in
the throne room:

> In the year that King Uzziah died I saw the Lord sitting on
> a throne, high and lifted up, and His train filled the temple.
> Above it stood the seraphim. Each one had six wings. With
> two he covered his face, and with two he covered his feet,
> and with two he flew. One cried to another and said: "Holy,
> holy, holy, is the LORD of Hosts; the whole earth is full of
> His glory." The posts of the door moved at the voice of him
> who cried, and the house was filled with smoke.
>
> —ISAIAH 6:1–4

Such a sight human eyes have rarely beheld. What immortal
sounds must have visited Isaiah's mortal ears! To say he was
"changed" would surely rank as one of the greatest understate-
ments ever uttered. These are his words:

> Woe is me! For I am undone because I am a man of unclean
> lips, and I dwell in the midst of a people of unclean lips.
> For my eyes have seen the King, the LORD of Hosts.
>
> —ISAIAH 6:5

Beholding the Lord of glory in worship has the effect of high-
lighting our own human frailty and failings. It is indeed *humbling*.
Its effect upon a church is exactly the same. When a congregation sets itself to worship, it quickly realizes that which Isaiah
perceived: we are "a people of unclean lips." At that moment the

certain response of every true believer is to, without haste, follow the Lord Jesus' closing command to the Laodiceans:

> Therefore be zealous and repent.
>
> —REVELATION 3:19

This is my explicit reasoning in describing authentic corporate worship in a chapter devoted to humbling ourselves before God. When a congregation in unity abandons itself in Christ-exalting worship and thereby enters into the magnificent, overwhelming, holy presence of God Almighty as a body, the inescapable outcome is the reverence of heartfelt humility. Because such abandonment in worship is the seed from which the fruit of humility is produced, a willingness, yea, a passion to worship in spirit and truth stands unavoidably as a key characteristic of a church prepared and positioned for revival. Yet there are other keys to be discovered as well.

ॐ

The proud heart will never serve others. Why? My question to many preachers and church leaders is, "You may have an MBA, but do you have a Mop Bucket Attitude?" Many cannot; their insecurities and image-consciousness will not permit it. The proud have a need to be served. Yet the inerrant Word of God makes it abundantly clear that humble servanthood is the hallmark of those redeemed by the blood of the Lamb. When Paul wrote, "By love serve one another," he was addressing the believers in the church at Galatia (Gal. 5:13). The night of Jesus' arrest, the Son of God apprised His disciples, "By this all men will know that you are My disciples, if you have love for one another" (John 13:35).

The Lord Jesus didn't make this observation from an elevated pulpit or lofty seat of honor. As He spoke those words the Prince of God was upon His knees, personally washing the disciples' filthy feet. While they debated among themselves about who would be the greatest in His coming kingdom, our servant Savior was stripping to the waist to take on the duty usually relegated to the lowest servant in the household—a servant to servants who was always the first appointed to the most demeaning and degrading of assignments. His illustration could be distilled to this: when they were seeking a throne, He offered them a towel.

This wasn't the first time the disciples had revealed their proclivities of self-interest, self-promotion, and selfish-ambition. A few weeks earlier the mother of James and John had come to Jesus seeking special status for her boys in what she assumed was an imminent earthly kingdom ruled by King Jesus. When the other ten were made aware, they were outraged by the parental power play. Christ Jesus responded with a stunningly paradoxical declaration regarding what constituted true leadership and divine advancement in His eternal kingdom:

> But Jesus called them to Him and said, "You know that the rulers of the Gentiles lord it over them, and those who are great exercise authority over them. It shall not be so among you. Whoever would be great among you, let him serve you, and whoever would be first among you, let him be your slave, *even as the Son of Man did not come to be served, but to serve and to give His life as a ransom for many.*"
> —MATTHEW 20:25–28, EMPHASIS ADDED

Pride—the genesis of Lucifer's infamous plummet from the highest echelons of heaven and the trap that triggered the fall of humankind—is antithetical to life and power in the kingdom of our God and of His Christ. It is therefore not coincidental that the people of that kingdom should "humble themselves," which constitutes the first requirement on the 2 Chronicles 7:14 road to revival.

Prideful and egocentric people are incapable and unwilling to don the towel and bend the knee to serve others in Christlike abasement. Conversely, authentic humility is invariably on display when we bow low to serve. This is especially true when those we're serving are not like us, or don't like us. The Lord gave the admonition, "For if you love [only] those who love you, what reward do you have? Do not even the tax collectors do that?" (Matt. 5:46, AMP).

Where are the humble gospel helpers? How gloriously revival would reverberate in the hearts and souls of the church if they could once more be found at their post. Oh, the great need for red-hot platoons of fire-baptized helpers facilitating a mighty outpouring of God's Spirit in the midst of the embattled hosts. What a bulwark of blessing they would be to the cause of Christ.

Oh, to hear that voice which fell upon the ears of captain Jonathan when he was vastly outnumbered against a mighty army. Those words came from a nameless servant, Jonathan's armor-bearer, who without even a sword, said to his leader: "Do all that is in your heart. Turn yourself, and I will be with you according to your heart" (1 Sam. 14:7). Our congregations that lay claim to the call of Christ are going to have to raise to a higher watermark than that of ruthless tax collectors if we truly desire to see the wind of God blow in a veritable outpouring of Holy Ghost rain upon the parched ground of our cities.

The incomparable Charles H. Spurgeon preached, "One sign of a true revival, and indeed an essential part of it, is the increased activity of God's laborers."[3] The mighty evangelist Charles Finney also wrote about the importance of God's servant-hearted laborers "There must be a waking up of energy, on the part of Christians, and an outpouring of God's Spirit, or the world will laugh at the church."[4] Both Spurgeon and Finney were referring to the harvest spoken of by Jesus Himself: "Lift up your eyes and look at the fields, for they are already white for harvest" (John 4:35). Yet as our Lord also pointed out, there can be no harvest without servant laborers: "The harvest truly is plentiful, but the laborers are few. Therefore, pray to the Lord of the harvest, that He will send out laborers into His harvest" (Matt. 9:37–38). God, grant us Holy Ghost–filled laborers—those who will, with reckless abandonment of self, thrust themselves into the now-white harvest fields. Send servants to pray and plead, to wail and weep, to go and give—to cut and mow, to cook and clean, to greet, to care…to love.

Our review of the revival's history revealed that a broken heart and abounding love for the lost and dying have characterized the greatest past moves of God. Pride looks inward. Humility looks outward. We must now focus our vision, efforts, mission, and finances upon stooping low to scour the highways, byways, and high-rises—from gated communities to alleys and ditches—seeking someone to serve.

During my nearly fifty years of gospel ministry I have been, and remain, deeply concerned and even grieved as I witnessed fields of souls in every city and town white for harvest, but the local harvesters had tunnel vision, and those souls were abandoned by those who either refused to reach down or were unable to reach up. More recently, most churchgoers have become isolationists—refusing to leave their suburban neighborhoods and coffee shop sanctuaries. Hurting, bruised and battered, helpless and hopeless humans are neither difficult to find nor at a premium. How many homeless shelters, soup kitchens, and homeless people are we driving past on the way to church? Are we even aware of how many children in our kids' schools go hungry over the weekend after they leave school on Friday afternoon? There is likely a pregnancy center within driving distance of your church that could save many more babies and families if it received more volunteer and financial support from the servant leaders and churches nearby.

No community anywhere is not dominated by sin and its cultural curse. Pastor, do you have any idea how many lost people live within twenty miles of your property? Do you weep for them, visit them, reach them? Where is any true evangelistic thrust and energy being sent in sending laborers into our harvest fields? The single greatest service anyone can ever provide a fellow human being is to introduce them to the Giver of eternal life. Yet two-thirds of evangelical churches will never train anyone, much less everyone, in evangelism. And the reality is unbearable that

America is the fourth-largest mission field in the world, yet 95 percent of Christians will not bring one soul to Christ in their lifetime. This is spiritually grotesque.

Second Corinthians 7:14 announces our authority, that we, in Christ, are superior to the forces of darkness. James 4:7, Luke 9:1, and Luke 10:19 amen this fact. Yet we claim authority but take no meaningful ground. We compose songs about victory over evil more suitable for the playground than the battlefield. We are proficient in the dialect of culture but void of the voice of heaven. There has boiled to the surface of the seething cauldron of religion an unholy alliance—an amalgamation of the godly and the profane that our righteous God will not tolerate.

There must be birthed in God's church, and in each of us, a desire for change—a hunger for more—a thirst for rain. The church is nothing unless, and until, it becomes an agent of redemptive change in the culture into which God's Christ has by His Holy Ghost infused it. We must set ourselves on an irreversible collision course with the forces of darkness in unified strength. We must incite a spiritual riot, rout our archenemy, Satan, and impose the boundaries of his kingdom.

Thy kingdom come, thy will be done on earth here and now as it is in heaven. We are not here to take sides, but to take over in the glorious name of the Lord. The call of every believer and every true church is to effect such a divine disturbance of hot meeting cold that the inescapable result is a storm of Holy Ghost rain!

When rebuilding the walls of Jerusalem, each of Nehemiah's workers carried a hammer in one hand and a sword in the other (Neh. 4:17). Similarly, when the church serves its community, it must do so with the gospel in one hand and a power drill (or a soup ladle, a wheelbarrow, or whatever the situation requires) in the other.

Imagine if an entire generation of Finneys and Spurgeons dared to get up from their plush pews and kneel to wash the feet of the "least of these" in their communities, all while telling the life-giving message of a God who so loved the world that He gave His only Son. In my book *Ancient Wells, Living Water*, I wrote:

> This is no job for the faint-hearted or the self-absorbed. It is a job for real men and women of God whose sole credentials are the old rugged cross, the bloodied brow and the pierced hands and feet of their Savior and the empty tomb that declares their eternal hope!
>
> Dare to lay down every fear. Start snatching souls from the flames with supernatural love, burning zeal and unquenchable faith in your Lord. This is the stuff of true revival and nation-changing evangelism.[5]

Are you secure enough in your identity as a son or daughter of God to humble yourself before Him, humble yourself before your neighbors, and serve your community and the desperately despondent world with both your Holy Ghost–anointed hands and your compassionate and Christlike heart?

ᖇᎧ

Sin begets sin as surely as day follows night. For churchgoers and religious folks, the sin of pride invariably leads to the sin of hypocrisy. It is no accident that the Lord Jesus' sternest rebukes were reserved for the self-exalted Pharisees and the self-important instructors in the Law. The usually gentle Savior pronounced this railing judgment worthy of His most confrontationally forceful prophets, Elijah or Jeremiah:

> Woe to you, scribes and Pharisees, hypocrites! You are like whitewashed tombs, which indeed appear beautiful outwardly, but inside are full of dead men's bones and of all uncleanness.
>
> —Matthew 23:27

Oftentimes our matchless Master performed miracles of healing, restoration, resurrection, renewal, and multiplication. But when He proffered His only destructive miracle, prideful hypocrisy was the direct target. There He cursed rather than blessed. He chose to prosecute rather than acquit. In the eleventh chapter of Mark, Jesus was hungry and saw a fig tree topped with broad, green leaves. He was hoping, of course, to find something to eat; however, arriving at the tree, He found no fruit. Keep in mind that in terms of biblical symbolism the fig tree is frequently a symbol for Israel or its ruling class. Like those scribes and Pharisees, the tree was outwardly boasting of being healthy, strong, and fruitful when in reality it was completely barren.

He who was truth personified was not amused, nor was His reaction muted. Speaking in an unambiguous tone, His answer was straightforward: "'May no one ever eat fruit from you again.' And His disciples heard it....In the morning, as they passed by, they saw the fig tree withered from the roots" (Mark 11:14, 20).

Herein is revealed a sobering lesson for every would-be disciple of Jesus Christ. It is both tempting and uncomplicated to continue to play the part and quote the lines of false Christian fruitfulness long after we've stopped bearing real fruit. One must simply learn "Christian-ese," occasionally attend a religious gathering, and contribute a bit financially to the upkeep of the institution. Pride prods us to live off the embers of yesterday's fire; to survive with an understanding of someone else's revelation; to be satisfied with last month's or last year's breakthrough of faith. There is peer pressure to at least *appear* fruitful even when our hearts are cold and our spiritual wombs are barren.

Remember, anything alive desires to reproduce. In the words of Leonard Ravenhill, "Could a mariner sit idle if he heard the drowning cry? Could a doctor sit in comfort and just let his patients die? Could a fireman sit idle, let men burn and give no hand? Can you sit at ease in Zion with the world around you damned?"[6]

The charade continues every Sunday morning. Not everyone standing around you during the worship, hands upraised, with shouts or faint whispers of "hallelujah" on their lips is actually close to God. I doubt that surprises you, but the extended impli-cations of that truth might. The same is true of pastors and church staff (or "teams") and others in full-time ministry. In fact, for these, the masquerade to *appear* fruitful is far more intense. This means pride's pull to keep up through pretense, the parody of faux fruitfulness, is even greater among "persona" ministry.

I've often said that great liberty of exaggeration is taken in pulpits. And if everything on the back jacket covers of Christian books were true of the authors, we'd have won the world to Christ decades ago. The hard truth I am compelled to speak is that many churches today are Christian in name only. These have wholly rejected the clear, historic tenets of the faith and replaced them with soft, trendy, modern, therapeutic platitudes that previous generations of long-suffering saints would not rec-ognize. They have abandoned the historic and pure message of the gospel in favor of something far less demanding, less strin-gent, less offensive to sinners. They find images of the cross and the demands of cosmic justice too crass, too disturbing to be spoken of in polite company. Something less convicting, a softer message that's more palatable is called for. Messages less insistent and reliant upon terms like *sincere repentance, authentic humility, biblical holiness*, and *righteous lifestyles* are required. The mantra is "We're trying to reach this generation!" It seems to me that the attempt to reach them is much more an excuse to join them.

Others have not completely abandoned the faith but have nev-ertheless compromised, commercialized, and consumerized their way into lukewarmness. Leonard Ravenhill foresaw this trend many decades ago and wrote:

> We may have an all-time high in church attendance with a corresponding all-time low in spirituality....Has great preaching died? is soul-hot preaching a lost art? have we conceded to the impatient modern's snack-bar sermons (spiced with humor!) the task of edging men's jaded spiri-tual appetites?[7]

Such counterfeit churches are concerned, above all, with being culturally "relevant." Of course there is a place for framing the ancient and eternal truths of God's Word in terms any intended audience will understand. We translate the Bible into local languages for a reason. The problem arises when we misunderstand what it means to be relevant. Some folks seem to believe that relevance means little more than the pastor wearing designer eyeglasses he doesn't actually need, denim jeans that cost the equivalent of a manual laborer's weekly wages, a worship team that exudes "cool," and a fog-filled sanctuary that looks more like a warehouse or a 7-11 than a holy edifice built to the glory of God. It is important to mention here that along with all of our new and improved décor, dress, and decorum has come an overwhelming diminishing of reverence and respect for the house of God, as well as an increase in adoration for the vessels of God and an esteem for the fivefold ministry gifts. I cringe as I witness blatant disrespect for demonstrations and manifestations of God's Holy Spirit. Is there no longer a place for piety; for honor and veneration; for esteem, devotion, and spellbound awe? God save us.

More troubling is when relevance requires tossing aside the most basic premises and proclamations of the gospel of the living Christ—precious, life-giving truth handed down from the apostles and prophets. Truths personally received from the Lord Jesus and transmitted faithfully through the millennia, often in the face of torture and death. Some feel compelled to muzzle or even reject the Bible's clear message of man's sinful nature and desperately wicked heart, and his need to repent of sin and walk in holiness. They refuse to speak about the reality of hell and eternal torment. For these, relevance comes at the price of apostasy.

In truth, relevance is a trite and pitiful goal for any church. The concern should never be whether the church is *relevant*; rather is it *revenant*?

In the first chapter of this work I introduced you to the word *revenant*, defined as "someone who has been dead but has been made alive once again." A revenant is literally a revived person. Upon hearing the term you may have thought of a 2015 movie starring Leonardo DiCaprio. The film is a fictionalized telling of the real-life story of Hugh Glass, a fur-trading frontiersman who, in 1823, was viciously mauled by a bear and left for dead in the winter wilderness by his companions while on a hunting expedition. Glass awakened and proceeded to travel the nearly two hundred miles back to the nearest fort. It took him six weeks.[8] The screenwriters, in Hollywood's characteristically perverse fashion, turned Glass' story into a revenge tale, depicting Glass as hunting down his former companions and killing them. In reality, when he finally reunited with the men who had abandoned him, Glass forgave them all, which would have made a much more positive and uplifting story than Hollywood's version.

As I noted in the opening pages of this book, real revivals produce an army of revenants. When the Father of life opens His heaven and pours out His refreshing, renewing rain, the dry desert of a congregation spontaneously combusts, exploding with new life.

Perhaps your current relationship with Christ (or your church) appears as dead today as Hugh Glass did to his companions. Have you and your family (or your congregation) lost your hearts for the lost and dying multitudes shuffling toward their eternal doom right outside your doors? How long has it been since the baptismal waters were stirred by a wave of repentant sinners? Have all the church programs turned inward, focusing on the comfort and entertainment of the members? Have the hundreds comfortably settled in luxurious surroundings inside forgotten those hurting thousands outside the doors? Are you and your fellow members leisurely reclining at God's sumptuous feasting table when the Master of the feast has ordered us to go into the highways and hedges and compel the downcast and downtrodden to come and dine (Luke 14:23)?

If any of these symptoms apply, do not despair. Remember, history reveals that revival among a people frequently begins with only a handful of believers or even a single saint. One just like you. If... Only *if!*

Pray that your church will follow the advice offered by Jesus in His indictment of the Laodicean church. Pray that together you would begin to purchase through humility of worship and self-abandoned service what the risen, ruling Christ identified as "gold, refined by fire."

Only a prophecy of apostasy can be the dreadful alternative. An American church that continues to say, "I am rich and have stored up goods and have need of nothing," while from heaven's perspective we are "wretched, miserable, poor, blind, and naked." Oh, that our churches and their people would humble themselves before almighty God and find true revival, rather than be spewed from His mouth having nauseated their righteous King.

That same glorious King is longing to pour out a revival, a national awakening upon America. There is a phenomenal flood of His mighty power available to every church and nation. The first step is to simply humble yourself. If... Only *if!*

Chapter 8

IF MY CHURCH...
WOULD PRAY

THE US GOVERNMENT's endangered species list is long. It includes the California condor, the Carolina northern flying squirrel, the Florida panther, and the Roy Prairie pocket gopher. But there is a majestic and mighty entity that should be added to another "endangered" list immediately. There was a time not too long ago that this living, breathing entity could be seen across the country—in major bustling cities, picturesque small towns, and scenic rural villages. Regrettably, it now teeters on the razor's edge of extinction.

I am referring, of course, to the irreplaceable prayer meeting. There was a day when believers across America gathered daily, at midweek, or on Saturdays to lift their voices together to labor fervently in prayer. In countless convocations of supplication the Holy Ghost was given freedom to inform and lead, to animate and illuminate the entreaty. The saints of God repented, petitioned, travailed, wept, and—when, by the Spirit, they sensed they had "prayed through"—were released, and rejoiced. I am old enough to have been an active participant in many of these concerts of prayer. Some are indelibly imprinted on my soul as the most profound and significant encounters with heaven of my life.

Yes, it was my privilege to spend my key formative years of spiritual growth among silver-haired saints who believed in the efficacy of prayer and understood the multiplied heaven-moving, earth-shaking, revival-producing power and intrinsic value of united corporate intercession.

I used the term "concerts of prayer" above with intentionality. The living Christ made this extraordinary statement regarding the power and authority of believers assembled in agreement:

> Truly I say to you, whatever you bind on earth will be bound in heaven, and whatever you loose on earth will be loosed in heaven. Again I say to you, that if two of you agree on earth about anything they ask, it will be done for them by My Father who is in heaven.
>
> —MATTHEW 18:18–19

The Greek word translated here as "agree" is *sumphóneó*, the root of our word *symphony*. Paul the apostle is describing a concert of prayer in which the Word of God provides the sheet music and the Holy Ghost is the conductor. Every individual believer represents a unique "instrument" in that holy orchestral army, and the Spirit of God is the wind that provides each instrument its expression. As Paul told the believers at Corinth, "There are varieties of effects, but the same God who works all things in all persons. But to each one is given the manifestation of the Spirit for the common good" (1 Cor. 12:6–7, NASB). If that is true—and it most certainly is—then our deep desire must become that more saints enlist their authority and Holy Ghost giftedness together in kingdom-advancing intercession.

The stunning message Jesus delivered is that when two or more (two being the smallest number possible for agreement) believers come together in unified faith, they jointly operate in multiplied levels of authority. From our earthly position, we wield mighty influence in heaven. Believers together have the ability to direct divine activity. This is judicial, law-enforcement jurisdiction from the high court of heaven bestowing the capacity to both "bind" and "loose." This is divine authorization to bind sin, deception, ungodliness, sickness, and the combined effects of Adam's fall. It is the supreme permission and directive to loose angelic hosts and to loose humanity from their prisons of darkness; the capability to loose protection and provision, healing and deliverance from sin, sickness, and Satan, from demons, depravity, and disease. Perhaps most importantly, it is the unction and anointing to produce the awakening we ache for. This is precisely what I witnessed over and over in my youth, and what I witness today in the congregation it is my profound privilege to serve as pastor.

This privilege is presented according to the testimony of Jesus to "two *or more*." Two is good, but more is better! This compounds the calamity that so few churches ever gather for the express purpose of unifying in prayer in this day of prime opportunity. As I stated at the beginning of this chapter, praying churches are an endangered species. Few today can muster more than a handful of elderly widowed women for a season of prayer for revival or any other purpose. Churches have traded seasons of travailing, repentant prayer for trendy self-improvement sessions or fashion shows and healthy-living pyramids of all stripes. To our deep shame, the modern church has abandoned tarrying in the holy presence of God in favor of hosting dating mixers for singles and wine tastings for empty nesters. With prophetic perceptivity Leonard Ravenhill spotted the trend way back in 1959:

> The Cinderella of the church of today is the prayer meeting. This handmaid of the Lord is unloved and unwooed because she is not dripping with the pearls of intellectualism, nor glamorous with the silks of philosophy; neither is she enchanting with the tiara of psychology. She wears the homespuns of sincerity and humility and so is not afraid to kneel![1]

The sin of prayerlessness has produced the curse of spiritual barrenness and lifeless wastelands where growth is accomplished only at the expense of the church across town and never because the sighing, crying, dying lost are being drawn to the cross. "If My people will humble themselves and pray," He said. If... Only *if*!

Did the Lord Christ Himself not inquire loudly in righteous anger proper to His outrage only days before lying down on that cruel, biting beam, that cross, "Is it not written, 'My house shall be called a house of prayer for all nations'?" (Mark 11:17). There is no satisfactory substitute for the united prayer of agreement and Holy Ghost supplication rising to heaven from God's saints. Prayer and prayer alone will generate an authentic move of God. We have become indifferent, uncaring, and unconcerned about those around us facing eternity in hell. Only prayer will cure that indifference. By the way, when did you last get on your knees and petition heaven for a gut-wrenching, sleep-depriving burden for your lost and dying family? That same Holy Ghost intercession in agreement will bring relief of that burden by moving heaven to release God's convicting revival.

We have clearly forgotten what sisters Peggy and Christine Smith from the Hebrides Islands knew. As we saw earlier, moved by a vision of their church overflowing with young people, they fell upon their sainted, tear-stained faces and entreated the God of heaven from their tiny cottage for long hours every night. These two agreed together for an outpouring of revival in their remote island corner of Scotland. Heavily burdened down under the weight of intercession yet overflowing with faith and expectancy, they shared their Holy Ghost–inspired vision of a sweeping revival with their pastor. His bewildered reply was, "Well, what do you want me to do?"

"What do we want you to do?" the physically impaired sisters repeated incredulously. "Pastor, we want you to pray!" With that challenge, the pastor and other church leaders began gathering twice a week in a barn to contend for the very thing the sisters had been wrestling in prayer for in their meager cottage. "Oh, Lord, would You rend the heavens and pour Your Spirit upon us?" You know the rest of the story. The Lord God Jehovah stands ever eager to honor His promise given in 2 Chronicles 7:14.

The fact is, if the righteous prayers of just "two or more" can become the spark that ignites revival, should we expect it to be any less efficacious when an entire congregation collectively falls to its knees to implore heaven for Holy Ghost rain? Oh, if... Only *if*!

Might I be so bold as to ask: What emphasis does leadership in your church place on prayer? I have heard it said that the typical American evangelical pastor—even a pastor with tens of thousands hanging on his every word—spends on average around half an hour each day in prayer. I shudder to compare the true figure regarding the amount of time our pastoral shepherds spend each day on social media. Just a thought to ponder...if this is the pitiful reality of those gracing our pulpits, then what of those in our pews? Even more pointedly, what of you? Renewing prayer is key number one in my Twelve Keys to Revival:

1. Renew prayer

2. Rediscover the Word

3. Revive Bible doctrine

4. Reintroduce conviction and repentance

5. Rebuild the altars

6. Remove idols

7. Restrain false doctrine

8. Restore God in government

9. Return God to the education system

10. Reassemble the people of God

11. Reactivate biblical praise and worship

12. Release financial abundance

It was Thomas Armitage in his work *Preaching: Its Ideal and Inner Life* who gives us our marching orders: "A sermon steeped in prayer on the study floor, like Gideon's fleece saturated with dew, will not lose its moisture between that and the pulpit. The first step towards doing anything in the pulpit as a thorough workman must be to kiss the feet of the Crucified, as a worshipper, in the study."[2]

Given the promise of 2 Chronicles 7:14, how could any true shepherd or leader not submerge every biblical and gospel-minded preaching opportunity as well as every plan and project in layers of prayer upon prayer? I call every pastor who truly believes what is written in the Book, which is his only foundation, to gather his fold for regular seasons and spontaneous occasions of Holy Ghost–orchestrated intercession!

Despite multiplied biblical commands and exhortations to pray consistently and persistently, I suspect we are likely to find more email forwards between church staff members than prayers of agreement, petition, and faith being lifted before Emmanuel's mighty throne. May God help us. An exorbitant number of modern preachers spend more time searching for cute jokes and clever Tweet-able and silly quips than on their faces beseeching the Holy Ghost to infuse and envelop their every word with heart-penetrating power born in a contrite place of prayer. It is possible. Consider which would be more life altering and history making for any congregation: an entertaining pep talk or a corporate encounter with the very glory of the living Christ of God? The latter is only probable when a pastor's investment of prayer time and agenda reflect that reality. If... Only *if*!

As a new recipient of the baptism of the Holy Ghost, the apostle Peter knew this secret. Peter spent ten days in prayer in preparation for ten minutes of preaching. The "new breed" of celebrity pulpit occupants pray for ten minutes and preach for ten days. No wonder we have so many failures. The true self-sacrificing shepherd knows that at times one must lead from the front, and when necessary, be willing to drive from the rear. Where are the pastors whose preaching, praying, and personal holiness and devotion compel their congregants to bombard the courts of heaven with weeping appeals to pour out the blessed rain of revival upon their barren souls and sin-scorched communities? Where are the all-night prayer vigils where brothers and sisters anoint the altar with tears of anguish for the fate of their lost neighbors and those they love most? Where, oh where are the church mothers walking around the tabernacle before services crying out, "Have Thine own way, Lord, have Thine own way"? Where are the church fathers joining them, praying, "Give us souls today lest we die"? Where are the churches willing to stop worshipping the idols of comfort and convenience and instead put God in remembrance of the conditional promise He made to Solomon to "heal the land"? After all:

> God is not a man, that He should lie, nor a son of man, that He should repent. Has He spoken, and will He not do it? Or has He spoken, and will He not make it good?
> —NUMBERS 23:19

> God will make this happen, for he who calls you is faithful.
> —1 THESSALONIANS 5:24, NLT

> I am God, and there is no other....."My counsel shall stand, and I will do all My good pleasure,"...Indeed, I have spoken it; I will also bring it to pass. I have purposed it; I will also do it.
> —ISAIAH 46:9–11

E. M. Bounds made this riveting statement: "Prayer is perfectly at home in the house of God. It is no stranger, no mere guest; it belongs there. It has a peculiar affinity for the place, and has, moreover, a Divine right there, being set, therein, by Divine appointment and approval. The inner chamber is a sacred place for personal worship. The house of God is a holy place for united worship."[3]

A true house of prayer—a church positioned for an outpouring of revival—will routinely engage in various types of prayer, including four key types. Let's briefly explore each member of this quartet of unbridled Holy Ghost potency.

1. THE PRAYER OF AGREEMENT

This form of prayer may well be the greatest power and yet the most underutilized potential available to God's church. As I noted previously, in Matthew 18:19–20 the Lord Jesus revealed the supernatural effectiveness that becomes available when even just two believers are united in prayer: "Again I say to you, that if two of you agree on earth about anything they ask, it will be done for them by My Father who is in heaven. For where two or three are assembled in My name, there I am in their midst."

On the day when Father God and Mother Time brought forth the church of Jesus Christ on earth, 120 freshly anointed fire-brands faithfully followed their ascended Savior's final instructions. They gathered for prayer in unity, sacrifice, and harmony, thereby aligning themselves for the manifestation of what He who cannot lie had promised in John 14: "I will pray the Father, and He will give you another Counselor, that He may be with you forever: the Spirit of truth, whom the world cannot receive, for it does not see Him, neither does it know Him. But you know Him, for He lives with you, and will be in you" (vv. 16–17). We find the fulfillment of that covenant in the events described in the Acts of the Apostles:

> When the day of Pentecost had come, they were all together in one place. Suddenly a sound like a mighty rushing wind came from heaven, and it filled the whole house where they were sitting. There appeared to them tongues as of fire, being distributed and resting on each of them, and they were all filled with the Holy Spirit and began to speak in other tongues, as the Spirit enabled them to speak.
> —ACTS 2:1–4

This is not the final time the believers of Jerusalem would witness the power of the whole church praying in agreement. Later in the narrative of Acts, King Herod, alarmed at the exponential explosion of the Jesus movement in Jerusalem, had James, one of the sons of Zebedee, murdered. James and Peter were essentially the primary leader-pastors of the church in Jerusalem. Right on the heels of this atrocity Peter was arrested as well and found himself, "between two soldiers, bound with two chains" (Acts 12:6). The believers of that church were in a near panic. It stood to reason that if Herod—"that fox," as Jesus once called him (Luke 13:32)—brazenly had James killed, he would surely not hesitate to murder Peter as well. The local believers of this fledgling movement were facing the prospect of losing both of their leaders in a very short span of time.

In response to this most dreadful development, they did precisely as they had been taught. They did not circulate a petition. They did not issue a press release. They didn't throw their hands up in despair, cry "the end is near," curl up in a ball, and desert their call.

Rather, they gathered in a home spacious enough to accommodate them and began to bombard the courts of heaven with a petition to intervene (Acts 12:12). They prayed with fervent fire and in undaunted unity. They prayed no "now I lay me down to sleep" prayer but interceded all night long. We know that this was their response because we have the evidentiary report:

> The very night when Herod would have brought him out, Peter was sleeping between two soldiers, bound with two chains. And the guards before the door were securing the prison. And suddenly an angel of the Lord approached him, and a light shone in the prison. He struck Peter on the side and woke him up, saying, "Rise up, quickly." And the chains fell off his hands.
>
> —Acts 12:6–7

Any and every body of believers willing to pray all night long if necessary is a church poised for an outpouring of miracles. Or it is one already in revival! The prayer of agreement is the birthplace of the supernatural. When Holy Ghost, consecrated people of God unite their voices as one and lay hold of the promise of God and refuse to be refused and deny to be denied, miracles will result. You're far too late to talk me out of this. I have been a witness to it a multitude of times.

2. THE PRAYER OF FAITH

The adversary of our souls has the American church exactly where he wants it—as the church at Laodicea mentioned in the previous chapter, she believes that she has virtually everything she needs, and whatever she does not have, there is always a convenient way to get it. Have you ever wondered why there are far more miraculous healings in Africa than there are in America? Perhaps the cause is they don't have a clinic on every corner or a vast array of medicine bottles in their cabinets. Most of us consume three meals a day and snacks in between, while in many parts of our world Christians have no choice but to pray literally for their daily bread. Americans exist in a world of abundance that would have astonished the wealthiest kings two centuries ago.

We surmise that we are rich, but from heaven's perspective and description we are "wretched, miserable, poor, blind, and naked." We are destitute of faith. We are deprived of the heavenly currency of expectancy and confidence in God's ability and willingness to change circumstances and soften hearts.

Yet Jesus commanded us,

> Have faith in God. For truly I say to you, whoever says to this mountain, "Be removed and be thrown into the sea," and does not doubt in his heart, but believes that what he says will come to pass, he will have whatever he says. Therefore I say to you, whatever things you ask when you

pray, believe that you will receive them, and you will have them.

—MARK 11:22–24

Here, the One to whom all authority in heaven and on earth has been given has directly delegated that authority to His church. We have been commanded to declare His decree, to speak His law and literally bring heaven to earth—Thy kingdom come, Thy will be done as in heaven so on earth. Where is our fearless confidence? It has been cast away by our shameful cowardice.

The One whose words are Spirit and Life declared, "with God nothing will be impossible" (Luke 1:37). So where are His miracles among us? Jehovah Sabaoth—God of the angel armies through our Risen King—charges us to pray in faith for His enemies to be made a footstool for His feet. So why are His enemies given free rein, unhindered in our schools and halls of government, unrestrained in our city streets and our own homes? Our mighty Savior once beheld His frightened, cowering inner circle and in frustration exclaimed, "Where is your faith!?" I'm sure, if you'll listen as I have, you'll hear Him addressing that same question to millions of church attenders today.

If we do not learn to prevail in the prayer of faith, the devil will continue to deceive the church into believing all is well because there's a surplus in the budget, we've got a "cool" preacher and a "rock star" worship leader, and vacation Bible school is full.

There is little, if any, point in gathering to pray if those gathered are weak in faith—the confident expectancy that arises from glimpsing God's mercy and might, His goodness and grace revealed in the living Christ's finished work on that cruel cross. So just how does a congregation receive these extraordinary gifts of insight? They are preached. They are boldly and directly declared from the pulpit without exception or apology or fear of contradiction—for "faith comes by hearing, and hearing by the word of God" (Rom. 10:17). If… Only *if*!

When that gospel preacher's life backs his language, God allows none of his words to fall to the ground. Then, formidable faith arises in the hearts of God's people. That faith becomes multiplied without measure through the power of agreement, makes Satan himself tremble, and sends his demonic horde fleeing in abject horror to seek cover among the rocks and crevices. Even so, agreement and faith are not the only two weapons of prayer waiting in our arsenal of dominion.

3. THE PRAYER OF THANKSGIVING

We tend to think of gratitude as an obligation as opposed to a weapon of warfare. A nicety, not a ferocious force for transformation. We are wrong. From our earliest days we are trained that polite people say "thank you." Certainly, this is true and proper. Those of us who were raised correctly instinctively say "thanks" when the barista hands us our three-dollar cup of coffee or a stranger hands us something we unknowingly dropped. But a heart of gratitude toward God is far more than a requirement of polite social interaction. It wields enormous benefits to its beneficiary.

There is a large and growing mountain of secular research revealing the power of gratitude in the human soul. Study after study reveals that thankful people—individuals who focus on the many blessings they have been afforded rather than what they don't currently possess—are healthier, happier, and more successful. None of this is surprising to the faithful student of Scripture. Our Bibles overflow with exhortations and promises concerning a grateful heart and positive attitude. And with good reason. Being mindful of and focused upon how good and gracious, how merciful and faithful our great God has been to you resets your posture, raises your expectancy, and opens your heart to approach God's holy presence and receive His abundant blessings—spirit, soul, and body—and all that pertains to life and godliness. The psalms repeatedly suggest both our deep need for and the benefits of our coming to God with our hearts abounding generously with thanksgiving. Oh, that we might—with happy heads, hearts, and hands uplifted—join with the psalmist in the 100th division and:

> *Enter into His gates with thanksgiving*, and into His courts with praise; *be thankful to Him*, and bless His name. For the LORD is good; His mercy endures forever, and His faithfulness to all generations.
> —PSALM 100:4–5, EMPHASIS ADDED

The final half of that stirring lyric contains words that are repeated many times throughout Scripture. Again and again we discover some variation of the ancient hymn of thanksgiving: "O, give thanks to the Lord, for He is good, and His mercy endures forever."

We see the first recorded appearance of these Holy Ghost–inspired words in a song penned by King David to celebrate the return of the ark of the covenant (and therefore the holy presence of God) to the epicenter of the Israelites' life. The incomparable warrior-poet placed them as the crescendo of a lengthy, exuberant hymn of praise. (See 1 Chronicles 16, particularly verse 34.)

In 2 Chronicles chapter 5 these awe-inspiring lines rise in effervescence from the combined harmonic voices of thousands singing aloud in resounding gratitude, resulting in the very glory of the living God of heaven and earth filling the room. So intense was His presence, so thick was the cloud, that those present could not remain upright upon their feet. In the twentieth chapter of that same book, the Israelites were called to go to battle to face an overwhelmingly superior enemy. The tiny army of Israel was preceded by the unmistakable sound of worshippers singing David's Holy Ghost–anointed lyrics of thanksgiving. Without warning, the mighty armies of their adversary fell into a deep delusion of confusion and disarray, turning upon and slaughtering each other. The attackers were destroyed and the victory won without a single Israelite sword being unsheathed. Such is the weapon of thankful praise!

This same unparalleled song appears repeatedly in the psalms of David and in one of the weeping Jeremiah's prophecies. Little wonder that they may very well be the most frequently repeated phrases in all God's Word. Why are they so obviously important and so clearly powerful?

Surely it is because thankfulness is without exception the most appropriate posture when approaching the Most High God. Not fear. Not greed or selfish desire. Not even hopelessness. The humility of gratitude. David's anointed declaration then offers us two decisive reasons why this is without rebuttal.

First, we have access with a grateful heart "for He is good." A faith rooted in God's fundamental goodness is the foundation upon which all sound theology must rest. It is the presupposition, the underlying premise from which all accurate logic and reasoning concerning God is anchored. There is simply no more important revelation available to you than the absolute understanding that God is unceasingly and unwaveringly good. And it is the ultimate impetus for us to be thankful—to God, and for God.

Second, gratitude is of supreme importance because God's "mercy endures forever."

The Hebrew word translated "mercy" here, or in some translations "lovingkindness," is *chesed*. It speaks of the covenantal nature of God's love for us. It means God's love is no mere emotion or disposition. God binds His love to us through an immutable, unchangeable, and unbreakable covenant. When you contemplate the truth that God loves you with a love that is relentless, tenacious, and impervious to your frailty, flaws, and wavering faithfulness, the heart has only one rational response: to cry out from every part and portion of your triune being, "thank You."

And when we shout that grateful cry together, it rends the very veil separating heaven from earth, allowing a deluge of glory like lightning flashing from a dark-throated storm cloud that causes the thunder to roll and releases an outpouring of refreshing rain upon our waiting hearts and parched souls.

Do you sense it? The prayer of thanksgiving is a weapon, not an obligation. It is a force, not a formality. Where the church of the living God unsheathes this sword, demonic principalities fear to tread. Even so, there is yet another arrow in the quiver of a praying church.

4. THE PRAYER OF CONSECRATION

More than likely, when your local church was founded, the pastor, leaders, and everyone involved in its planting gathered together to consecrate, dedicate, and separate the new work to the kingdom of God and His Christ. Perhaps they did so again with each new building the church acquired or built through the years. This is as it should be. There would be great gain in an awareness of spaces and places consecrated to God. These should be holy, set apart, distinguished from the contamination of everyday activities. But these rare and momentous special events of dedication must not be the only occasions wherein we—individually and corporately—pray prayers of consecration. Certainly, such prayers must never be confined to buildings and foundings. These are temporal and will pass away.

The call to follow, to be a disciple of the Lord Jesus, demands the complete and consistent cleansing and purifying effect of true consecration. Romans 12:1 instructs us to present our "bodies as a living sacrifice." Communities of believers are called to the same lifestyle of holiness and separation. Just as our faith in Christ as individuals absolutely requires a daily dying to ourselves and a continued and purposeful surrender to the Word and will of God, so it must be also in our local churches.

Though few would ever have the intellectual and spiritual honesty to admit it, the founding prayers of consecration in many churches carry an unspoken expiration date. "God, this is Your church...until You decide to reinvent and reimagine our church and Your gospel." "Lord, let Your gospel always be at our core... until we're large enough for our super-powered programs to become our heartbeat." "Father, we'll do things Your way...unless

'Your way' makes us appear old-fashioned, outdated, or uncool in the eyes of the community."

I doubt that even 20 percent of church attenders (i.e., sinners) have ever heard the term *consecration*, much less understand it and apply it in their daily lives. Yet it is on glorious display and in living color throughout our Bibles. Consecration looks like Abraham binding his miracle son's hands on a pile of firewood. Consecration looks like David picking up five smooth stones. It looks like Daniel facing hungry lions as a result of his refusal to cease praying to the one true and living God out loud, in public, three times a day despite the government's command and threat of facing certain death. Consecration looks like three Hebrew young men holding out their hands to be bound by ropes as a furnace is heated to a glowing red. Consecration looks like the Lord Jesus firmly setting His face toward Jerusalem to keep an appointment with torture, shame, wrath, and abandonment. I can also tell you what consecration does not look like. It bears no resemblance to the faux Christianity perpetrated in celebrity culture cult churches of this modernistic, humanistic, narcissistic hour.

Any group of believers willing to sanctify themselves for God's plans and purposes not only as individuals but also as a body is a group positioned for revival. This is a people about to be used mightily of the Lord and to be witnesses to Him as He works with them, confirming His Word with signs, wonders, miracles, and the greatest harvest of souls the world has ever beheld.

&

Is your church a house of prayer? It can be. God desires for it to be. Like most revivals, prayer revivals begin with one person. Pray for a prayer partner, and when God answers that petition—and He will—pray the prayer of agreement for the spirit of intercession to fall upon the people of your fellowship. A house of prayer is a place God will fill with the glory of His perfect and perfecting presence. Becoming a house of prayer fulfills one of the key stipulations of God's conditional 2 Chronicles 7:14 promise.

Where there is true biblical consecration, one will never hear the mantras of the selfish: "Why me?" "I want." "I have a right." "I deserve to be happy." "How could God?" We have exchanged "that convicts me" for "don't condemn me." We are among a perverse generation that constantly demands their rights and forsakes their responsibilities, always asking "What does God have to offer me?" rather than "What can I do to serve God?"

Gone are the days of holy living spawned from Bible preaching from texts like Hosea 8:12, "I wrote for him the ten thousands precepts of My law, but they are regarded as a strange thing [which does not concern him]" (AMP). May Christ be merciful to those who refuse to preach or live by the laws of holiness. Hear with clarity the thundering voice of the Almighty: "If the foundations (of prayer) be destroyed, what will the righteous do?"

Away with modernists' teaching, false doctrine, and producing a warped, self-indulgent generation. They are rolling in luxury, reveling in excess, rollicking in pleasure, revolting in morals, and rotting in sin. What can be expected from a generation where passion is a riderless horse and self-indulgence a runaway train? Where accountability has been rebranded as judgment, man is magnified above his Maker, and creation is worshipped above its Creator?

We must become those crying out, "Where truth lies fallen in the streets, we must insist upon moral integrity, physical purity, and spiritual intensity." We must speak up and speak out when holiness is neither preached nor expected. We must declare God's truth of eternal severity and never stutter. We must not be silent when hucksters in pulpits entice the unthinking, undiscerning, prayerless masses into the perpetuation of their own perversions. These have fallen victim of their own flesh-fueled desires, their emotions enticed and their souls seduced by a silly gospel delivered in sweet, syrupy, soft, whispering tones. Beware the serpent's hiss! Beware his promise, "You shall be like God."

As a generation creates an idolatrous gospel conducive to whatever abominable lifestyle they have chosen for themselves, we must love God's law in this age of lawlessness. We must live lives of character and conviction born in the crucible of consecration. May our intercession of dedication be laced with anguish and our hearts never grow cold. May our knees not be smooth nor our hands weak.

Chapter 9

IF MY CHURCH...
WOULD SEEK MY FACE

MY SPIRITUAL GRANDFATHER, the extraordinary, miracle-working preacher Smith Wigglesworth, had a set daily routine that he followed faithfully when conducting a revival meeting. Between the hours of 8:00 a.m. and noon each morning, he would pray for thirty minutes, read the Word for thirty minutes, then pray for another thirty minutes and read for another thirty minutes, and so on. That's four hours, not four minutes. In this purposeful alternating between prayer and meditation upon holy Scripture, this giant of the faith was seeking the very face of God. After a break for tea, he would then retire to a quiet room and simply wait in the presence of God until it was time to dress for the evening service.

Wigglesworth had discovered what so few have: a pathway of entering the very presence of God through multidimensional disciplines. He realized the wisdom and power available in seeking the Holy One's face through His infallible Word, as well as in prayer—seeking His face in quiet consecration and meditation, listening intently for his immutable God to speak by the Holy Ghost.

How many preachers in this bleak and dark hour approach the sacred honor of delivering the gospel of Christ with even a fraction of that desire, discipline, and dedication? Being called of God and having accepted the heavenly assignment of rightly dividing the Word of truth to rescue the perishing, reach the desperate and dying, as well as teach and train God's people? How many are willing to completely sanctify themselves from worldly pursuits and selfish ambition long enough to focus on the face of the living Savior? Do our worship leaders spend as much time Saturday fine-tuning their hearts as they do their instruments, sound systems, and lighting panels—or watching Netflix, for that matter?

Where are those who will sanctify themselves, for tomorrow the Lord will do wonders among them? (Josh. 3:5). Such challenging questions as these must be asked and answered of church leaders. "For to whom much is given, of him much shall be required" (Luke 12:48). Woe to those who have been charged with these sacred tasks and count it a light thing. So very few are actually called to gospel ministry. Most today simply made a career choice. If you recall, James warned would-be teachers of the Word about a "heavier judgment" (Jas. 3:1, ASV).

The fact is that no one, myself included, is fit to speak to the people of God until they've first spoken to God about the people.

"The fish rots from the head down," the old maxim dating back to the 1600s tells us. And churches grow stagnant, stiff, and cold from the top down as well. Rigor mortis regarding evangelism is a telltale indicator of spiritual death. According to Psalm 133, the anointing flows downward from the head. Yet this does not mean that a pastor bears the sole responsibility for the spiritual health of the body. We must no longer expect the church leadership to provide everything for our spiritual success from the cradle to the grave. If Paul the apostle pleaded with the churches he oversaw to fervently pray for him, how much more do our true pastors need our prayers and those of our fellow members? A church body hungry for revival must individually and collectively seek the face and presence of Jehovah God Shammah.

To the church at Colossae, Paul commanded, "Set your mind on things above, not on things on the earth" (Col. 3:2, NKJV). Sadly, things above have become eclipsed by "things on the earth," which have become no longer a distraction but rather the very focus of churchgoers and their uninspired leaders. Rather than being in passionate pursuit of God's face, a multitude of "believers" spend their time, talents, and treasures seeking the things of this carnal world. We have watered down and adulterated the gospel in a fruitless, foolish quest for "relevance" and people-pleasing popularity. Yet the Lord Jesus clearly warned that no man (or church body) can serve two masters (Matt. 6:24). We will either serve God or we will bow and grovel in the perverted hope of a little approval from Mammon, which is but one of the myriad of idols in this culture. Paul spoke in paralyzing directness when he asked, "For am I now seeking the approval of men or of God? Or am I trying to please men? For if I were still trying to please men, I would not be the servant of Christ" (Gal. 1:10). Did that arrest your attention? This is not Burger King. You can't have it your way. Nor can you serve the living God and cater to the whims of men.

Every congregation in America has made this fateful choice. I wonder how many have chosen poorly.

While in exile on the island called Patmos, John, being in the Spirit on the Lord's Day (now that's a thought), was transported to heaven and visited by his Savior, resplendent and terrifying in His resurrected glory. The first thing the risen, gloried Christ directed the aged disciple to do was to deliver seven specific messages to seven separate first-century churches. Each was founded by Paul on his third missionary journey and was located in a beautiful Greek city in the Roman province of Asia Minor. They also represent the church through the ages. These messages contained commendation and encouragement where deserved, but also correction. Back in chapter 7 we examined the modern implications of the letter to the Laodicean church. Now consider these rebukes the Lord Jesus gave to some of the other individual fellowships of believers in that day:

[To the church in Ephesus:] You have abandoned the love you had at first. Remember therefore from where you have fallen. Repent, and do the works you did at first, or else I will come to you quickly and remove your candlestick from its place, unless you repent.

—REVELATION 2:4–5

[To the church in Pergamum:] You have there those who hold the teaching of Balaam, who taught Balak to cast a stumbling block before the children of Israel, to eat things sacrificed to idols and to commit sexual immorality. So you also have those who hold the teaching of the Nicolaitans. Repent, or else I will come to you quickly and will war against them with the sword of My mouth.

—REVELATION 2:14–16

[To the church in Thyatira:] You permit that woman Jezebel, who calls herself a prophetess, to teach and seduce My servants to commit sexual immorality and eat food sacrificed to idols. I gave her time to repent of her sexual immorality, but she did not repent. Look! I will throw her onto a sickbed, and those who commit adultery with her into great tribulation, unless they repent of their deeds.

—REVELATION 2:20–22

[To the church in Sardis:] You are dead. Now wake up! Strengthen what little remains, for even what is left is at the point of death. Your deeds are far from right in the sight of God.

—REVELATION 3:2, TLB

Each letter was bound to the others, like a book, and then circulated to all seven. How illuminating are these words from the Great Shepherd for these local flocks! Some were guilty of abandoning their love for God and one another. Others followed false doctrine and teaching. The Sardisians were near spiritual death. The priests in Thyatira were sleeping with prostitutes! Yet surprisingly, God did not, by any means, consider any of these the worst church of the group. That infamous shameful title of indistinction went to the church in Laodicea, indicted by none other than the King of kings and undisputed ruler of heaven and earth, Jesus Christ Himself, with these words that we examined earlier:

> I know your works, that you are neither cold nor hot. I could wish you were cold or hot. So then, because you are lukewarm, and neither cold nor hot, I will vomit you out of My mouth. Because you say, "I am rich, have become wealthy, and have need of nothing"—and do not know that you are wretched, miserable, poor, blind, and naked—I counsel you to buy from Me gold refined in the fire, that you may be rich; and white garments, that you may be clothed, that the shame of your nakedness may not be revealed; and anoint your eyes with eye salve, that you may see.
>
> —REVELATION 3:15–18

The worst of the churches in Revelation was not the one near death or even the one with a brothel of prostitutes frequented by priests in its temple. The lowest was the one so blinded by its visible yet worldly success, personal prestige, and fame that it could not see how "wretched, miserable, poor, blind, and naked" it was. They believed they were the best of the best. Why, I'm sure they were complimented by the press and entertained celebrities on the front row every week, sitting beside local dignitaries and visiting politicians. How tragic; what an indictment. It parallels another biblical warning from 2 Thessalonians 2:11–12: "Therefore God will send them a strong delusion, that they should believe the lie: that they all might be condemned who did not believe the truth but had pleasure in unrighteousness."

The Laodicean church had it all with nothing on the side. They had lots of people but no presence. They had refreshments in the foyer but no revival. They had fun at their fellowship outings but no outpouring. In response to their self-induced, blind igno-rance, the Word made flesh in plain, unvarnished, unapologetic speech said, "I will vomit you out of My mouth." For the errant church He had mercy. For the corrupt church He offered for-giveness. Even to the dead church He offered resurrection power. But to the self-righteous, unrighteous, worldly church He offered only the lye soap and washbasin of self-crucifying, heartrending repentance.

Given all of this, what rational believer would ever want to be part of a church meriting such a stinging rebuke from the Head of the church? Yet the bulk of churchgoers from sea to shining sea in this vast "Christian" nation gather, if they attend church at all (the average is once every six weeks), in places that fit to a tee the description of one or more of these seven churches. How can that be? It is quite obvious to those with eyes to see; it's because the prince of this world "disguises himself as an angel of light" (2 Cor. 11:14). He "does not stand in the truth, because there is no truth in him" (John 8:44). The deceiver has beguiled the American church into kneeling to the idols of this present age. We have allowed what God would not. We have insulted and abandoned the very message proclaimed by the Christ of Calvary.

Just as the Israelites did after entering the land of promise when they erected the idolatrous golden calf because they wanted a god they could see, we too have gone after the false gods of the surrounding pagan culture and defiled ourselves at their altars. (See, for example, Judges 2:12–13 and Judges 10:6.) In their day, the false gods went by names like Dagon, Baal, and Ashteroth. The false gods of our day go by different names, yet they seduce God's people to their altars all the same. These blasphemous pagan altars are legion, but let us examine some of the most popular.

৪১

THE ALTAR OF KNOWLEDGE

God has always and does yet delight in using the uncreden-tialed. Jeremiah Lanphier, the human spark that ignited the Fulton Street Revival, was a common salesman who sold other businessmen on the idea of praying with him. Evan Roberts was still a young student when he abandoned his classwork to fan the embers of the Welsh Revival into a nation-transforming conflagration.

The students at Asbury experienced revival while they were receiving their education, not after they had become pastors and theologians with master's degrees and doctorates.

Another tremendous example is Dwight L. Moody (1837–1899), who was known as the apostle of laymen (meaning the people in the pews) evangelism. He was the instrument of God to show what one single consecrated layperson could accomplish when filled with the Holy Ghost and a desire to experience a renewing, restoring revival in their generation.

How is it that a non-ordained shoe salesmen became one of the greatest evangelists of the nineteenth century? How is it that a young man with no formal training or denominational backing could come to reach over one hundred million people with the gospel? The answer: five pews.

That's right. It's not a misprint. Just five pews. Five rows of seats reserved for the unsaved. The broken. The downtrodden. The misfits. The outcasts. The sinners. Well, a few wooden benches couldn't have possibly birthed a worldwide evangelistic revival, could it? I'm glad you asked. Because Dwight L. Moody would want me to tell this story—*his* story that made history.

Moody was one of nine children, and his father died when he was just four years of age. College wasn't an option because he never made it beyond a fifth-grade education. At the age of seventeen, he left home to seek employment in Boston. After he failed to secure a desirable position, his uncle reluctantly hired him in his shoe shop. Everything changed for Moody when, at age eighteen, he gave his heart to Christ in that very store. Shortly thereafter he moved to Chicago, opened his own shoe business, and was given God-ordained ideas to increase sales. As success in selling shoes came, so did a passion for saving souls and a determination to never let a day pass without telling at least one person about the saving grace of Jesus Christ.

While working fifty to sixty hours a week selling shoes and exponentially growing his business, Moody got involved in a local church. He even asked his pastor if he could teach a Sunday school class. When the pastor declined, Moody asked if he could have five empty pews reserved every Sunday and promised he'd fill them with the lost. He was determined to become the greatest lay minister and individual recruiter of souls that local church had ever witnessed.

With no office, no desk, no funding, no salary or stipend, no vehicle, no social media, no telephone, and no help, Moody managed to fill every one of those five pews every Sunday morning for five years. And he never allowed anyone to sit there twice. He singlehandedly grew that church and the kingdom by the hundreds.

And soon Moody would preach to crowds of twenty thousand up to five times a week in revival meetings that would last fourteen days or more—but not until he built his own Sunday school. He recruited the students with candy and free pony rides, paid for out of pocket, and Moody himself led every song, taught every lesson, and dismissed every child by name, week after week.

Please do not misunderstand. I am a relentless and tireless advocate of education, especially when the curriculum is firmly anchored to biblical truth. I have founded and funded Christian schools, Bible colleges, and universities. Charles Spurgeon said once, "Bible study is the metal that forges a Christian,"[1] and I agree. A person could study the Bible every day for the rest of his or her life and barely obtain a glimpse of the revelation knowledge, beauty, and power of our sovereign God. Although the dual witnesses of Scripture and history testify that credentials don't qualify a person to be used by God, they don't *disqualify* either.

Nevertheless, much of Western Christianity has embraced a pointy-headed but powerless brand of the faith. This credentialed cult's leaders exalt the academic over the anointing. They are book-smart in every text except the one that truly matters. When they do address the Bible, it is only to analyze it into meaninglessness. Frankly, a lot of exegesis simply x's out Jesus. It seems the more they learn, the less they believe. Paul warned Timothy about such leaders, describing them as "always learning, but never able to come to the knowledge of the truth" (2 Tim. 3:7). Pointed.

The altar of knowledge has led to a church-paralyzing pandemic of intellectual, philosophical, analytical preaching that loads church members with information but drains them of zeal. They absorb facts but experience no impartation. God's people get clever arguments but no conviction. In short, they are worshipping at the altar of knowledge.

Given the prevalence and popularity of this type of preaching, it is no coincidence the American church has not experienced a genuine move of the Spirit for two generations. Man's love affair with knowledge in the twenty-first century has resulted in countless plaques and degrees on the walls but no culture-shaking revivals. While our churches proliferate and some grow to stunning size, the cities in which they have exploded continue to implode in a relentless slide into demonic depravity.

Near the end of his life, Solomon admitted, "I set my heart to know wisdom and to know the folly of ideas and to know foolish behavior, and I know that this as well is like chasing the wind. For in an abundance of wisdom is an abundance of frustration, and he who increases in knowledge also increases in sorrow" (Eccles. 1:17–18).

We cannot seek out knowledge in the futile hope of discovering the almighty God. Rather, let us seek Him with our whole heart, mind, soul, and strength, who will then grant to us the knowledge with which we may wholly glorify Him and His great name.

THE ALTAR OF NUMBERS

"Bigger is always better." "Scale it up." "Attract more customers and add more locations." "The winner is the one with the biggest number at the bottom line." As I pointed out in chapter 7, these are the mindsets and values of America's entrepreneurial culture. They are fantastic values in the world of commerce. One of the many exceptional attributes of this miracle of a nation is that it has always been a place where any individual—no matter how humble his or her origins—can begin with nothing but drive, creativity, and character and build something that straddles the whole world. We are a culture whose greatest heroes and icons are those who founded businesses. On Wall Street and on Main Street, numbers define success—particularly the numbers associated with gross revenue and customer counts. The problem is that our pastors and churches have wholly adopted identical values and this exact mindset.

My dear pastor, I am in no way interested in nor impressed by the size of your crowd. Forgive me if I am not awestruck by your "numbers." I was privileged and honored to preach to crowds of more than fifty thousand in my early twenties. I have learned a difficult lesson now, in my mid-sixties, that more is not necessarily better. Especially after I got a good look at the spiritual quality of those exciting throngs.

In speaking some years ago with a preacher, I pointed out that their style and content of preaching had changed drastically. Having acknowledged my assessment in the affirmative, they explained why with this heartbreaking admission: "I know, but I've learned how to move the crowd, and I'm intoxicated on the applause." With a crushed and compassionate heart I pray for them—and for us. God, send revival.

Healthy things grow. But Jesus said that often a severe pruning is necessary along the way. (See John 15:2.) In kingdom mathematics, addition often requires subtraction. Let me emphasize what I pointed out in chapter 7. Far too many pastors view themselves as founders and chief executive officers of startup businesses rather than shepherds of a flock. Put a group of pastors in a room together and the first question most will ask of others is, "What is your attendance running on Sunday morning?" Or, "How many services and locations do you have now?" In the eyes of our Savior, a far better question would be, "How consecrated to the will and ways of God is your congregation these days?" And the first question should never be "How many do you have coming?" but "How many do you have going?" (See Mark 16:15–16.) The higher objective is spiritual quality, not numerical quantity. Again, the apex of all Christian endeavor must be to place the jewel of a soul in the crown of our Savior that the Lamb of God slain may receive the reward of His suffering.

I ask you to please read the following closely. I believe Satan's goal is *not* to empty out our churches; it is to fill them to overflowing with lukewarm believers attracted by milquetoast preaching that coddles the ego, excites the emotions, numbs the conscience, and dulls the spirit.

This I believe to be the strategy of the great deceiver. Sadly, if I'm counting, far too many are bewitched by it, kneeling and worshipping at the pagan altar of numbers. Perhaps we need to stop putting so much effort and emphasis on attempting to get larger numbers of people in and instead build around the church a nine-foot fence with razor wire around the top and dare people to try to get in. Those who would scale that barrier and ignore the pain as they gain entry and fall prostrate at the altar would be those who would shake this generation for the kingdom of God and of His Christ.

By the way, I believe that the only way to be born again is...to die. Oh, I'm sorry, is that too graphic? Does it offend our delicate sensibilities? If so, please read John 3:1–7. The words in red are our Savior's own.

THE ALTAR OF COMPROMISE AND COMFORT

In the introduction, I mentioned a classic comment by my late friend, John Osteen: "The church has become so worldly and the world so churchy, you can't tell the difference." For as much grief as we've given the world for hating the church, to me the true reality is in all this culture's pain and distress; its agony and misery; its darkness, debauchery, and despair, they still—though they may not admit it—look to the church for refuge. But to their chagrin, they find no agape love, no abundant life, no Holy Ghost–fueled hope of happiness. We must stand upright, turn our backs, and walk away from the idolatrous altars of compromise, comfort, and complacency that we may be revived by God's mighty power. We must once again offer a valid, biblical alternative. It is ours to extend to those hurting hordes of humanity just outside our doors.

Where is our witness? Our fire? Our energy? When did we lose our passion and power? Why are people not showing up Sunday morning an hour early because they can no longer constrain their flaming hearts from diving toward the altar and worshipping their Savior? I fear the day when men and women of this generation will stand and confront such an anemic church and cry out, "You never told me the truth!" They were entertained. They enjoyed the jokes. They were comforted in their sin, excused from their iniquity. Their iniquity was renamed their problem, and their worldliness was redefined as their spiritual journey. All the while, those charged with bringing the truth of the gospel of Christ to them week in and week out failed miserably. Jesus warned of a day like this.

> Not everyone who says to Me, "Lord, Lord," shall enter the kingdom of heaven, but he who does the will of My Father who is in heaven. Many will say to Me on that day, "Lord, Lord, have we not prophesied in Your name, cast out demons in Your name, and done many wonderful works in

Your name?" But then I will declare to them, "I never knew
you. Depart from Me, you who practice evil."
—MATTHEW 7:21–23

"Depart from Me," the risen Lord will say. Or, framed in
the language of the letter to Laodicea, "I will spit you out of
My mouth." As I stated in the preface of this book, Leonard
Ravenhill, one of my greatest spiritual mentors and friends, once
exclaimed that he does not believe even 5 percent of modern
church attenders will make it to heaven. What an indictment!
What a sorrow! The mere suggestion itself should be enough to
cause church leaders and members alike to crumble in horror,
scrutinize every priority, and reevaluate everything they think
they know. As basketball coach John Wooden, baseball coach
Earl Weaver, and President Harry S. Truman were all famous
for saying, "It's what you learn after you know it all that counts."
Connect the dots. A compromised, false gospel leads to false
conversions, which results in more souls damned to an eternity
without God. The witness of sacred Scripture reveals that the
Lord Jesus has no tolerance for the lukewarm church, and the
church that prefers the altar of complacency and comfort may be
the most tepid of all.

We have a cancer of compromise in the church, and its root
lies here: entertainment has replaced Bible preaching. Today's
church attender demands production value rather than preaching
that convicts. They want showmanship, not sanctification. Here
is the devilish trap in that. If you have to put on a show to get
them in the sanctuary, you'll have to put on ever-more-enthralling
shows to keep them. Therein lies the reason most churches have
as many people slipping out the back door as coming in the front
door. We ask them to make zero commitment to get in and then
are confused as to why they don't come back.

There will be no awakening when the church puts people
in a stupor produced by the opiate of cheap Christianity. Self-
sacrifice is entry-level Christianity. A church that allows the

winds of popular culture to drive it to the pagan altar of compromise and comfort ultimately ends up worshipping self rather than the risen Christ. *Seek your most successful life! Find your truth! Feel better about yourself!* This will attract a crowd and, more importantly, avoid offending anyone with a gospel that calls for repentance, self-denial, and cross carrying. Indeed, any mention of the cross at all is minimized, if not mocked. The very existence of Calvary's cross shouts of man's depravity and our utter helplessness to save ourselves. The shame and suffering endured by the guiltless Son of God forces us to acknowledge our darkened hearts and filthy garments. As I wrote in my book *The Cross: One Man. One Tree. One Friday*:

> But more often than not the admirers of Jesus the teacher and Jesus the prophet shrink back in horror and embarrassment from Jesus the Lamb of God. This Jesus was slain for the sins of the world. Spat upon. Nailed to a tree. Writhed in His own blood.... The scene at Calvary is too ugly. Too shame-soaked. Its implications about sin, sin's toll, and the severe demands of cosmic justice too troubling to ponder for long. "No, you can keep your shattered Jesus of the cross," the spirit of the age seems to say. "If we must have a Jesus, and we'd prefer not to, we'll take the pretty Sunday school illustration version with children on His lap."[2]

The church that pays homage at the altar of compromise and comfort is not building on the foundations of faith, hope, and love, with Jesus Christ as the chief cornerstone. Instead they attempt to build on the shifting sand of secular humanism and a flattering self-help gospel. They place their hope not in the work of the cross but in pastoral pundits who have manipulated the masses. As a result, the modern church has produced a warped generation that is motivated by convenience, not commitment. One that makes decisions based not on principle but on popularity.

Churches become dry and (spiritually) barren for three reasons. First, they lose their evangelistic zeal. They become single-mindedly focused on the people warm and comfortable inside the walls rather than those shivering in Satan's icy grip outside the walls. Second, they lose their tolerance and respect for the immutable Word of God, preaching with compromise and apology. Third, they exchange seeking the face of God for seeking the face in the mirror. I weep for the tens of thousands of churches and their blind, "blessed all the way to hell" members that in our day have committed all three idolatries.

Yet even in the spiritual drought and death grip of this late hour—only minutes before a midnight of judgment—God stands ready to pour out the warming, reanimating fires of revival upon His people. "If... Only *if* My churches would seek My face, I would hear from heaven and heal their land."

Chapter 10

IF MY CHURCH...
WOULD TURN FROM
ITS WICKED WAYS

WRITE THIS FINAL full chapter with an anguished heart of deep sorrow—and yet abiding hope. The message here will, in all probability, infuriate a few and even offend many. It may well be denounced on internet podcasts and mocked by a myriad on social media. I am at peace with that. Long ago I abandoned seeking the approval or applause of men. As Dr. Lester Sumrall taught me over thirty years ago, "Other people's heads is a terrible place to keep your joy." Here in my sixties, having practically returned from the dead and having been healed of cancer, I am not intimidated, and I write and speak with only one audience in view—the One who sits on a great white throne. I seek only His smile. My sole ambition is to hear Him say, "Well done, good and faithful servant."

Over the years, I have discovered you don't attain celebrity status when you, as did the Lord Jesus, preach the truth regarding repentance from sin. That is OK. They picked up rocks to stone Jesus too, and the mob attempted to catapult Him over a cliff. This servant is not better than his Master. As the British revivalist Joseph Parker once observed:

> The man whose little sermon is "repent" sets himself against his age, and will for the time being be battered

mercilessly by the age whose moral tone he challenges. There is but one end for such a man—"off with his head!" You had better not try to preach repentance until you have pledged your head to heaven.[1]

To preach God's glorious gospel in the current culture is an extremely serious endeavor. If you are fearful and faithless, do not attempt it. If you are not endued with His power from on high, don't try it. If you are not called and anointed, turn from it. If you seek comfort and companions, flee it. If you can do anything else and live, under God, do it!

I write to tell you we have reached the final and utterly unskippable waypoint on the 2 Chronicles 7:14 journey to revival. "If my people...will turn from their wicked ways." Again, what is true for individual believers is true for the collections of believers we call churches. In fact, that original promise was made to "My people, who are called by My name." This a collective call to collective groups who claim the name of Jesus. And as we saw in John's letter to the seven churches, He holds the pastors particularly accountable.

It has become our responsibility to defend gospel truth in a secularist, humanist culture and most distressing churches. So much of what passes as Christianity in these dark days has been spawned from the modernists or liberal theologians. It is from these false doctrines and philosophies that we must cleanse ourselves or fall by our own weight. They are the doctrines of devils that have seeped as raw sewage into the minds and sermons, the doctrines and philosophies—indeed, the worldview—of cold, religious morgues once known as the church.

There were and are fountainheads of these which church leaders adhere to by their deafening silence on the key tenets of biblical Christianity and the gospel of the living Christ. Consider this infamous quote by H. Richard Niebuhr, former professor of Theology and Christian Ethics at Yale Divinity School, which sums up this virus of liberal theology: "A God without wrath brought human beings without sin into a kingdom without judgment through the ministrations of a Christ without a cross."[2]

May I remind us that silence denotes agreement. Though messages against the doctrines of God's wrath, sin, judgment, and the cross may not yet be heard in our circles, how many messages have been heard that are foundational to a true understanding of their absolute necessity in order to keep God's people from being lured away from biblical truth? Never forget that to permit is to participate. As I wrote in my book *Culturally Incorrect*:

> In the eighteenth century, a generation fought for America's independence from British rule. In the nineteenth century, a generation fought to preserve the Union from those who would tear it asunder. In the twentieth century, a generation fought to defend democracy from the forces of tyranny and oppression in both Europe and the Pacific. In the twenty-first century, a generation will fight for the preservation and propagation of a culture based on truth.[3]

A mighty revolution must be fought for. It is not free.

When worldviews collide, nations hang in the balance.[4] So I must urge every true believer to engage in the battle of ideas, of thoughts, of mindsets, of worldviews.[5] The question is, will we fight or slink passively into irrelevance and isolation? Will we simply sit by, horrified spectators?[6] I intend to call the church to nothing less than another Great Awakening.[7]

The church's present impotence, compromise, and failure stems from a fundamental misunderstanding about what it really means to be a Christian. The very gospel we preach is a mere shadow of the real thing. As a result, we have been a midwife to the births of entire generations of believers ill-equipped to engage the culture; unprepared for the rigors of the call of Christ; and unwilling to fight for their King.[8]

There is a price to pay to rescue a generation, restore a nation, and revitalize a civilization. Many on the other side hate us but regardless, our biblical mandate is to love and bless in return.

Challenge them? Yes. Argue for the superiority of our worldview? We must. You see, when worldviews collide, nations hang in the balance. So let me urge you to engage, to lead, to influence.[9]

Under God, we must "fight the good fight of faith" (1 Tim. 6:12) that we may have this testimony, that we "will be a good minister of Jesus Christ, nourished by the words of faith of good (sound) doctrine" (1 Tim. 4:6).

Sound doctrine. Now there's a thought. I fear that neither the church nor its preachers have much knowledge of nor perceived need for any form of doctrine. This is to our great shame and detriment. W. E. Vine made it plain: "The 'new church' model is to be inoffensive, not to speak on sin or mention the cross or suffering, thus avoiding anything that would make people uncomfortable. Consider this quote: 'This subject of sin the preacher must face and bring his hearers face to face with it.' The truth has ever been exposed to the liability of attempts, on the part of many who handle it, to render it palatable to the natural man, and so neutralize its power. Against this the faithful ministry of Christ will always be on his guard."[10]

And then jabbering from national television stars—excuse me, preachers—comes this broadcast of blasphemy: "I don't think anything has been done in the name of Christ and under the banner of Christianity that has proven more destructive to the human personality and, hence, counterproductive to the evangelism enterprise than the often crude, uncouth, and un-Christian strategy of attempting to make people aware of their lost and sinful condition."[11]

May we at least learn this solid doctrine and preach it again?

> And you were dead in your trespasses and sins, in which you formerly walked according to the age of this world and according to the prince of the power of the air, the spirit who now works in the sons of disobedience, among them we all also once lived in the lusts of our flesh, doing the desires of the flesh and of the mind, and we were by nature children of wrath, even as the rest.

—EPHESIANS 2:1–3

"I was brought forth in iniquity, and in sin my mother conceived me" (Ps. 51:5). Therefore, human persons are born into sin. They are by nature wicked, corrupt, vile, and vain. Who has ever had to teach a child to lie? One would sooner be required to plant weeds in a garden.

J. Rodman Williams teaches us that "Man the creature is also man the sinner. It is the actuality of sin that has blighted the human situation since the beginning of history. It is to this critical situation that the Christian faith primarily addresses itself, for Christianity is at heart a way of salvation."[12]

In the corrupted and errant doctrines of the modern church, whether preached or accepted by silence, man has no sin problem but rather has a few flaws that teaching him to have a better self-image will correct. They say man came from a lower species and in a few more million years he'll be just fine. Evolution takes a while, after all. Or, man is simply uneducated and simply needs to be taught.

I think I have the greatest disdain for this one: man has simply been suppressed and needs to be freed from the taboos of religious guilt and the bondage of authority.

In the midst of this cesspool of religious and philosophic numbheadedness, where is the church of the living God? The church stands silent about the things that matter most while exalting those that are both petty and childish; coddling the emotions and flesh while missing the heart blackened by sin. Remember this and mark it well: man is not a sinner because he sins, but rather he sins because he is a sinner.

The blood of Calvary's crucified Lamb did not just save us "from" sin but saved us "in" our sin. Oh, how desperately depraved we were, verifiable enemies of God. We were—in His holy sight—criminals, traitors, and rebels. Your Bible speaks over and over of us being at enmity with God, which means deep-rooted anger, irreconcilable hostility, or to be at war. Understand this and weep for every faux church and backslidden preacher as you pray in desperation for revival. Sinners are not people to invite to a Sunday morning show and then attempt to teach them to be better people. This is humanism at its corrupt core. Rather, let us with the fervor of the Holy Ghost, the victory of His blood-soaked cross, proclaim as did the apostle Paul to the church at Ephesus, "that He might reconcile both to God into one body through the *cross*, thereby slaying the *enmity*" (Eph. 2:16, emphasis added).

Take a cursory glance at Romans 5:8, and get ready for a deluge of Holy Ghost rain: "While we were yet sinners..." That prophesies we shall not always be so because God Almighty has demonstrated His love toward us as a result of the unspeakable gift and supreme sacrifice of His only begotten Son. The blood of the Son of God was the propitiation (the price paid) to reconcile us to God and God to us. This is the gospel we must adhere to, not that of self-help gurus and life coaches posing as gospel preachers. The modern church must quit with its emphasis on positive thinking and emotional singing and "it's all about my happiness" on this cursed planet. It must cease its emphasis on this life and become conscious of eternity. If revival is sought... If... Only *if*!

Paul warned his apprentice pastor, Timothy, of a day like ours. "For the time will come when people will not endure sound doctrine, but they will gather to themselves teachers in accordance with their own desires, having itching ears" (2 Tim. 4:3), he wrote.

Oh, how desperately we need gospel preachers. Men and women with the spiritual unction and fortitude to, in the words of Joseph Parker, "set themselves against the spirit of this age"[13] and call sin, "sin." In the place of fearless, fire-breathing, Holy Ghost preachers we have a generation of timid "teachers" ready, willing, and eager to scratch the itching ears of the compromising and compromised. Please note that the teaching gift, while vital and biblical, is the only one of the fivefold office gifts—apostle, prophet, evangelist, pastor, teacher—with no innate ability to convict the heart of sin. It is no wonder modern American churchgoers flock to the teachers and shun the preachers.

Can unashamed proclamation of biblical standards of holiness really convict and soften hearts of stone? Is it possible that preachers with hearts aflame and a clarion call of the true gospel on their lips actually bring reprobates and rebels to their knees at a tear-stained altar of repentance? Oh, yes. It's not only possible; it's probable for those petitioning God's throne for revival.

I recall the night my uncle, thirty-five years in hopeless, helpless bondage to alcohol, staggered into one of my services so intoxicated that two ushers had to hold him upright as he got to his seat. This calloused, timid, and bound man had long stood as the only member of my maternal family who had resisted surrendering his life to Christ.

That night, the atmosphere was pregnant with the presence of the Holy Ghost. Eternity was in the room. I had asked evangelist Dwight Thompson to preach that evening. He opened his Bible and preached about a holy God who hates sin yet so loves sinners that He sent His only Son to die for them. He preached about a sinless Savior who willingly bared His back to the slicing, flaying scourge of a trained Roman lictor. He preached under a powerful anointing, describing the Lord Jesus gladly laying His mangled back down upon a rough-hewn wooden cross and giving His outstretched arms and wrists to the flesh-nailer. He then related a story of a sinful man crying out, "Enough is enough!" in response to sin's toll on his life.

Midway through the masterful message, my uncle struggled to his feet, raised his shaking hand, pointed his bony finger, and began to say, then shout, "Enough is enough!" He had come to the point of total surrender. My family and I went to him and shouted with him, "Enough is enough!" My beloved Uncle Willie fell to his knees and prayed a repentant sinner's prayer. (Remember those?) We gathered together in prayer until Willie claimed victory. (That's difficult to do in an hour-and-fifteen-minute service.) He arose from that altar a new creature. Born again. Transformed and translated from the kingdom of darkness to the kingdom of God. There was a decision, a choice between two alternatives. Then there was a confession, which is an admission of guilt, followed by a heart conversion. My precious uncle lived another thirty years and never missed church nor ever touched alcohol again.

Please don't attempt to tell me that unabashed preaching on the subject of sin and repentance will not prick consciences, pierce hearts, and convict souls. You are far too late. I have witnessed the glorious power of the Holy Ghost convict men of sin and convince them of righteousness in every service I've ever conducted. But what if my uncle, on what was likely his final opportunity, had instead walked into the church down the street and encountered the three platitudinous points and a poem about sunsets and kittens that passes for preaching in our day? He would have stumbled out (or been escorted out) of that service unchanged and destined for an eternity in hell.

Recall God's complaint to the church in Thyatira from Revelation 2:

> But I have a few things against you: You permit that woman Jezebel, who calls herself a prophetess, to teach and seduce My servants to commit sexual immorality and eat food sacrificed to idols. I gave her time to repent of her sexual immorality, but she did not repent. Look! I will throw her onto a sickbed, and those who commit adultery with her into great tribulation, unless they repent of their deeds. I will put her children to death, and all the churches shall know that I am He who searches the hearts and minds. I will give to each one of you according to your deeds.
> —REVELATION 2:20–23

The leaders at Thyatira were convinced that through their super-powered plans and programs that were always new they could make the gospel more palatable—not so brash and insensitive, so loud and boisterous—and in so doing, they could bring the values of the church to the surrounding pagan culture. To their shame, the values of the godless, pagan culture made themselves at home in the church. Sadly, just as in our day, in some quarters of Christendom, flagrant sexual immorality was initially ignored—then tolerated—and ultimately endorsed. This merited the sternest of rebukes from the King of kings. Indeed, there is no sterner rebuke than a threat of death. This should serve as a sobering wake-up call to the lascivious, sensual American church, for He remains "He who searches the hearts and minds" (Rom. 8:27).

John the Baptist called out sexual sin in the political leadership and offered his neck to the executioner's ax rather than retract and compromise. Yet we rarely hear even the mildest cautions against sexual sin from our pulpits today. Cowards. How many pastors know there are young people in the pews who woke up that morning next to someone with whom they do not share a marriage covenant, and refuse to stay silent on the matter? How many shepherds have the backbone to proclaim the Bible's clear position on same-sex involvement? Where are the prophets who, in the midst of a wicked and perverse, "gender-confused" generation, are willing to stand up and cite Genesis 5:1–2: "In the day when God created man, He made him in the likeness of God. He created them male and female"? Revival? If... Only *if*!

The numbers are far too few. The greatest indictment is not that there is sin in the camp but that no one seems to care.

In Joshua chapter 7 we discover how the sin of one man, Achan, among the vast throng of an entire nation, drained the entire Israelite army of power to secure victory over tiny Ai. Just a little sin in the camp rendered it powerless. Yet we marvel that our churches lie impotent and helpless before the enemies of Christ in our twisted culture. We wring our hands in bewildered despair as our communities and schools slide relentlessly into the gaping maw of hell, all while gross sin is routinely winked at, excused, and frequently rationalized from our pulpits and in our pews.

As Peter concluded his revival-igniting sermon at Pentecost, the crowd's first impulse was to cry: "What shall we do?" The apostle had a ready answer: "Repent and be baptized, every one of you, in the name of Jesus Christ for the forgiveness of sins.... Be saved from this perverse generation!" (Acts 2:37–38, 40). Open, heartrending confession of sin remains the consistent prescription for what ails us. Both James and John, the sons of thunder, agree:

> Confess your faults to one another and pray for one another, that you may be healed.
>
> —JAMES 5:16

> If we say that we have no sin, we deceive ourselves, and the truth is not in us. If we confess our sins, He is faithful and just to forgive us our sins and cleanse us from all unrighteousness.
>
> —1 JOHN 1:8–9

These prophetic proclamations were provocative to the cold-hearted churchgoers, as their intended audience was not godless pagans but Christians. As were the pointed and powerful words of the late Leonard Ravenhill, who wrote:

> This is an hour in need of burning hearts, bursting lips, and brimming eyes! If we were a tenth as spiritual as we think we are, our streets would be filled each Sunday with throngs of believers marching to Zion—with sacks on their bodies and ashes on their shaking heads, shaking at the calamity that has brought the Church to be the unlovely, unnerved, unproductive thing that she is![14]

Jeremiah could rightly ask and answer concerning this generation, "Were they ashamed when they had committed abomination? They were not at all ashamed, nor could they blush" (Jer. 6:15). The most flagrant of sins festering in plain sight no longer even make us blush. We hold no sorrow for them, nor are we even surprised. Perhaps many have seen the open flaunting of such flagrant sin performed and displayed for their entertainment and enjoyment on television, theater, computer, and cell phone screens so many times that we do not recoil when we see them in our own fellowships. Or homes. Or hearts. May God have mercy on their souls, and may He send a revival to our lives and to our land. If… Only *if!*

&

Why does the refreshing, life-giving rain of revival tarry? Why does heaven withhold its life-resurrecting downpour of renewal from us? As you now know, it is no mystery. The answer is right before us, in the timeless conditional promise of 2 Chronicles 7:14:

> If My people, who are called by My name, will humble themselves and pray, and seek My face and turn from their wicked ways, then I will hear from heaven, and will forgive their sin and will heal their land.

If revival comes to our shores once more, it will be only because our churches have relearned the impulse to feel sorrow and shame for our sin and rebellion. Two hundred years ago a revived revenant of saints sang this now-forgotten hymn:

> Blest are the humble souls that see
> Their emptiness and poverty;
> Treasures of grace to them are given,
> And crowns of joy laid up in Heaven.

> Blest are the men of broken heart,
> Who mourn for sin with inward smart;
> The blood of Christ divinely flows,
> A healing balm for all their woes.[15]

Altars filled with broken hearts that mourn over their sin and their condition, lost without Christ and therefore without hope in this world or that world to come: this and this alone is our only hope of revival. Our patient Father, full of mercy and grace, will ever and always stoop low to hear and comfort the truly repentant souls. The psalmist knew what we have too soon forgotten: "The sacrifices of God are a broken spirit; a broken and a contrite heart, O God, You will not despise" (Ps. 51:17). Yet as I look across the current spiritual landscape and take its pulse and temperature, I see countless churches filled with dry eyes and drier hearts. Where are the tears of saints pierced to the core of their being over their own sin, and over a church whose pews are filled each week with members bound by alcohol and drug abuse, quasi-pornographic video streams, gossip and envy, covetousness and strife, lying and lewdness and every other form of wickedness? We can—we must—"turn from our wicked ways."

All of this is true, which is why I began this chapter with the admission that I write in deep sorrow. But I also mentioned abiding hope—and I am indeed hopeful. For I have studied the history of revival and have come away with the understanding that it is never too late for a move of God. That the driest, deadest, most barren of spiritual deserts can explode with life once more. *If...*

Which is why I am contending for something even greater than revival in my lifetime. What can be greater than a full-fledged Holy Ghost outpouring of revival? You are about to discover.

Conclusion

TOWARD A NEW AMERICAN AWAKENING

RAIN REVIVES. IT refreshes. It cleanses. It releases renewed life and fruitfulness. And now, here at the end of our journey together, you know...

You know that no matter how deep the drought of your soul; no matter how long you've gone without the life-giving rain of the Holy Ghost (you realize it's been so long since your eyes have been washed with tears); regardless of how barren, fruitless, and parched the soil of your heart is today, you have discovered a dynamic truth—all of this is subject to change. You are only four simple acts of humble obedience away from becoming certified and qualified to become the beneficiary of a promise that God still honors and heaven supplies supernaturally today. What God has promised, He will do. He is faithful. He remains forever the Holy One who "keeps covenant to a thousand generations" (Exod. 20:6; Deut. 7:9; Ps. 105:8).

As Paul reminds us, in words that can serve as either stern warning or hopeful encouragement:

> Be not deceived. God is not mocked. For whatever a man sows, that will he also reap. For the one who sows to his own flesh will from the flesh reap corruption, but the one who sows to the Spirit will from the Spirit reap eternal life.
> —GALATIANS 6:7–8

It is a spiritual illegality for you to compliantly "sow" the four directions of 2 Chronicles 7:14 and not "reap" the promise of healing and restoration. For your spirit. For your soul. For your entire life and the wholeness of your being.

You can experience a personal outpouring revival at this moment, right where you are. Alone wherever you may be reading right now, the Holy Spirit of God can revive your heart for the kingdom of the living Christ as you have never before experienced. You can fall upon your knees with your bed, chair, or sofa as a holy altar and humbly confess to God Almighty your deep need as you seek His face with dogged determination; you can with fervent intention ask Him to forgive you for having not been His living temple as He has called you to be—He is the only One who can offer this forgiveness.

We know something else now as well. Revival need not begin and end with you, an individual believer. The greatest outpourings of divine demonstration, of salvation, of prayer repeatedly took place in history as the result of a single, surrendered soul who obeyed those four commanded opportunities. Often that personal revival gave birth to a relentlessly unsatisfied passion for lost and dying souls and a weighty burden for God's church. Becoming a revived revenant will do that. It turns you outward. You are no longer the object of your focus and energy, and you begin to sense the very heart of God pounding in your chest to reach those around you with the gospel.

Nevertheless, I firmly believe that every broader revival must begin with the individual before it can spread in the wind of the Holy Ghost. Asbury College experienced a very significant revival on its campus after the Lord God sent fire from heaven into the hearts of its young students. The tiny church in Cane Ridge experienced a supernatural outpouring when Barton Stone and a handful of others in the community opened wide their waiting hearts to a deluge of everything the glorious Holy Spirit would manifest in the hills of eastern Kentucky. And the stunning Welsh Revival ignited when one young girl bravely stood up to profess and confess her life-altering love for Christ Jesus. However, what the inhabitants of Wales experienced in 1905 and the Hebridean farmers and fishermen in 1949 was more than a revival. It was an *awakening*.

An awakening is revival so wide, so deep, so strong that it bleeds into the fabric of society. It refuses the normal boundaries of church buildings and scheduled services. It takes no thought of time or place, for its time is always now; its place is always here. It steps over boundaries of race, class, economics, and institutions of all human restraint. It transforms culture. It is inescapable. It needs no advertisement other than changed lives. It requires no publicity but its own miracles, signs, wonders, and demonstrations of the Holy Ghost. The unchurched and unsaved sense it and benefit from it. There is a palpable atmospheric rearrangement. No one is outside its divine influence and grasp. No one remains dry in such a drenching storm. One realizes the transformative power of such a Holy Ghost hurricane because after it passes, nothing is left unchanged in its wake.

When those arriving in the Hebrides stepped off their boats, without warning many fell on their faces under heavy conviction of the Holy Ghost. In the streets, people would suddenly collapse to their knees, crying out, weeping for the forgiveness of God's Son. When attending the accompanying revival meetings, the people would become upset not because the preacher had gone beyond the allotted twenty-eight minutes but because he had stopped due to sheer physical exhaustion! Across the length and breadth of Wales everyone and everything was affected by the manifested tangibility of God, including the night life and the donkeys in the coal mines. The Welsh people became intensely interested in the things of God's kingdom with little, if any, affection for the affairs of this world. Even the local press began printing special revival editions.

When an awakening falls upon an entire community as it did in Wales and the Hebrides, every person knows it. There is a dynamic explosion of God's Spirit, and the effects are like shockwaves pulsing through a town, a city, a region, a nation. Even those few with hearts so hard and black that they resist the drawing of the Holy Ghost still reap benefits from such an outpouring; they benefit from the drop in the crime rate and the overall elevation of the society from the sewers of self-destructiveness and decay that sin invariably fosters upon any community and which festers in its people.

So I will spend my closing words and thoughts with you here, endeavoring by God's grace to stir within your heart a hunger, a hope, a Holy Ghost expectancy for a true, life-altering revival and history-changing awakening in the nation you love. I have such a divinely driven hunger and expectation. You see, I've detected rustling in the mulberry bushes. I sense a rumbling just below the surface of church normalcy. It's very much like the one some spiritually attentive American believers likely heard and felt just over a century ago.

There is an old maxim frequently attributed to Mark Twain: "History doesn't repeat, but it often rhymes."[1] As you're about to discover, our current moment is rhyming perfectly with an earlier one.

ಬಿ

It was March 1918 and the Great War, known to posterity as World War I, was mercifully nearing its end. It would drag on eight hellish months more before the official armistice was signed by all parties. The assassination of Austria's archduke on June 28, 1914, served as the spark that lit a fire that engulfed the entire world, ultimately involving more than one hundred nations in a brutal, blood-drenched affair. More than twenty million people lost their lives in this largely pointless conflict before the exhausted, war-weary parties finally laid down their arms.

As history records, the Allies—including the United States, Great Britain, and France—were destined to prevail. Mercifully, the "War to End All Wars," as it came to be known, was winding down. Soon the world would be able to begin rebuilding itself from the cataclysmic destruction and once again live in peace. Or so those living at the time sincerely believed. "Surely no nation will ever again dare to engage in war after all of this appalling horror," says the conventional wisdom. Of course, we now know that only twenty-one years into the future, Germany invaded Poland, triggering a cascade of atrocious events that plunged the planet into all-out war once again. Twenty-one years. How tragically soon we forget.

But then, as the world neared the end of one unprecedented tragedy, another equally grievous global calamity was already underway.

Among the first to discover that horror was a US Army Private named Albert Gitchell. He was stationed at Camp Funston located at Fort Riley in Junction City, Kansas. Upon waking on the morning of March 4, 1918, Gitchell assumed he would be eating breakfast in the mess hall as he usually did. Instead, he reported to the camp's hospital complaining of cold-like symptoms that included a sore throat, fever, and headache. Soon after, more than one hundred of his fellow soldiers were reporting similar symptoms. Though doctors could not have known what was happening at that moment, this was the beginning of the 1918 Spanish flu. Almost immediately it began spreading unabated like wildfire through other military camps and US prisons.[2] Wherever large numbers of human persons lived in close proximity, this viral infection spread with swift, deadly efficiency.

Though its origin is disputed, what no one can deny is that the 1918 influenza pandemic was horrendous and lethal worldwide.[3] It is estimated that from March 1918 through the summer of 1919, roughly 500 million people—a staggering one-third of the world's entire population at the time—became infected with the deadly H1N1 virus. Worldwide, at least 50 million deaths resulted from this killer pandemic, including 675,000 fatalities in the United States.[4]

I'm certain that this scenario is sounding quite familiar to you. The worst of the pandemic arrived during the summer of 1918, when soldiers returning from battle quickly and easily spread the deadly disease to the general population, especially in the world's most densely crowded cities.

With no vaccine and very few antibiotics, efforts to control the spread were limited to non-pharmaceutical methods like educating the public about personal hygiene, using disinfectants and face coverings, imposing quarantines, and limiting public gatherings.

The population was encouraged to stay at home and avoid any and all physical contact. Libraries stopped lending out books. The city of St. Louis, Missouri, closed its schools and movie theaters and banned all public gatherings. Citizens of San Francisco were actually fined if they were caught in public without masks and were often criminally charged with disturbing the peace. (California seems to have always had its own set of rules.) The media lambasted the city of Philadelphia when it refused to cancel its parade to support and encourage the public to get behind the war bond effort. Businesses were forced to shut their doors because so many employees were becoming infected. Agriculture production slowed and crops spoiled in the field simply because there weren't enough farmers to harvest the crops.

Bill Sardo was a funeral director in Washington, DC, during that pandemic. He saw countless bodies in that season. But years later it was the fear and dread that he would recall most vividly. Writing in remembrance he said:

> From the moment I got up in the morning to when I went to bed at night, I felt a constant sense of fear. We wore gauze masks. We were afraid to kiss each other, to eat with each other, to have contact of any kind. We had no family life, no church life, no community life. Fear tore people apart.[5]

So is any of this sounding eerily familiar to you? Is history "rhyming" in this moment?

I must pause here and interject that "there is nothing new

under the sun" (Eccles. 1:9), and Satan has no new tricks, no new strategies, and no new objectives. In 1918, as they are doing now, legions of demonic forces endeavored to divide us. A polarized people is a weak people. We must never succumb to the demonic spirit of division. There is strength in unity. There is great power in agreement. Recall that the Holy Ghost fell in power on 120 individual souls when they "were all with one accord in one place" (Acts 2:1, KJV). Note also that in the Old Testament narrative, when God wanted to destroy an invading army, He frequently sowed confusion in their ranks, causing them to turn upon one another. On more than one occasion, Israel won a battle against her enemies without ever even having to draw a sword. Such is the destructive capability of division.

Mercifully, in 1919, by the close of its second summer, the unprecedented influenza pandemic dissipated, leaving behind 50 million bodies to bury and a devastated economy to rebuild. All while the rubble of a devastating global war was still smoldering.

The pandemic had departed. God Almighty, however, had not. In fact, Jehovah Sabaoth, the God of the Angel Armies, was just about to release upon a reeling planet a divine response to devastation, destruction, helplessness, and hopelessness.

Allow me now to take you to a remarkable service already in progress. It is December 31, 1918, as we enter Victoria Hall, a Pentecostal mission on South Spring Street in downtown Los Angeles. In one hundred years, the *Los Angeles Times* building will sit on this very spot. But tonight, those in attendance are seeking a different kind of news. The meeting hall, with an official capacity of 650 seats, is packed to the rafters. As we approach the building we see a large crowd assembled out front, disappointed that they were unable to gain entry but far too energized and expectant to go home. Others crowd around the open windows on each side of the hall, straining to hear the words of a young woman named Aimee Semple McPherson. At twenty-seven years of age she is already well known in many parts of the country for her powerful preaching. One reporter of that era wrote of her, "Never did I hear such language from a human being. Without one moment's intermission, she would talk from an hour to an hour and a half, holding her audience spellbound."[6]

As we enter the hall, every seat is filled, as is every available place to stand. People are seated on the steps of the platform and even on the platform itself. At the center, and the focus of every eye gathered, is a dark-haired young lady dressed head-to-toe in dazzling white in what seems like a cross between a nurse's uniform and a woman's military attire. She is preaching with a fervor and intensity that few have ever witnessed. Yes, she is fiery and eloquent, but there is something more than talent here. Those with the spiritual sensitivities to discern it feel the presence of a powerful anointing. Let us listen in for a moment.

Her text is Ezekiel's valley of dry bones. Like an Old Testament prophet she is calling dry, sinful, backslidden Christians to be brought back to life by the breath of the Holy Spirit. She is calling for them to repudiate and confess their sin, their connection to worldliness and ungodliness (re-vived!), to repent of apathy and complacency concerning the lost and hell-bound around them. She will cite Jesus' own words to the church of Ephesus: "Nevertheless I have somewhat against thee, because thou hast left thy first love" (Rev. 2:4, KJV).

She will proclaim, "I have been sent here tonight to point the way back to the place of power and blessing."[7]

Heaven clearly endorsed that message. A few months later she would write of that night:

> When the call for the altar service was given the prayer room was filled to overflowing, the rostrum, the entire altar (and even though the seats were moved back to make room) all round the building and in the aisles scores were praying for salvation, believers receiving the Baptism of the Holy Ghost, sick healed and such dancing and rejoicing as

the lost came home!...Strong men and women wept like children; a broken, contrite, mellow spirit seemed to fill everybody.[8]

The meeting continued hour after hour through the night. As midnight approached, even as drunken revelers all over Los Angeles prepared to welcome in the New Year, someone in the meeting returned to the piano and began to play a Pentecostal hymn titled "Victory Ahead." Aimee and the assembled throng instantly joined in singing the exuberant, exultant song. By the time they got to the chorus, it seemed the roof might lift off:

Victory ahead! Victory ahead!
Through the blood of Jesus, victory ahead;
Trusting in the Lord, I hear the conqu'ror's tread,
By faith I see the victory ahead![9]

Aimee recalled of that moment:

Saints joined in and marched round and round the building in such numbers that the aisles were choked as they took the place for God. All joined hands, forming one unbroken circle about the entire hall and prayed with such fervor and zeal that it seemed the very heavens dripped fatness and honey.[10]

This New Year's Eve event sparked a full-blown revival in Southern California that spilled over into the early part of 1919. Word of the outpouring that began in the meeting spread like lightning upon a blackened sky, not only across the city but across the nation. Newspapers reported it as telegraph services carried the news across North America. Aimee herself recalled that "Missionaries, evangelists, ministers and Christian workers heard of this great outpouring hundreds of miles away and came by train and boat that they might themselves be revived and be a blessing to others."[11]

In mid-January, Sister Aimee began preaching at nearby Bethel Temple. Soon the crowds were so large that the meetings had to be moved to a larger venue. Even there, the auditorium's seating capacity of thirty-five hundred proved inadequate for the growing masses. Revival seekers would stand in line for hours hoping for a seat when the doors finally opened. Young people would sit on the floor and even on the stage as that mighty vessel preached. All the remaining rooms of the building were used for overflow.

In the services that followed in that season, people would come hours before the advertised start time. Spontaneous worship would break out. People would experience the baptism in the Holy Ghost or miraculous healings just sitting there waiting for the actual service to begin. This, dear friend, is what a revival in and among churches looks like. If you have not seen this, I suspect you have not seen nor experienced true revival. But you can! I am praying and believing that you will. If... Only *if*!

That tremendous move of God came in the aftermath of a global pandemic and in a time of great cultural turmoil and polarization in the country. So why not us? Why not now?

Perhaps *if* today's church leaders and attenders were more concerned with the pitiful, powerless state of our hearts regarding the lost, suffering, sighing, crying, and dying helpless, hopeless hordes of humanity all around us than with "convenient," nondemanding hour-and-fifteen-minute tips of their time to God on every other Sunday or Saturday...*if* they were sufficiently grieved by the reality that their families, neighbors, and coworkers face eternal judgment and final incarceration in hell forever without God, we would have such a revival. If... Only *if*!

Could it be that conditions like those we face today have always been the catalyst for revival? Don't we all have the tendency to look up for God when our faces are in the dirt, to turn to Him only when it seems there is no one else to turn to? Perhaps that's the problem with the American church. We are too comfortable, sitting at ease in Zion. Just too coddled in the most prosperous, overfed nation on earth. Too spiritually spoiled. Like the prodigal son, we are too full of the husks that the swine did eat after a long binge of living just as this pagan, demonized, cursed world lives—zombies; the walking, singing, church-attending dead. Our churches have become little more than a reflection of Ezekiel's vast valley of dry bones.

When nothing is required—when no personal investment must be made—nothing is expected. Yet the atmosphere of expectancy is the breeding ground of miracles!

If... Only *if* the people of the living God, called by His name...

What a multigenerational impact one revived individual can have in this world! In 1921, while leading a revival in Oakland, California, Aimee McPherson began preaching what she would call "the four-square gospel"—Jesus as the only Savior, the Great Physician, the Baptizer with the Holy Spirit, and the coming Bridegroom. Shortly afterward, a ministerial conference collected signatures from one thousand people to whom this foursquare gospel appealed, and on January 1, 1923, the first church of the Foursquare Gospel opened its doors in Los Angeles. It seated more than 5,300 people. By 1925, 32 branch churches had sprouted up in Southern California, and within just another four years, 100 churches had been established, leading to the birth of the International Church of the Foursquare Gospel (ICFG), which today boasts nearly 9,000,000 members in over 90,000 churches across 146 nations![12]

All this leaped into existence because one young lady still in her twenties, in a pandemic-ravaged, war-weary nation, chose revival as her lifestyle and God's kingdom as her passion.

I can't help but wonder: Could we be standing at the threshold of something quite similar today, as our world begins to see the decline of the worst pandemic since the 1918 Spanish flu? I know the answer to that question because I know in whom I have believed. Rather than saying, "Where is the Lord God of Elijah?" I heard God asking, "Where are My Elijahs?" Hear and mark these words well. It is the sin of idolatry within the modern church that is withholding heaven's raining revival, the same as stopped heaven's rain when Elijah prophesied against Ahab and Jezebel. But I believe we are on the brink, the edge, the fringe of that repentant and obedient surrender—that return to the discarded values of the past, which will result in a glorious revival. The clouds full of rain are already forming over our heads, and the spray is already being felt upon the faces of God's revenant remnant. In the depths of my spirit I know God yearns to open His heavens and rain down glory upon the dry, parched, barren landscape of this current secular church culture. His heart is to raise up revived and prophetic men and women who will declare His decree to the dry bones that litter our demonized and devastated, once-great cities.

It is His will to answer the prayers of the righteous and release upon us even more than a revival, as glorious as that will be. He is ready, He is willing, He is able to send us that "awakening" for which our hearts cry out—a move of His own mighty power and resplendent glory so wide and so deep that it reshapes and remakes America. But awakenings begin with revived churches. And revived churches begin when individuals like you and me refuse to be refused and deny to be denied. When we begin to cry out in desperation and plead for personal revival.

With deep sadness I must speak of our lost, those without God and with hell awaiting them; family, friends, neighbors, and coworkers who have no interest in what passes for spiritual life in most churches right now. The lost—in all of their dysfunction, in all of their pain and shame, in all of their darkness and debauchery, in all of their sin and iniquity, lost in a world of lies, hypocrisy, and evil—even now are searching for the living Christ. Their lives are full yet oh-so-empty. Full but not fulfilled. Successful but without joy. Popular without peace. Rich yet in poverty of soul. And I wonder about the words of Romans 10:14, "How then shall they call on Him in whom they have not believed? And how shall they believe in Him of whom they have not heard? And how shall they hear without a preacher?"

Where are those beautiful feet who preach the gospel of peace, who bring good news of good things? We must reverse that order. There must be the "sent ones" who will then preach so the lost can hear the true gospel. Only after having heard can they believe upon Him, and therefore call upon Him and be saved from the wrath to come.

I pray once again that God's people would now embrace the life-transforming truth of this Holy Ghost–inspired proclamation:

> The apex of all Christian endeavor must become to place the jewel of a soul in the crown of our Savior, that the Lamb of God slain may receive the reward of His suffering.

If we actually believed that, really *believed* it, it would ignite and change our prayers. It would mold and change our will. It would change our hearts.

We can have an awakening in America. But if… Only *if.*

℘

God is not a man that He should lie. We have His sacred and solemn promise:

> If My people, who are called by My name, will humble themselves and pray, and seek My face and turn from their wicked ways, then I will hear from heaven, and will forgive their sin and will heal their land.
>
> —2 Chronicles 7:14

If we take Him at His immutable Word, might we indeed reignite a roaring fire?

When I was a young boy, my father was the master of keeping a fire going. Come bedtime during one of those frigid Ohio winters, I watched as he scooped up that day's ashes and piled them on top of the fire. I immediately questioned why he was extinguishing such a warm and beautiful fire. He explained that he in fact was "banking" it so that it was safe to leave unattended for the night.

He continued this life lesson. "I don't want to allow the fire to burn out," Dad said. "I want to preserve it for tomorrow." When my dad smothered the fire with ashes, he was depriving it of oxygen, causing it to extinguish immediately. The next morning, however, Dad would fan away those lifeless gray ashes on top and begin blowing on the coals underneath. Ignited by his breath, the embers of the previous day's fire would once again glow red and then burst into flame.

I am certain the glowing embers of a roaring fire are lying under what appears to be the mound of cold, gray ash that is the church today. Concerning those concealed, glowing embers Paul the apostle said, "We do not look at the things which are seen, but at the things which are not seen. For the things which are seen are temporal [subject to change], but the things which are not seen are eternal" (2 Cor. 4:18). You may not perceive those red-hot coals containing the fuel for the flames of revival fire in your church, or even in your heart, but they are there waiting— waiting for the breath of God's blessed Holy Ghost to blow away the useless religious ashes that have not buried but banked His embers of revenant believers. The winds of Pentecost are blowing again! Adjust your sails and catch the wind.

The world is desperate for an awakening so revolutionary that cultural shifts take place that affect far beyond the boundaries of any single church, denomination, or organization. I believe that in the post-COVID world, those around us have been primed to receive the true gospel of the living Christ in this light and purpose of our calling—to reach the one (Luke 15:4). Could our glorious and gracious God be offering us one last opportunity to allow the blessed Holy Ghost to be poured out without measure upon the earth before His Son's return? Could He be preparing us for the greatest harvest of souls the world has ever witnessed? He is!

So we shout together, "Father, send revival upon us again!

Lord, in the name of Your Son, our Savior Jesus Christ, send forth an awakening the likes of which this world has never seen, and place us right in the middle of it!"

He can. He will. *If...*

NOTES

PREFACE

1. Dr. Aubrey Malphurs, "The State of the American Church: Plateaued or Declining," The Malphurs Group, accessed June 23, 2022, https://malphursgroup.com/state-of-the-american-church-plateaued-declining/.
2. Tim Keller, "Why Church Planting?," January 9, 2012, https://www.acts29.com/why-church-planting/.
3. Bob Smietana, "Southern Baptist Decline Continues, Denomination Has Lost More Than 2 Million Members Since 2006," May 21, 2021, https://religionnews.com/2021/05/21/southern-baptist-decline-continues-denomination-has-lost-more-than-2-million-members-since-2006/.
4. "Do You Really Know Why They're Avoiding Church?," Barna, accessed June 23, 2022, https://www.barna.com/churchless/.
5. "The Gospel Truth: Quotes of Leonard Ravenhill," GospelTruth.net, accessed June 23, 2022, https://www.gospeltruth.net/ravenhill.htm.
6. Daniel W. Whittle, "There Shall Be Showers of Blessings," 1883, https://www.hymnal.net/en/hymn/h/260.

INTRODUCTION

1. Rod Parsley, "If My People Pray / Joni Parsley / Joni's Journal / Pastor Rod Parsley," YouTube video, 9:22, April 9, 2012, https://www.youtube.com/watch?v=c8V6D8-vDHU.

CHAPTER 1

1. Charles Haddon Spurgeon, The Metropolitan Tabernacle Pulpit: Sermons Preached and Revised by C. H. Spurgeon, During the Year 1874, vol. 20 (London: Passmore & Alabaster, 1875), 16.

2. *Merriam-Webster*, s.v. "revive," accessed June 23, 2022, https://www.merriam-webster.com/dictionary/revive.

3. *New Oxford American Dictionary*, s.v. "revive," Oxford University Press, 3rd edition (September 2, 2010).

4. W. P. Mackay, "Revive Us Again," 1863, https://library.timelesstruths.org/music/Revive_Us_Again/.

5. Arthur Wallis, *In the Day of Thy Power: The Scriptural Principles of Revival* (Fort Washington, PA: CLC Publications, 2010), 25, 30.

6. Leonardo Blair, "Most Adult US Christians Don't Believe Holy Spirit Is Real: Study," Christian Post, September 10, 2021, https://www.christianpost.com/news/most-us-christians-dont-believe-holy-spirit-is-real-study.html?uid=1916f97344&utm_source=The+Christian+Post+List&utm_campaign=CP-Newsletter&utm_medium=email.

7. Anugrah Kumar, "60 Percent of Adults Under Forty Say Jesus Isn't Only Way to Salvation; Equal to Buddha, Muhammad," The Christian Post, August 22, 2021, https://www.christianpost.com/news/60-of-young-adults-say-jesus-isnt-the-only-way-to-salvation.html?uid=1916f97344&utm_source=The+Christian+Post+List&utm_campaign=CP-Newsletter&utm_medium=email.

CHAPTER 2

1. Oswald J. Smith, "The Moravian Revival (1727)," Women of Christianity, May 16, 2011, https://

womenofchristianity.com/the-moravian-revival-
1727-by-oswald-j-smith/.

2. Oswald J. Smith, "Moravian Pentecost,"
   Women of Christianity, May 16, 2011, https://
   womenofchristianity.com/moravian-pentecost/.

3. John Greenfield and Mark S. Mirza, *Power From
   On High* (Atlanta: CTM Publishing, 2017), 20.

4. Evelyn R. Hassé, *The Moravians* (London:
   National Council of Evangelical Free Churches,
   1913), 123.

5. Smith, "Moravian Pentecost."

6. Smith, "The Moravian Revival."

7. Smith, "The Moravian Revival."

8. Janet and Geoff Benge, *Count Zinzendorf:
   Firstfruit* (Seattle: YWAM Publishing, 2006), 81.

9. "Herrnhut (The Lord's Watch)—1727," The
   Hidden Ones, July 30, 2012, http://hiddenonesmi
   .com/2012/07/30/herrnhut-the-lords-watch-1727/.

10. Stephen F. Olford, *Heart-Cry for Revival* (Westwood,
    NJ: Fleming H. Revell, 1962), 68.

11. "1801 Cane Ridge Revival," Beautiful Feet, accessed
    June 24, 2022, https://romans1015.com/cane-ridge/.

12. Matt Pettry, "Dreaming at Cane Ridge: A Strategy
    for Awakening and Reformation," *Charisma*, May 20,
    2015, https://charismamag.com/revival/dreaming-at-
    cane-ridge-a-strategy-for-awakening-and-reformation/.

13. "1801 Cane Ridge Revival," Beautiful Feet.

14. Wayne Johnson, "The Fulton Street Revival," Leben,
    January 1, 2017, https://leben.us/fulton-street-revival/.

15. Johnson, "The Fulton Street Revival."

16. "Jeremiah Lanphier, US, Businessman," 365
    Christian Men, accessed June 24, 2022, https://
    www.365christianmen.com/podcast/jeremiah-
    lanphier-us-businessman/.

17. G. Campbell Morgan, *The Welsh Revival* (Michigan: Reformed Church Publications, 2015), 42.
18. Solomon Benjamin Shaw, *The Great Revival in Wales: Also an Account of the Great Revival in Ireland in 1859* (Chicago: S. B. Shaw, 1905), 65–66.
19. Shaw, *The Great Revival in Wales*, 11.
20. Shaw, *The Great Revival in Wales*, 19–20, 65.
21. Shaw, *The Great Revival in Wales*, 98.
22. Morgan, *The Welsh Revival*, 84.
23. Dante Alighieri, *Inferno*, vol 1. (London: Cassell, Petter and Galpin, 1866), 26.
24. *The Homiletic Review*, Vol. 44, Issues 1–5 (New York: Funk & Wagnalls, 1902), 382; "William Booth Quotes," Quotefancy, accessed June 24, 2022, https://quotefancy.com/strong-quotes.
25. Rume Kpadamrophe, "When God Came Down— The Hebrides Revival," Christian Today, accessed June 24, 2022, http://christiantoday.com.au/news/when-god-came-down-the-hebrides-revival.html.
26. Kpadamrophe, "When God Came Down."

CHAPTER 3

1. "51% of Churchgoers Don't Know of the Great Commission," Barna, March 27, 2018, https://www.barna.com/research/half-churchgoers-not-heard-great-commission/.
2. Leonard Ravenhill, *Why Revival Tarries* (Minneapolis: Bethany House, 1987), 22.
3. Charles H. Spurgeon, "If You Have to Give a Carnival...," QuoteFancy, accessed July 19, 2022, https://quotefancy.com/quote/786352/Charles-H-Spurgeon-If-you-have-to-give-a-carnival-to-get-people-to-come-to-church-then.
4. Rod Parsley, *The Cross: One Man. One Tree. One Friday* (Lake Mary, FL: Charisma House, 2013), 6.

5. Mark Fackler, "The World Has Yet to See…," *Christianity Today*, accessed June 24, 2022, https://www.christianitytoday.com/history/issues/issue-25/world-has-yet-to-see.html.

6. C. S. Lewis, *Mere Christianity* (New York: Macmillan, 1952), 125.

7. Alcoholics Anonymous, "The 12 Steps of AA," accessed June 24, 2022, https://www.alcoholics-anonymous.org.uk/about-aa/the-12-steps-of-aa.

8. Rod Parsley, *Could It Be?* (Columbus, OH: Results Publishing, 2002), 156.

9. "A Revival Account Asbury 1970," Messiah Missions, accessed June 24, 2022, https://messiahmissions.org/asbury-revival/.

10. A. W. Pink, "It Is Not the Absence of Sin…," QuotesLyfe, accessed July 19, 2022, https://www.quoteslyfe.com/quote/It-is-not-the-absence-of-sin-178046.

11. Watchman Nee, *The Spiritual Man* (New York: Christian Fellowship Publishers, 1968), 91.

12. Winkie Pratney, *Revival: Principles to Change the World* (Lindale, TX: Agape Force, 1984), 190.

13. Judson W. Van DeVenter, "I Surrender All," 1896, https://library.timelesstruths.org/music/I_Surrender_All/.

CHAPTER 4

1. Shaw, *The Great Revival in Wales*, 60–61.

2. E. M. Bounds, *The Classic Collection on Prayer* (Orlando: Bridge-Logos, 2001), 490.

3. Jim Reeves, "How Long Has It Been," 1958, https://genius.com/Jim-reeves-how-long-has-it-been-lyrics.

CHAPTER 5

1. Rod Parsley, *Gone: One Man. One Tomb. One Sunday* (Lake Mary, FL: Charisma House, 2016), 125–127.
2. Thomas C. Brickhouse and Nicholas D. Smith, *Plato's Socrates* (New York: Oxford University Press, 1994), 201.

CHAPTER 6

1. Ravenhill, *Why Revival Tarries*, 48.
2. James Melvin Washington, ed., *A Testament of Hope: The Essential Writings and Speeches of Martin Luther King, Jr.* (New York: Harper One, 2003), 220.
3. Oswald Chambers, "December 7: Repentance," My Utmost for His Highest, accessed June 24, 2022, https://utmost.org/classic/repentance-classic/.
4. Rev. Fr. Peter Obinna Umekwe, *240 Inspirational Quotes on Humility: Quotes That Lead to Humility* (Bloomington, IN: Xlibris, 2009), 37.
5. Parsley, *Could It Be?*, 129.
6. James C. Humes, *The Wit and Wisdom of Winston Churchill* (New York: Harper Collins, 1994).

CHAPTER 7

1. Cindy Walker, "Child of the King," 1967, http://baptistsearch.blogspot.com/2017/05/child-of-king_19.html.
2. *Merriam-Webster*, s.v. "humble," accessed June 24, 2022, https://www.merriam-webster.com/dictionary/humble.
3. Charles Haddon Spurgeon, *Spurgeon's Sermons Volume 06: 1860* (Woodstock, Ontario: Devoted Publishing, 2017), 79.
4. Charles Finney, *Lectures on Revival of Religion* (New York: Treasures Media, 2007), 20.

5. Rod Parsley, *Ancient Wells, Living Water* (Lake Mary, FL: Charisma House, 2003), 188.
6. Ravenhill, *Why Revival Tarries*, 92.
7. Ravenhill, *Why Revival Tarries*, 64.
8. Hugh Glass, HughGlass.org, accessed July 19, 2022, http://hughglass.org/.

CHAPTER 8

1. Ravenhill, *Why Revival Tarries*, 17.
2. Thomas Armitage, *Preaching: Its Ideal and Inner Life* (Philadelphia: American Baptist Publication Society, 1880), 170.
3. E. M. Bounds, *E. M. Bounds on Prayer* (New Kensington, PA: Whitaker House, 1997), 184.

CHAPTER 9

1. Charles Haddon Spurgeon, *Spurgeon at His Best* (Grand Rapids, MI: Baker Book House, 1988), 25.
2. Parsley, *The Cross*, 7–8.

CHAPTER 10

1. Joseph Parker, *These Sayings of Mine: Pulpit Notes on Seven Chapters of the First Gospel, and Other Sermons* (New York: I. K. Funk & Company, 1881), 62.
2. H. Richard Niebuhr, *The Kingdom of God in America* (New York: Harper & Row, 1959 [1937]), 193.
3. Rod Parsley, *Culturally Incorrect* (Nashville: Thomas Nelson, 2007), vii.
4. Parsley, *Culturally Incorrect*, xvii.
5. Parsley, *Culturally Incorrect*, xv.
6. Parsley, *Culturally Incorrect*, xvi.
7. Parsley, *Culturally Incorrect*, xxi.
8. Parsley, *Culturally Incorrect*, xxi.
9. Parsley, *Culturally Incorrect*, xxii.

10. Rod Parsley, "This I Believe: Jesus Paid It All," speech transcript, October 14, 2012, World Harvest Church, 2012.

11. Lisa Singh and Adelle M. Banks, "Crystal Cathedral Founder Robert Schuller Dies at 88," *Washington Post*, April 2, 2015, https://www.washingtonpost.com/national/religion/crystal-cathedral-founder-robert-schuller-dies-at-88/2015/04/02/61b96702-d970-11e4-bf0b-f648b95a6488_story.html.

12. J. Rodman Williams, *Renewal Theology: Systematic Theology From a Charismatic Perspective* (Grand Rapids, MI: Zondervan, 1996), 221.

13. Joseph Parker, *Things Concerning Himself* (New York: Funk & Wagnalls, 1884), 127.

14. Ravenhill, *Why Revival Tarries*, 95.

15. Isaac Watts (1674–1748), "Blest Are the Humble Souls That See," c. 1710, http://ehymnbook.org/CMMS/hymnSong.php?id=pd12637.

CONCLUSION

1. Brian Adams, "History Doesn't Repeat, But It Often Rhymes," HuffPost, January 18, 2017, https://www.huffpost.com/entry/history-doesnt-repeat-but-it-often-rhymes_b_61087610e4b0999d2084fb15.

2. This Day in History—March 4, 1918: First Cases Reported in Deadly 1918 Flu Pandemic," History, A&E Television Networks, last updated March 3, 2021, https://www.history.com/this-day-in-history/first-cases-reported-in-deadly-influenza-epidemic.

3. The 1918 pandemic came to be known as the Spanish flu not because it originated in Spain but because Spain was the first country to report on it. Spain had declared itself a neutral country during World War I, so they felt free to cover

news of the virus from the start of its regional outbreak in Madrid, Spain, in May 1918. Both Allied and Central Powers had covered up news of the outbreaks to that point in order to keep soldier morale high.

4. J. K. Taubenberger and D. M. Morens, "1918 Influenza: The Mother of All Pandemics," *Emerging Infectious Diseases* 12, no. 1 (January 2006): 15–22.

5. "Lessons From the 1918 Influenza Epidemic: Part 4—Conclusions—'Such a Big Event, So Little Public Memory,'" *History Is Now*, June 16, 2020, http://www.historyisnowmagazine.com/blog/2020/6/16/lessons-from-the-1918-influenza-epidemic-part-4-conclusions-such-a-big-event-so-little-public-memory.

6. "Aimee Semple McPherson: Foursquare Phenomenon" *Christianity Today*, accessed June 24, 2022, https://www.christianitytoday.com/history/people/denominationalfounders/aimee-semple-mcpherson.html.

7. Aimee Semple McPherson, *This Is That: Personal Experiences, Sermons and Writings of Aimee Semple McPherson, Evangelist* (Los Angeles: Bridal Call Publishing House, 1919), 232.

8. McPherson, *This Is That*, 232–234.

9. William Grum, "Victory Ahead," 1905, https://hymnary.org/text/when_the_hosts_of_israel_led_by_god.

10. McPherson, *This Is That*, 234.

11. McPherson, *This Is That*, 234.

12. "About Us," Union Foursquare, accessed July 5, 2022, http://foursquareunion.org/aboutUs.html.